Library of
Davidson College

THE *Middle East* COLLECTION

THE *Middle East* COLLECTION

Advisory Editor
John E. Woods

Editorial Board
William R. Polk
Speros Vryonis, Jr.
John C. Campbell
Mostafa Ansari

MODERN SONS OF THE PHARAOHS

BY

S. H. LEEDER

ARNO PRESS
A New York Times Company
New York—1973

916.2
L484m

Reprint Edition 1973 by Arno Press Inc.

Reprinted by permission of Hodder and Stoughton Ltd.

Reprinted from a copy in
 The Princeton University Library

The Middle East Collection
ISBN for complete set: 0-405-05310-X
See last pages of this volume for titles.

Manufactured in the United States of America

Library of Congress Cataloging in Publication Data

Leeder, S   H
   Modern sons of the Pharaohs.

   (The Middle East collection)
   Reprint of the 1918 ed. published by Hodder and
Stoughton, London, New York under title: Modern sons
of the Pharoahs; a study of the manners and customs of
the Copts of Egypt.
   Bibliography: p.
   1. Copts. 2. Egypt--Social life and customs.
3. Coptic Church. I. Title. II. Series.
DT70.L4 1973   916.2'03'4   73-6288
ISBN 0-405-05346-0

75-3349

The author acknowledges his great indebtedness to the following Coptic gentlemen :—

> MARCUS H. SIMAIKA BEY (who has since become a Pasha), whose influential and authoritative help was unstinted.
>
> KYRIAKOS EFFENDI MIKHAIL, who spent valuable weeks in making possible the many journeys in out-of-the-way Egypt.
>
> AMIN PASHA GHALI.
>
> ZAKI BEY WISSA (of Assiout).
>
> AZIZ BEY HANNA SALEH (of Fayoum).
>
> DR. GEORGY SOBHY, of Cairo, who put all his special knowledge at his disposal.

Dr. NAGEEB MAHROUS (of Fayoum).

IBRAHIM EFFENDI ZAKY.

ABADEER EFFENDI HAKIM (of Assiout).

HABIB EFFENDI BASTA, A.R.I.B.A., A.Inst.C.E.

NASHED EFFENDI HANNA.

LOUIS EFFENDI FANOUS.

MARCOS EFFENDI SIDAROUS.

FOAD EFFENDI NAGUIB.

Preface

IT was the intention of the publishers that this book should appear in the autumn of the year 1914, and the author completed the MS. by the very last day of July, the day that seems to us now to have been fated to mark the close of a world epoch. In the uncertainty of the upheaval a postponement of publication was agreed upon; "till the end of the war," was at that time a phrase fresh and hopeful. Three years have more than passed; the war goes on, and after what perhaps has been a surfeit, readers are seeking for books unconnected with translations of the doctrines of Hunnish savagery and German philosophy, or even of the allied politics and the history of the war itself. Moreover, Egypt and its native people (although the exigencies of war have sealed the country to the mere tourist) have become the centre of new interest through a realisation of its vital importance to the very existence of our Empire, and by reason of the great armies which have assembled there from every part of the Empire to assert and protect our rights. And so the publication of this study of the Coptic people of Egypt has been decided on for the early days of 1918.

The writer has not been in Egypt during the period

of the war, though the pleasure of correspondence with many native friends there—Moslem and Coptic—has happily not been interrupted. When he left the valley of the Nile, after the last of several prolonged visits, the "Coptic question," to which he refers in the last chapter, was in an acute stage provoking much controversy. The advent of war put an end, of course, to all agitation of that nature. As the days of strain and trial to our Empire multiplied, the disposition increased on the part of the Coptic people to assist the Government in every possible way—in the realm of politics as well as philanthropy.

The author has thought it would best serve the Coptic people and the responsible Government of Egypt to leave his work exactly as the beginning of the war found it. After the long truce, which will end with the war, it may be useful to be able to turn to a clear and unbiased record of the things these ancient dwellers in the land of Pharaoh have regarded as necessary for reform, and to have the original statement of their reasons and arguments for a different treatment, side by side with the official answer to their claims. It is not unlikely that in the light of the revelation which may come from the tremendous experiences of the world war the mistakes of both sides may stand out plain and clear—the suppliant may see that he has asked too much, and the governing power that it has been willing to accede too little.

Preface

There is promise of a new era for Egypt when the days of normal government are resumed. A corrupt Court has been scattered, and the firm authority of Britain has been established in the place of counsels feebly divided with Turkey. The thousand social and administrative scandals arising from the Capitulations have been removed. Mosque and Church alike have been freed from the chance of internal corruption and bribery through the exercise of national control over their considerable revenues. In view of all the hopes which will herald the new day, is it too much to trust that a way will be found to satisfy the Coptic aspirations, which I would ask those in authority in Egypt to believe —whatever may be said of their political value—are as honest and sincere as they are heartfelt?

Contents

BOOK I

THE PEOPLE AND THEIR CUSTOMS

CHAPTER I

	PAGE
A VISIT TO THE VILLAGE OF A COPTIC SQUIRE	3

CHAPTER II

THE HOME-LIFE OF THE SQUIRE 27

CHAPTER III

COUNTRY RAMBLES AND CHATS WITH BEDOUINS AND FELLAHEEN   45

CHAPTER IV

AMONGST THE COUNTRY-FOLK. THEIR BELIEFS AND SUPERSTITIONS. THE INTEREST AND HUMOUR OF THEIR TALK . 63

CHAPTER V

BIRTH AND ITS ATTENDANT CELEBRATIONS . . . 82

CHAPTER VI

BAPTISM AND CIRCUMCISION 95

CHAPTER VII

How a Wife is Chosen, with an Account of the Ceremonies of Betrothal 104

CHAPTER VIII

The Coptic Wedding 112

CHAPTER IX

The Oriental in Grief; and the Coptic Burial Customs 122

CHAPTER X

The Marvels of the Saints' Tombs, and their Birthday Fairs 136

CHAPTER XI

Oriental Shopkeepers and Handicraftsmen . . 146

BOOK II

THE PEOPLE AND THEIR ORIENTAL CHURCH. THEIR GREAT DIGNITARIES. THEIR SOCIAL AND POLITICAL POSITION

CHAPTER I

The Oriental Christian in his Church. The Church Itself 169

CHAPTER II

The People at Worship 183

CHAPTER III

Of the Bread and the Wine, of Holy Water, and the Extraordinary Coptic Fasts 209

CHAPTER IV

THE BELIEFS OF THE COPTS 228
                            PAGE

CHAPTER V

A SKETCH OF THE AGED COPTIC PATRIARCH, CYRIL V. . 245

CHAPTER VI

A VISIT TO THE VENERATED BISHOP OF THE FAYOUM . 265

CHAPTER VII

DOES THE ANCIENT RACE OF THE PHARAOHS STILL SURVIVE IN EGYPT? 305

CHAPTER VIII

THE EGYPTIAN CHRISTIANS AND BRITISH RULE . . 327

ADDENDA—
    THE BURYING OF THE PICTURE IN THE ALTAR . . 345
    THE BREAKING OF THE BREAD 346

BIBLIOGRAPHY 347

INDEX 349

Illustrations

ONE OF THE MOST GORGEOUS COPTIC WEDDINGS OF RECENT YEARS . . . . . . *Frontispiece*	
	FACING PAGE
A MONASTERY IN THE REMOTE DESERT . . .	32
THE HEAD OF A DESERT MONASTERY (LEANING ON HIS STAFF) AND HIS YOUNGEST ACOLYTE	32
THE CHIEF NAZIR OF THE PASHA	32
THE MONASTERY OF JEREMIAS AT ASSOUAN . . .	32
BUTTER CHURNING IN THE VILLAGE	48
THE OLD BEDOUIN, AGED 112 YEARS, AND HIS WIFE .	48
IN THE HOT DAYS OF SUMMER	64
A VILLAGE SCENE IN EGYPT	64
A HOLY TREE OF GREAT AGE	80
THE SCENE AT THE FARM IN THE DELTA . . .	112
THE DISTANT VILLAGE IN UPPER EGYPT FROM WHICH IT IS SAID THE MAGICIANS CAME WHO PITTED THEIR ARTS AGAINST THOSE OF MOSES AND AARON . . .	112
IN THE BAZAAR OF THE CAULDRON SELLERS . . .	144
THE HARNESS-MAKER AND THE WORKER IN PALM-FIBRE .	160
A FRUIT SHOP IN THE WATER-MELON SEASON . .	160
THE SCREEN DIVISIONS IN THE COPTIC CHURCH OF ABU SERGEH, OLD CAIRO	176

	FACING PAGE
THE PULPIT AND MIDDLE-SCREEN OF THE CHURCH OF ABU SERGEH	176
THE PORTICO AND THE INTERIOR OF A COPTIC CHURCH	192
THE EGYPTIAN VILLAGE OF KENEH, LARGELY COPTIC	240
WHERE THE DRINKING VESSELS ARE MADE	240
THE BEAUTIFUL BANKS OF THE NILE	240
THE DOMES WHICH ARE CHARACTERISTIC OF ALL COPTIC CHURCHES	272
ON THE ROOF OF A COPTIC MONASTERY	272
THE SAINTED BISHOP OF THE FAYOUM WITH HIS WONDERFUL HAND-CROSS	304
A COPTIC WOMAN OF THE POORER CLASS	320
A COPTIC PRIEST	320
THE GREAT COPTIC CENTRE IN EGYPT—ASSIOUT	336

S. H. Leeder

Book I

CHAPTER I

A Visit to the Village of a Coptic Squire

TO me the village life of Egypt has an irresistible fascination. I have had the privilege of staying in several of the out-of-the-way hamlets, and the more I have seen of the fellaheen, the more I have appreciated the charm of their simple courtesies, their unaffected hospitality, and a certain native grace, even in the common people, which shines through all the ways of a life so primitive as to belong to the days little removed from those when man was driven out of the Garden to eat bread by the sweat of his brow all the days of his life.

In recent years this primitive life has been tempered in some villages by the increase of wealth on the part of the landed classes, and by the return of much of the land into the hands of the people from whom it was confiscated by a succession of tyrant rulers, ending with the earlier Khedives, who had declared themselves the owners of the whole country. Much of this wealth is in the hands of the Copts, who have prospered exceedingly under the security of British rule.

There is on the part of some few of the wealthy Copts a genuine desire in increasing and improving their estates, to rule their domains in such a way as to gain the esteem and affection of their many dependants.

Nothing could make for the lasting good of Egypt so surely as the enthusiasm for skilled farming these men are showing. They are encouraging the study of scientific agriculture, by which means the productivity of their country is being enormously increased; and at the same time, by the introduction of every sort of modern appliance, they are rapidly bringing into fuller cultivation vast areas which have until now been dependent on the annual flooding of the Nile for a single crop, but which is now made by artificial irrigation to yield a succession of crops throughout the year.

In the Delta—especially by great systems of levelling of the soil—these landowners are rescuing immense tracts of pure desert and brine-logged earth, and making it to smile under the waving corn which, as by magic, springs up where once the sea reigned or the hot dry sand refused to yield a single green blade.

Lower Egypt, in a very true sense, is the gift of the Nile. There was a time when the Delta was a bay of the Mediterranean Sea, and before the Nile deposits filled it up, the limestone ridge of the famous Mokattam Hills, behind Cairo, was washed by the sea.

In addition to the wide tracts that have been recovered, there are still in the Delta a million and a half acres of land lying waste, waiting to be freed from the salt which has impregnated it and rendered it sterile for ages. Experience shows that it can be brought into cultivation, and will then grow not only rice but cotton.

Speaking broadly, from the deductions of the geologist, it may be said that the mighty river, since modern time began, made itself the generous servant of mankind by its never-ceasing task of pushing back with its rich deposits the Mediterranean Sea; in early times the gift grew in magnitude as the population increased to receive it; and at the present day history is repeating itself.

The part that man has played in supplementing the work of the river has always been an important one. It may be doubted if the skill used to-day far exceeds that of the early Egyptians, who applied themselves to develop this rich gift of the sacred river. There is ample evidence that they understood the science of irrigation, as well as that of construction in wood, brick, and stone.

It only needs a glance at the figures of the fabulous increase in the population of Egypt, under its present conditions of justice and security, to show how necessary for the support of human life the work of men, such as I have spoken of, is, even in supplementing the activities of the Government, in the way of reclamation by immense systems of irrigation and drainage.

It is scarcely realisable that while the population of Egypt about seventy years since was roughly two millions, it is now nearly ten, and that the greater part of this increase has come under British rule, which only dates from the year 1882.

Forced labour no longer condemns tens of thousands of men to a slavery which often proved a quick road to death. It is a strange reflection, that an august lady is still living for whose pleasure a Khedive made a road—from Cairo to the Pyramids—in such brutal hurry that many thousands of lives were sacrificed in two or three weeks.

There are many works in Egypt gained at a like cost in human agony and blood. In the days of the *corvée*, so comparatively recent, the villages used to echo with the piercing cries of demented mothers whose sons were snatched away from them, either for forced labour or for the army. Well those poor mothers knew that from either service the chances of seeing their loved ones again were less than faint.

Under Lord Cromer the *corvée* came to an end, and to-day the army service causes no wailing; the mother, and the youthful wife, look forward to seeing the lad again, strong and straight, a travelled man with many things to tell, and even with a little money in his pocket.

Having an invitation from a Coptic squire to visit his domain, we are, as the Eastern custom ordains, taken in charge by our host, from the time we leave our own dwelling in Cairo to the moment when he will bring us back to the same threshold. I know that I must not insult an Egyptian host by offering even to pay my own railway fare, and can only console myself in submitting to such an un-English custom by the promise he has made me to visit me at my home in England, when it will be polite for me to show him equal consideration.

Arrived at the country station, we are met by several servants, with an odd collection of camels, mules, and donkeys, on which our party are to ride across the country to the out-of-the-way village. The salaams and greetings between the folk assembled to meet us are instinct with genial courtesy on all sides, and we all call down the blessings of peace, with wishes for a bright and happy day, upon each other.

It is a glorious morning in January, the sun having dispelled the coldness of the night (it has only just escaped actual frost) and the white mists of early dawn.

After many delays, all so characteristic of Egypt to those who know its casual habits, our cavalcade starts, and leaving the little town we are soon travelling single file along the raised bank of the canal, almost the only sort of road known in the country.

How exhilarating it all is—the dry, sun-warmed air, the blue sky, the vivid colouring all touched with a pale golden glow so peculiar to the land of the Nile. The fields are green now with the *burseem*, a sort of indigenous clover, and the beans, filling the air with that delicious scent which speaks so subtly to an Englishman of the first warm days of summer at home. The scents here are not the elusive whiffs of the English countryside, but take us in full and warm embrace—the earth is transformed into a very paradise of delicate perfumes. We draw deep breath; the air is not only delicious, but full of exhilarating and health-giving powers, with suggestions of an eternal youthfulness in which care falls away and the spirit of man becomes free and untrammelled.

The bird life by the waterside is enchanting. Here the kingfisher, whose glory of colour and sheen have never been known to those who have not seen him boldly flitting about in such sunlight as this, shows little trace of any fear of man. I have seen twenty of these birds together at one moment, darting about over a canal. In Egypt it has never occurred to the boys, small or large, to disturb the pleasures of the birds.

Small owls, too, fly in and out of the banks, having apparently forgotten the night habits of their species; or, if they choose to sleep, we pass them on the bare boughs of the few small trees, nestling together in couples.

The lark is here, with a little song of its own, where nearly all the birds are silent; and the busy wagtail. The beautiful hoopoe is as tame as the pigeons of

St. Mark's, while other tiny specks of vivid living colour flit to and fro like animated flowers.

One of the features in the landscape of Egypt is the procession of natives along by the waterways, the men in their blue cotton robes, and the women swathed in dusty black, a procession which, from the rising till the setting of the sun, seems never ending.

Because we are riding, we give, by immemorial custom, the salaam to those who walk, and in return receive the greetings and the smiles of the passers-by.

Soon we leave the canal, and take one of the paths cutting across the fields, worn hard by the countless feet that have passed over it.

There is a market to be held to-day, at the nearest town; and as we come within its range we are met by great numbers of men, women, and children, all leading animals—camels, oxen, asses, goats, and sheep, the young lambs being sometimes carried across the shoulders, or literally in the bosom of the shepherd.

By the wayside, a number of youths, on the way to market, have stopped to play at the word-games in which they delight, and which provoke them to subdued bursts of merriment.

Here again a group of schoolboys, released from their morning studies, are playing a very ancient game, something like rounders. One of the smaller ones has shed all his clothes, and is chaffed by his companions because a Frangee has seen him naked. "Oh," he replies in a flash, "he will think that I am the *ginn* of the noonday"—a familiar *afreet* of the Nile valley.

In one field a young fellah is guiding one of the primitive ploughs, drawn by a great ox, the while he sings in a pleasant monotone a very ancient song of the soil, the words of which I afterwards secured from another labourer in the fields. This is a very free translation :

> Warm is the sun,
> The flood waters run;
> Safe is the seed I have sown.
>
> Soon I shall reap,
> The young lambs will leap;
> Glad will be harvest home!
>
> In wet sand will the cool melons grow,
> And green cucumbers hang from the bough,
> And the grape, and the peach, and the red pomegranate,
> Will gladden the days when the waters run low.

The sounds that rise from the sunlit fields in Egypt create an impression of natural gladness unlike that of any other country. Whether it is the lowing of the contented cattle at this time of the year when the *burseem* is in crop, or the laughter and shouts of the dancing children who attend them, or the twittering of the birds, that gives to the great anthem its special note, I do not know, but here one seems to be listening to the primeval song of seething young life in the first Garden before the sunshine had ever been overcast.

In Egypt every animal is considered to have the right to a course of *burseem*, which has a name signifying "taste of the spring." By this name it is called by the man who sells it in the streets of Cairo, for the benefit of the horses and donkeys on hire there. The drivers feed their beasts with it at every opportunity, and the green litter of *burseem* is a characteristic of the Oriental city which all visitors will remember. Our host tells us that his city horses are all sent by train into the country every year for their "taste of the spring"; we are, indeed, bringing with us two or three of the animals at this time.

You cannot of course turn a number of animals loose into a clover field to feed. Each beast, whether it is a goat or a buffalo, is tethered at the edge of the crop, the stake being placed with nice discrimination as to the amount of clover to be allowed in a given time.

Our cavalcade passed through two or three villages, having to take the narrow passage-ways in single file. The huts are built of unbaked bricks of mud from the Nile banks, and have flat roofs, generally stacked with the yellow sticks of Indian corn which is used as fuel.

The huts are windowless; but as all things that love the sun are out of doors, one sees all the life of the village going on in the small open spaces.

Here some women are churning for butter, the milk being simply thrown from side to side in a goat's skin, suspended from a bamboo tripod—a group of women and girls sitting round, of course, to discuss the operation.

Here a mother sits in the sun, with her back to the wall of her hut, nursing her babe. Other women are coming up from the river with the water-pots on their heads. The women are all swathed in the black robe of Egypt, so unsuitable where every pathway is a track of dust; as we appear, their faces are covered until the men of our party have passed.

It would be most improper for men to address the women, but my wife generally rides behind so that she may have the pleasure of greeting them. For her, they drop the covering from their faces completely, and smile as they offer all sorts of compliments and good wishes. Will she not stop and drink of their milk? Can they bring her food? Having been in Algeria, she recognises a form of greeting which is in general use by the Arabs there, but which in Egypt is used only by the women—*sabah el khayr*.

The ordinary sight-seer who visits Egypt will learn with surprise that off the tourist tract the word *backsheesh* is never heard, however poor the people may be. Indeed, on every side they are anxious not to take, but to give of their humble best to the visitor, who by ancient tradition is the guest of all.

As it is noonday there is generally a group of men, returned from the fields, who are resting on the village "green." The fact that it is not green, but dust-grey, seems to have no effect on the activities of the great flock of fine-looking geese who forage upon it to good result.

The fellah, like all classes of men in the East, delights in conversation, and it is allowable by the strictest rules of politeness for all men to forgather where talk is going on.

The news of the day naturally goes by word of mouth, and no man who has the advantage of being able to read would be so churlish as to deprive the great majority of his neighbours, who cannot read, of the benefit of his enviable gift. The passer-by will always stop and quietly take a seat near a group of men who are talking, his presence never being resented.

The Eastern laws of politeness, almost as old as time, are so well understood that there is rarely anything unseemly in these casual gatherings. The good breeding which prevents a man from addressing directly another man with a recognised claim to higher respect, also dictates to the man of better position a gentle consideration of his lowly companion. It is not good to presume on superiority of education or wealth; and boisterousness of voice or manner is universally deprecated for all men. For this reason no one ever whistles with his mouth in the East.

The politeness of Egypt is far deeper than any sort of ceremonial observance. I have read of an old Coptic monk whose rules for eating were very strict, but with visitors he would eat against these rules when he thought that it would put them at their ease. It is such courtesy as this that gives a foreign visitor at the present day the perfect repose in strange society which makes for social enjoyment. A *faux pas* is impossible, in this way, that whatever a visitor does (no matter how contrary to the custom of the country) it is excused without a sign. If any apology is made, it is met with a gentle smile and the words, "We knew that what you did was polite in your own country." The only time I have ever known an English visitor to give deep offence was when a lady, after attending one of the Coptic church services, insisted on buying as a souvenir the cymbals that had been used. Fortunately the politeness which allowed the lady to have her way was rewarded by the intervention of a man who understood the nature of the wound so thoughtlessly inflicted, and the church's property was restored.

The fellah is a being full of curiosity, as a lover of gossip will always be. Quietly, but tersely, our servants are questioned again and again all along the journey, as to who the strangers are! Why they are visiting a part of the country where tourists never go; how long are they going to stay; above all, has the gentleman any connection with the Government?

And the news travels forward in all directions, by those magic means only known in the East. As in scriptural days, the watchman on the housetop, and the guardian of the fields on his mound, send out their signals.¹

At last we see in the distance, across the emerald fields, the village in which we are to stay. It is, as all the hamlets are, a picturesque huddle of mud huts, built all over a slight eminence so as to be lifted out of the flood at high Nile. It is dominated by the graceful minaret of the mosque, and by the one great white house, or *gasr*, to which we are going, and by the small domes which distinguish the Coptic church. In any other country the dirt surrounding the villages would be insufferable. It is one of the wonders of Egypt how the sunshine redeems everything.

In the hieroglyphic annals of ancient Egypt, mention is frequently made of houses which were distinguished from the ordinary dwellings by the title of "white ones." The treasury of Pharaoh was called "the double white house." It is just the same to-day. The greater number of buildings of the Egyptian Government are whitened by lime, and may be recognised afar off by the traveller. The dwelling of every Egyptian of standing in the country has its walls whitened. Now that there is no need to hide the Christian churches, they too are whitened as of old. Even the chapels attended by those many Copts who have been won to Presbyterianism by the American Mission, stand out from the dull yellow mud colour of the dwellings of the people in gleaming whiteness.

Arrived at the house, we are bidden welcome with delightful courtesy by our host, who introduces us to his chief *nazir*, or factor; and to other im-

---

¹ "The watchman went up to the roof over the gate unto the wall, and lifted up his eyes, and looked, and behold a man running alone" (2 Sam. xviii. 24).

portant servants, who all from that moment devote themselves to our comfort and entertainment.

It is interesting to find that this house, though it dates only from the early days of the British occupation which brought the security and much of the wealth on which the fortunes of its owner are founded, yet follows a plan closely corresponding to that of the ancient Egyptian dwellings of like importance.

The unbaked bricks of the Exodus are its material, and the inner courtyard surrounded by chambers used for the reception of visitors, for court-room or *mandara*, and for household and general stores, are much the same as in those days.

This large courtyard has leading from it the workshops, the estate offices, the servants' sleeping-rooms, the kitchens, the lumber-rooms, and even the stables of those animals in immediate use by the family. It is in the courtyard that visitors dismount. Most courteous are the servants who hurry to his assistance, and offer him the eloquent greetings which custom requires.

The folding doors of the courtyard, with wooden lock, are very like those of ancient days, and so are the tall conical pigeon-houses which flank the entrance. The doors have been strengthened with metal plates, which may well remind us of how the doors of the Pharaoh's temples were plated with gold or bronze—to be stolen by foreign foes without any respect to the deity.

The pigeon towers are of great interest. The pigeon is a very important item of food in all country places. The origin of the towers, ages ago, was doubtless the discovery that the pigeon in this hot climate likes to hide itself for sleep during part of the day in any cool pot or pitcher it can find. These conical towers are built up simply of mud with old pots stuck into it. No one thinks of buying pigeons in Egypt; to supply these cool retreats is always enough to attract as many birds as you can provide for in this way. The towers are seldom disturbed even to be cleaned out, except to remove the guano, which is of great value. It is, however, characteristic of the dove to show no trace of the dust and dirt of its surroundings. When, towards sunset, the pigeons come out in circling flights, and catch the golden light of the sun, it seems that the poetic line of the Psalmist must have been inspired by just such a sight—" Though ye have lien among the pots, yet shall ye be as the wings of a dove covered with silver, and her feathers with yellow gold."

In the interior decoration of his house the ancient Egyptian showed great taste: applied ornament was greatly used, the walls were all painted, and the furniture was decorative. The modern country house in Egypt, like this one we are visiting, is usually without mural decoration of any sort, the walls being left roughly plastered. The furniture is scanty and hideous, but for the divan coverings, which are sometimes of good material, and the rugs and carpets—generally of great value. It is an interesting point, however, to those who believe that the Copt is directly descended from the people of the Pharaohs, to see how, with a return of prosperity, an extraordinary love of elaborate decoration of the home is growing up. I know several Coptic houses on which a great amount of wealth has been spent in the ornamentation of all the principal rooms. Nothing, indeed, but the ancient skill and taste is lacking in these costly attempts to adorn the home. It is hoped that, as a result of the care that is being given by the Government in the teaching of handicrafts, in the excellent technical schools, the old talents may be found to be only dormant and not utterly lost.

On the part of the peasantry, the only attempts at any sort of decoration are the crude drawings, made round the doorway of the huts to show when one of the inhabitants has been on a pilgrimage. If the man is a Moslem, his journey to Mecca gives him the title of *hadj*, and his friends prepare for his honoured return by painting hideous representations of the camels, trains, and ships, by which he is supposed to have travelled, on his house wall round the doorway.

But it should be remembered that sacred pilgrimages in the East are not confined to the Moslems. The Copt should strive equally to visit Jerusalem, and to bathe in the Jordan. In Egypt they are both unconsciously carrying on a custom of the ancients, for the pilgrimage to a temple was an earnest obligation and a sacred adventure; also to be painted on the houses.

When guests arrived in ancient days they were offered a small cup of wine and a nosegay of flowers. Now there is the inevitable cup of coffee and the cigarette. It is the very modern and travelled Copt who departs from this custom, universal to Moslem and Christian alike, and orders the whisky bottle and the syphon.

The Copt should be jealous of preserving the coffee-drinking custom, for it was to a Coptic monk, so says a tradition, that its discovery is due; his experiments to find something that would enable him to keep awake for his long devotions in the night, led him to decide that the coffee berry was the very thing he sought.

It is impolite to offer a full cup of coffee, and I have only rarely seen a second cup offered; I have been told that to offer a third cup would be taken as a studied insult—"the third for the sword," as the saying has it.

Our host is of the old-fashioned order, so that we sip our coffee on the sunny side of the courtyard, where seats have been placed and rugs spread for us, while all the uninterrupted life of a feudal stronghold goes on around us.

In the middle of the great courtyard is a beautiful spreading sycamore tree, in the branches of which numbers of birds are chattering. One or two groups of the children of servants are sitting under its shade, gazing at the visitors and exchanging amusing comments about us. Their highly coloured garments make a gay note in the scene. A few of them are negroes, born of the *bowabs*, the gatekeepers who sit silently on guard by the entrance, having their home in the small single rooms on each side of the doorway. Service in Egypt never means celibacy; the significance of the fateful word "encumbrances" is unknown either to master or man. It is this sort of life that we read of in early pages of the Bible, where there are so many references to the children of the servants—"the son of thine handmaid."

The primitive Eastern people hold celibacy in the utmost detestation, as childlessness is a terrible infliction. Religious monasticism, although it was the early growth of the Coptic Church, has made no impression on the views of the people on this matter. The Oriental also hates a hairless masculine face.

The position of our host is like that of a feudal lord, and the people look to him for countenance and protection, and give him reverence, as did the serfs of old. The negro *bowab*, who keeps the gate, has little to do, for entry to the courtyard is practically free, not only for those who have even a pretence of business, but for any one who desires to feast his eyes on the grandeur of his overlord, or merely wishes to enjoy a drink of water from the great *gulah*, or *zir*, under the shade of the tree, and to rest, in a squatting position, on one of the mats on the ground; or, if he chooses to sit on one of the wooden seats provided, the slippers are dropped off and the legs are almost always drawn up on to the seat with the arms clasped round them. It was so that the ancient Egyptian sat, as the monuments illustrate.

There is one form of resting, which Christianity and Mohammedanism have alike made impossible. On the ancient monuments men are seen resting on one knee, especially in the presence of superiors; but since the Prophet's day it has been universally held that it is wrong for any man to prostrate himself except to God alone.

I have seen a poor man who in distress was humbly suing for favour from a Pasha, take dust from the ground of the courtyard and press it to his lips as a form of deep obeisance; but the same man would not prostrate himself, even to the Khedive.

All day the courtyard is the meeting-place of all in the neighbourhood who have any leisure—the men, the women, and the children. Old men who are past work spend many hours here every day, enjoying a sight of the activities of the place, telling their beads if they are Moslems;[1] muttering their prayers, "Our Fathers," and "Kyrie Eleisons," if they are Copts, also with a rosary; exchanging reminiscences of days long past, when life was a sterner thing than now, and every back of men of their order was scarred with the tyrant's whip.

The night watchmen, with their long staves, are here to make report; the fun-loving donkey-boys, with their whips, await orders.

Generally there is a group of young men and old lying on the ground playing those simple games with stones, which the ancients played. If we think them childish games, we may conclude that these simple folk are all children.

And always there reigns, however many people are assembled, a stillness and gravity peculiar to the Oriental. It must not be thought, because these people are not boisterous, that they are melancholy. There is a brightness about them which is no less joyous because it is subdued. Their appreciation of drollery and mirth is unquenchable. They show the greatest court to any man who can "give a good answer," or who excels in mimicry, or has any touch of wit or humour.

Perhaps it is because his mirth never depends on any degree of intoxication that the Egyptian fellah[2] is not boisterous: one hears the cheerful laugh, although it is seldom very loud; but the guffaws and the shouting of the common people who assemble in the beery resorts

---

[1] The Moslem does not use his rosary for prayer, but to mark his recitation of the ninety-nine excellent names of God, with which the very pious would always "keep their tongues moist."

[2] I use the word here in the sense accepted by Europeans, of the country labourer; fellah is, however, the name given to all engaged in agriculture in Egypt, rich or poor.

of Western lands are never heard. The Oriental is taught from early youth that every form of self-demonstration is impoliteness to be discountenanced.

The Egyptian of any wealth, never, under any circumstances, lives on the ground floor of any house or hotel, whether in town or in country; to sleep there, especially, he thinks highly injurious to health. It is therefore on the first floor that the reception-rooms are found, to which we are now taken.

Here are the broad and brightly covered divans of the East, running round the room, and the floor coverings of costly and beautiful rugs. There are many windows, often in a state of ill-repair; some will not shut, or odd panes are cracked or broken. This is an instance of how the Egyptian can make an excellent garment, but will not sew on the last button. Fortunately he likes fresh air in his apartments, and wrapping himself up in the evening when he sits indoors he inhales "the life-giving breath of the north," with the same pleasure as did his early ancestors, who used this exact expression in the hieroglyphics to describe the north wind. In the Book of Job it speaks of "fair weather cometh out of the north."

The Arab's hatred of wind, which the Prophet himself shared, is solely confined in Egypt to the *khamseen*, that hot and sand-laden breath of the desert, which is indeed a thing to dread, when its season approaches.

There are two great suites of rooms, traversing the whole length of the buildings; each room leading out of the other, so that to reach the apartment at the end one must go through the whole suite—an arrangement which to remotest times has been customary in Egypt. One suite is open to visitors, the other is *hareem*, or "reserved," to use the word which has been so mischievously distorted in the West. The hareem, in this instance, is merely the wing of the house in which the family lives; it is reserved for the wife and children, and no one of the male sex outside a certain degree of relationship may visit it.

It is often asked if the Copts follow the same customs in the seclusion and veiling of women as do the Moslems. The question needs a careful answer, because a certain number of educated and enlightened Egyptian Christians have broken away, since the British occupation, from the old customs which till then were universally followed by Copt and Moslem alike.

The rich Coptic ladies of Assiout, for instance, have entirely discarded the veil, and move about as freely as if they were in England, except for such slight compromise as is made necessary by the fact that it is still a matter of comment for them to be seen in public in a country where seclusion is the rule.

In Fayoum, again, a few ladies of the upper and middle class are banded together to advance their position on Western lines. In Cairo and Alexandria there are families where the home-life knows nothing of seclusion or reserved apartments: friends of both sexes are invited to the lunch and dinner table, and perfect freedom of intercourse has become the rule.

I have met in this way a number of very intelligent Coptic ladies. They are often beautiful, with a gentle charm born of the hidden life from which they have just emerged, enhanced by a pretty self-possession which their excellent education by foreign governesses from France and England has cultivated. They speak our language perfectly, and turn with easy fluency to the speech they use when on their yearly shopping excursions in Paris, where they buy all their clothes—indeed, their native Arabic does not go so far towards classical perfection as do these acquired languages.

A very accomplished and charming Coptic girl friend of my wife's writes not only English prose which would do credit to a graduate of Girton, but English verse, in which her Oriental imagination finds rich expression.

But interesting as it is to find this advance, it has to be admitted that it is confined to a very small class. Strict seclusion, and the closely drawn veil, must still be described as the Coptic rule; and that not alone amongst the rustic and the ignorant. There are young men who, in spite of education in the learned centres of Europe (perhaps because of it), have determined that the Oriental customs, so far as they are concerned, shall be conserved. I know more than one young Copt, graduates of English Universities, who have returned to Egypt, determined to keep their young wives strictly veiled and secluded.

With the great bulk of the people, rich and poor, the matter has scarcely been questioned. In the heart of Cairo I have visited Copts of all classes, from my wealthy country host in his town house to the government official, and from young professional men to the priests and singers of the church, without ever seeing a sign of the wives and daughters of the family. Just as in the Moslem households, my wife has been taken off alone to the Coptic hareem, and it has been through her that I have heard of all the interesting life that is going on behind those guarded doors.

It must not be supposed that the women, in their seclusion, are caged birds beating their wings against gilded prison bars. There has been more nonsense written about the hareem than about any other of the details of Oriental life, concerning which Western writers are so fruitful in the false (and often salacious) deductions with which they cover their want of exact knowledge.

It has always been one of the libels most readily accepted in Western lands, that the wearing of the veil and the seclusion of the hareem were the invention of the Prophet Mohammed, maintained by his debased followers, and that the Christians in Egypt had perforce to adopt the pernicious customs from their Arab conquerors.

It is rather to ancient Egypt, and to Old Testament times, that such a position of women as these things imply, must be traced. The Syrian women depicted by Renan, just as did the women of old Egypt, held themselves aloof from the general activities and social interests of their lords, content to look after his well-being at a distance, to receive him with gentleness when he visited them, and to find their pleasure in a thousand feminine ways, surrounded by their beloved children; to receive their friends, and return their visits, to discuss, as all women do, the clothes they will wear, and all the family news, in great detail.

The ladies of the hareem in such a house as this we are visiting are not idle, as is generally supposed. The care of their households occupies them a great deal; and their skill in certain details of cooking is a thing they delight in. They are worthy of their ancient ancestry in the perfection of the innumerable pasties they make for the great feasts in which their lords and their friends have pleasure.

In the matter of dress, there is prolonged and serious consideration of the rich stuffs, and of the costly jewels sent by the city merchants for inspection. The silks and satins chosen will be bright in colour, sheeny or iridescent, with tissues of silver and gold. As for jewellery, in no country is the artificer in precious metals and stones so important a personage; if you know where to look for them you will find rarer jewels and more beautiful settings in Cairo than in Paris. The favourite jeweller is kept continually at work for ladies with even moderate wealth; for if they are not adding to their possessions, they are having the costly tiara, or the heavy necklace, or bracelets, remodelled, so that they may renew their delight in their diamonds, and pearls, rubies, and emeralds—the favourite stones.

And when the lady of this class is not so engaged, the embroidery frame is in her hands, with skilful and beautiful results. The selection of the many Eastern perfumes which she and her daughters use is one of her minor occupations; she is a good judge, and as her husband also uses a favourite scent—probably it will be jasmine—she will select this for him. She uses henna to stain the nails of her feet and hands to add to their beauty (apart from its more lavish ceremonial use), and antimony to make the eyes look long.

If she retains her husband's affection, the Egyptian lady asks nothing more for perfect happiness; indeed, if he were to suggest a removal of the boundaries which are supposed to make a prisoner of her, she would think his care and love were deserting her, and all the world would seem for her to be falling in ruin.

Very many of the marriages are perfectly happy; and if the old suggestion is made that the women are mere toys of the men, I can say that I know of numbers of clever women whose intelligence and character are greatly respected by their husbands; of many a hareem which is the favourite resort at all times of the husband

and sons, who never take a single important step in life without seeking the wise counsel of the gracious lady who reigns there—the lady who, when the closing days of a long life are in sight, still retains the veneration and respect of all the men who have the right of entry to her domain.

When we had arrived in the courtyard, we were quite sure that behind the lattices of the women's apartments many curious eyes had observed us, and chattering tongues had acutely discussed every detail of our appearance, and our travelling possessions.

I was sure the ladies were delighted at the pleasure we showed in our greetings of the children, who had come down to join their father in our welcome, for we have long since learned enough of Oriental lore to know how to use discretion in conveying to proud parents our admiration of their beautiful offspring, so as not to scare them with all the awful fears of the envious eye, which have abated no whit with time's advance. The belief in "the evil eye" is both primeval and universal, and in many countries is as current to-day as it was in prehistoric times.[1] "Ma'shallah!" we say, as the children greet us; "Praised be God!" "May God

---

[1] What in English is called "the evil eye" has its equivalent in every written language. Shakspere calls it "overlooking." The mistake is often made of thinking this is an Eastern belief, and possibly Moslem. In Italy one cannot live an hour amongst the people without being confronted with the superstition. Modern science and education have done nothing to weaken the belief. Certain people have the power of casting a malignant spell through the glance of the eye, especially when they are displeased. At the root of the idea it will always be found that *envy* is the destroying spirit. Our English word *envy* means a malignant or hostile feeling arising from jealousy. When Saul envied David he "eyed" him from that day (1 Sam. xviii. 9), the same idea running all through the Old Testament envy being an evil to pray against. It is significant that a whole Commandment deals with covetousness. In the mercy of God, "His eye is upon man for good."

keep them for you!" "Ma'shallah! May God let them grow and bless them!" And we do not let the parents know but that we too have a quiverful of children, *almost* as beautiful as these, for only by such means will they have any delight in our admiration.

I have myself seen children of the rich, especially the boys, allowed to run about shabby and dirty, so as to escape the eye of envy—though this habit is dying out, especially in the cities, where the children are often nowadays beautifully dressed, and are cared for by French and English nurses and governesses.

CHAPTER II

The Home-Life of the Squire

LATER, as we rest in one of the suite of rooms, which are, we know, used as reception-rooms, or bedrooms, according to the needs of the moment (it only wants the spreading of mattresses and sleeping rugs to change them from one to the other), our host discreetly questions us as to our preferences in the matter of food, while he tries to find out what are our usual times for meals. A gentle battle of polite evasions arises between us, my desire being to follow the customs of the house, while courtesy demands of him to adapt his whole establishment to the predilections, however foreign, of his guests.

He claps his hands, and the servant whose chief care is the commissariat quietly appears, holds himself erect and with dignity, while he receives from his lord the softly muttered orders, making no response but the Arabic word which may be translated "Perfectly."

He then disappears, to translate the necessary details to Marcus the cook, a valued servant, of whom we later hear that he is a native genius, having gone, from a village near by, as an utterly illiterate youth, to Cairo, where his talent in cooking was developed in the kitchen of a great hotel. The powers of memory and of observation in Eastern people have always been wonderful: this man seems never to have forgotten anything he ever learned; he cooks equally well in the native or the Parisian way. If he is asked to provide a French meal, he will insist on a menu being written out, dictating correctly the French name of each item. To-day, by our special desire, Marcus is to cook a purely Egyptian meal.

While the food is preparing, our host invites us to stroll with him through his garden, to enjoy the cooler air now that the sun is setting. An Egyptian garden is at the same time an exquisite delight and an indefinable disappointment. There are at all times flowers in abundance, and the warm rich fragrance in which one is steeped at every turn is a revelation to the senses. The Egyptian counts everything that grows, however beautiful, a mere nameless weed, and no flower, unless it gives forth a pleasing scent.

Here are roses in rich abundance in January, bringing a wealth of colour to the scene; here is a great hedge of jasmine, white with its large blooms, breathing a delicate ecstasy; and orange trees in blossom, inviting us to delights embarrassing in their profusion.

When we reach the prosaic corner devoted to vegetable production, we find the fragrant bean deliberately cultivated for its scent, for our host has scores of acres of beans growing on his home farm.

But what is it about these gardens which, for all their varied delights, disappoints? For one thing, the sober repose of the well-tilled soil of England is impossible where a daily flooding and splashing of water, brought from the river, is the only way to keep anything alive—the splashing which turns the flower-beds into untidy muddy spaces. Then, the paths of an Oriental garden are, in the absence of anything like pavement or gravel, never pleasing to the eye which delights in contour and neatness.

And above all, there is nothing comparable to our English lawns to be found in this land, where in the hot days of summer all grass must perish, so that a new crop has to be cultivated every winter; and consequently it never makes anything but a green pretence of a lawn to those who know the richness of the English sward, sometimes centuries old.

Having thrown off the cares of the day, our host is now in a humorous and genial mood. As we wander about the garden, he invites us to gather and eat of the many fruits; knowledge of the length of Egyptian banquets, however, makes us discreet, and we leave such delicacies as ripe green figs, oranges, strawberries, and other rare fruits, untasted.

There is often occasion to remark on the fact that the Oriental always does everything in an exactly opposite way from the Western people. This applies equally to the things he eats. The same taste which leads him to prefer the green end of a radish, accounts for my host gathering the young flowers and the shoots of the green pea, which he commends to me as far more delicious than the peas which I persist in taking from the pod.

Laughingly he tells me one of those stories which are current in the East. The most sacred duty of any man, and of those of nomadic descent especially—and there are many pure Arabs wandering the deserts of Egypt, some of them of great wealth—is that of unstinting hospitality. It is as important as to be brave.

There was once a bedouin who, although he was not poor, had so far forgotten the traditions of his ancient race, that he meanly begrudged the refreshment of travellers, who in that remote region so confidently crossed the threshold of his tents. To say them nay was unthinkable to bedouin pride, but this man, in his meanness, cunningly sought to be rid of the hungry wayfarers at the least possible expense.

While the meal they expected was preparing, he would take them for a long-drawn-out visit to his garden, and as he talked with them he repeatedly gathered handfuls of beans[1]—the cheapest food in Egypt—for them to eat. Long delay, of which no man would complain in the dilatory East, made them hungry, and all unsuspectingly they became replenished before the more costly goods were ready; at which the man, whose meanness disgraced the noble race of those whose pride it is to dwell in tents, as their forefather Abraham did, was gratified.

With laughter in his eyes, my host declared that this was his reason for bringing us to the beans, while his feast was cooking!

We now return to the house, where in the great reception-room preparations are almost complete for the banquet.

It is easy to forget, at times, in such entertainments, that there is any distinction between Copts and Moslems; there is one thing, however, that will almost always come up to remind us. The whisky bottle and the liqueur decanter, even in the most temperate households, make their appearance in the last period of waiting for dinner, and some of the men drink, as an *aperitif*, nibbling the while at tiny dishes of Eastern *hors-d'œuvre*; for it is a belief of the Copts that it is injurious to drink spirits

---

[1] All Egyptians eat the young beans in a raw state, often in great quantities—they are tender, and delicious in taste.

without some sort of food. The choice is offered to the visitor of every sort of Scotch and Irish liquor, of all the famous brands.

Several large round trays have been placed on low portable stands; properly, we should seat ourselves on the floor, but a concession has been made to our different habits by the provision of chairs.

The first act of ceremony at a banquet is to go to the table and secure one's serviette, as large as a towel, and then withdraw again to the outer hall, where two or more servants are waiting with the water-jugs (the *ibreek*) so that we may wash our hands over the basin (called *tisht*) in running water. It is a never-failing source of surprise to the Oriental that any one can bring himself to wash, even his hands, in standing or "dead" water—to him the habit is too dirty to contemplate. We make a great lather with the soap, for it is polite to show particularity in washing the hands before food. We dry our hands on our serviettes, and at once return to the table, the host being the last to wash.

The company is now in merriest mood; we all beam with gaiety, and a charm steals over us which it is difficult to suggest to those who have never experienced it. One element of the sorcery which the Oriental wields in his hospitality, is a soothing feeling that one is amongst friends or brothers; the atmosphere is that of a form of good breeding which puts no check on good humour. It is subtly conveyed to you, that, as a guest, you are the object of every attention, while no sign obtrudes itself even of the solicitude of which you are the object, which might ruffle your peaceful enjoyment.

The Oriental is incapable of suffering sombre thoughts of the future; he indeed realises that sufficient unto the day is the evil thereof; that the morrow is in the hands of God, whose concern it remains.

The gravest of the Egyptians—and some Orientals of middle life can be very grave—are still by nature the children of a joyous sociability, able to surround their friends with such an atmosphere of good humour and a forgetfulness of the sterner claims of life, that even an Englishman finds it easy in such society to turn awhile from the displeasures of memory, and the irksomeness of duty, and even the claims of time itself, in the blissful content of the moment.

It has been told of the present Sultan of Morocco, that lately he gave a banquet at Fez, to the French Resident-General. The guest noticed that the clocks in the palace were all stopped, and hinted that he would like to present His Majesty with a timepiece that would keep time. The Sultan's answer was characteristic of the manners of the Orient. "The clocks were stopped by my orders," he said. "During your Excellency's too brief stay with us, why be reminded of the flight of the hours?" God made eternity; man invented the despotism of the timepiece.

With Moslems, the Eastern graciousness of manner is perhaps more marked than with my Coptic friends, and I can only think that something is sacrificed to the artificial stimulus imported from the stills of Northern Britain. The Koran prohibits all intoxicating drink.

A great deal of the charm which distinguishes the Oriental as a conversationalist comes from the picturesque language in which he instinctively clothes anything he has to say; and from the inherited wisdom that finds expression in the wealth of proverb always to hand. At such gatherings as this, I always note the proverbs that flow so easily into the conversation. I take these from my notes of this occasion :

A MONASTERY IN THE REMOTE DESERT.
"Deir Siriam" or the Syrian Monastery.

THE HEAD OF A DESERT MONASTERY (LEANING ON HIS STAFF) AND HIS YOUNGEST ACOLYTE.
The Monastery of Anba Bishai.

THE CHIEF NAZIR OF THE PASHA.
With some of the clerks, awaiting us at one of the farms. They have decorated the gateway in our honour.

THE MONASTERY OF JEREMIAS AT ASSOUAN.

"A man who is bitten by a serpent will be frightened by the sight of a rope."

"A man who has no brother is like a person who has a left arm, but no right."

"Stretch your legs according to the coverlet."

"He is your brother who shares your disaster."

"Be as friends in social life, but be as strangers in business."

"The devil is no match for an old woman."

"Without human companions Paradise itself would be an undesirable place." (This is the more remarkable because it is also a Moslem proverb.)

"The truest man on earth is he who remembers his friend when he is absent, when he is in distress, and when he is dying."

"An unmarried daughter has a broken wing."

"The central gate of heaven is open to the man who has been dutiful to his parents."

"Paradise is opened at the command of mothers." (This is a variant of the Moslem proverb, "Paradise is at the feet of the mother.")

It was interesting to find here a proverbial saying to denote a profitless character—You can do nothing with such a man, "his mind is salt." I remembered that it is recorded of one of the monks of Lower Egypt, as long since as the fourth century, that certain brethren entreated Abba Epiphanius on one occasion, saying, "Father, speak unto us some word of life, even though when thou speakest we may not grasp the seed of thy word, because the soil is salt."

A rich man of a neighbouring village was mentioned, with a guarded expression of disapproval, put in the form of an ancient proverb, "Grass grows on his fireplace." This was a familiar saying in Egypt fifteen centuries ago, applied to a man lacking in the virtue of hospitality.

Another saying was used, which I have heard before in Egypt. " He only loosed the tent-peg " was amusingly applied to a man present, who had, a few years since, created a great deal of strife in the Church, on the occasion of the visit of the Patriarch, when the ill-feeling between those Copts who had joined the American Presbyterians and those who remained orthodox, had led to a riot. The man protested that what he had said and done was so trifling that he should not be blamed. Our host quietly agreed that the man " had only loosed the tent-peg a little," the comment provoking such general merriment that I begged for the origin of the saying. It is this.

A young *afreet*, a very fiend for mischief, travelling with an older being, in passing through a peaceful encampment one night, set the whole place in a terrible uproar. When the old man accused him, he denied that he had done anything to account for the hubbub. "What then has caused it?" "I can't imagine unless the sheikh's stallion has broken loose. He was tethered to a tent-peg, and I thought I would just see if he was properly fastened. I may have loosed the peg a little."

Personal gossip, however, especially of a spiteful nature, is cautiously avoided, in conversation of this sort, lest any kind of offence, however indirect, should be given; though this does not say that the Egyptian is not a shrewd judge of character. The Government, on the contrary, in all conversation is criticised with astonishing freedom of speech; and weird alternative political schemes, from those before the country, are suggested in such terms as make one think of debates in Bedlam.

The Home-Life of the Squire 35

Comical stories and adventures are related, great feats are recalled, and blood-curdling ghost stories are told. To-night many incredible tales are related of the miracles of the venerable and sainted Bishop of Fayoum, to be capped by a Moslem present who relates legends of the magic powers of a sheikh who lives beyond Assiout. The conversation is at the same time polite and courtly, fanciful and eloquent, and always illuminated by simile and apt comparison; the accompanying gestures helping the speaker's meaning. I do not think I go too far when I assert that such conversation is brilliant, with a vein of native intelligence running through it which redeems it from the narrowness of information and from the reproach of the superstitiousness which characterise every remark.

On the table in place of cutlery we have only one wooden spoon; the only crockery consists of plates, and these are of modern introduction—they are unnecessary to the men of old-fashioned habits. We have great pieces of the thin flat cakes of the country, which we break into pieces small enough to dip into the round dishes (put on the centre of the tables) to secure the morsels we desire. In the case of soup, we use our wooden spoons, all dipping into the one tureen. When fowls and turkeys appear, the strong fingers of our host, assisted by his guests, tear them apart, and we are invited to appropriate the tenderest pieces.

The feature of all such banquets as this is a sheep roasted whole; it will have been killed that morning according to the rites which have been the custom in Egypt ever since, and even long before, the days of Moses. I cannot say I enjoy the sight of this whole sheep, but knowing that it is a tribute of honour to a guest, I join in its disintegration with what Dickens calls "impartial eyebrows." Fortunately none of the dishes stay long; it is the chief guest's privilege to waive them aside to the servants, though it is only an Egyptian who ever exercises the right. The European guest can never bring himself to accept the position of lord in another man's house, which the native knows is the right of a guest of honour. After a long succession of courses the welcome sweets at last arrive, signal that fruit will follow.

At last the end of the banquet is reached, and in the promiscuous way that is here polite we leave the table one by one, the moment we have finished, going straight to the same servants who are waiting without, to lave our hands again; our host being the last to leave the feast.

While we wash, other servants remove all sign of our repast, even to the tables, and when we return, we sit upon the broad divans, drawing our feet up under us, after slipping off our shoes. And then we sip a special coffee of Arabia—so delicious and scarce that the connoisseurs of the East take care that it is not wasted on the coarse palates of Europe—while we smoke the cigarettes for which Egypt is famed.

A native concert has been arranged for our entertainment, and soon we adjourn to the balcony leading from our apartments and overlooking the great courtyard, which is illuminated with modern lamps, and where great numbers of dependants of the house and fellaheen from the villages have already assembled, and are sitting on the ground in picturesque groups, every sound and gesture expressing pleased expectancy.

The intense soul-stirring pleasure which the fellaheen—indeed, the Egyptian of every class—derive from the native singing, is an experience outside that of the folk of more northern climes. It has been so from the time when history began.

The performers on this occasion are two men from different villages, between which an endless feud goes on as to the rival talents of their respective favourites, in whom the whole countryside delights. The performers trust to memory for an endless repertoire of native songs, and are entirely self-taught in the marvellous skill with which they play the instrument called the *kemengeh*.

The sounding body of this primitive viol is nothing but part of a cocoa-nut, but playing with his bow upon its two strings the performer will stir the whole gamut of primeval emotion in his audience, as he accompanies the Eastern songs, of love and passion, of mirth and pride, of the deep delights of the tent and the caravan, of running water and green oasis, of the thrill of battle, and the contest of wit and repartee.

In choosing such singers, no thought would ever be given by their employers as to whether they were Moslem or Copt; and in giving their entertainment, it would never occur to the singers that it was necessary to consider the religion of their host. This I discovered when one of them burst forth into that passionate pilgrim song in which the Moslems express the intensity of their longing for Mecca and the other holy places of their religion. My host and all his Coptic friends saw nothing at all incongruous in this. And once or twice when the minstrel sang those impassioned songs in praise of the Prophet, which one hears in all Islamic lands, the only answer to my remark on it was, " You see, he is a Moslem."

The men take it in turn to sing, and it is amusing to see the partisanship between the different groups favouring each performer. The people do not wait for the end of a song to show their approval; after almost every line they express their pleasure by intense and long-drawn ejaculations—"Al-*lah*! Al-*lah*!"

The faithfulness of the Egyptians to a singer who has pleased them is lifelong; the star performer in Cairo whose sweet monotones have commended him to the city audience is sure of an enthusiastic following so long as he has strength to face them, just as the village idol is secure in the affections of his countryside.

I could not resist the desire to leave the lordly company of the balcony, during an interval in the singing, to provoke the clans in defence of their favourites, by mischievously praising each in turn to the opposite camp. The hubbub was delightful; the partisanship was so childlike in its earnestness, and so picturesque in its expression. The singing of one was "less than the creaking of a broken water-wheel"; the other was "like the bellowing of the kine, or the baying of the dogs to the moon." Was I not pleased with *this* man; he should sing to me his song of the love of Yussef the potter, and then I should know purest bliss, and acknowledge that earth could not have a rival to such an artist.

And when I got back to the balcony the rivalry seemed to have stirred the singers to a greater intensity of expression; and I own to being deeply affected by the passionate recitatives, and the obbligato, which with weird emphasis supplemented the emotional appeal of the performer's voice. There were times when the tapping of the little drum, or *darabukeh*, alone accompanied the telling of a story, conveying a thrill which gives even a European a glimpse of that excitement which in the Oriental often leads to an unearthly ecstasy.

There is no doubt that the modern Egyptians of

The Home-Life of the Squire 39

the landed class are conscious of the dignity they gain from appearing to their dependants on these balconies, which every important house possesses, generally enclosed with the intricate lattice woodwork, in arabesque design, so wrongly called *mushrabieh* in such a case, for that Arabic word merely means "a place for drink," and applies only to that part of a hareem window-screen where the water-bottle is placed to keep it cool.

It is interesting to reflect that the "arabesque" designs are so little Arab in origin that in tombs dating more than three thousand years before our era, Egyptian art used these ornamentations for decorative purposes. The ceilings of some of the tombs show us finished examples of designs of the most delicate and graceful order, in which a rich fancy, given full play, has produced effects that charm the eye.

I think one may see, in this as in so many other details of Egyptian life, some support for the claim of the Copts to descend from the Pharaohs. They seem to have some right to assert that they have brought from the ancient civilisation some of the arts which, under their conquerors, have so greatly enriched the world, in Constantinople and even in remoter Spain, as well as in Egypt.

The Moslems have always admired this sort of decoration, which they probably saw first in the glorious examples in Coptic churches of Old Cairo. I have heard a friend say, in contemplating the rich effects wrought by it in one of the mosques, that the beauty of these designs could only have been imagined in heaven; and that it is a belief of the unlettered that man was first taught the art of inlaying of mother-of-pearl in ebony in such designs by the beneficent *ginn* who learned it in Paradise itself.

As for the balcony: there is in a tomb dated the XVIth century before Christ, a representation of one of these balconies, where the mysterious King Amenophis IV., in the company of his wife and daughter, is throwing jewels and decorations to one of his officers, as a reward for faithful service in a town recently founded in honour of the deity he worshipped. Our balcony to-night is decorated by costly rugs thrown over the sides, just as was that of the far-off king, who is shown resting his hands on the beautiful tapestry.

We eventually retire to rest in a chamber elaborately furnished in the style of a first-class Parisian hotel: our host regards all its costly elaboration of modern comfort with pride, as one who has understood and provided for the needs of European guests; though I know the bedsteads and other furnishings are to his habits totally unnecessary. In one detail, especially, the Oriental can never get over the astonishment which I have already mentioned, and which the provision of our European water-jugs and basins remind him of: we are pressed to say if we would not prefer a man-servant to come to us with the spouted brass ewer, so that our ablutions may be decently made with running water! We have to decline, of course.

As a final courtesy, it is pointed out that two servants will sleep on their mattresses within reach of our door, ready to serve us if any sort of necessity should arise during the night.

In the morning, after a simple breakfast, of which the tiny eggs of the country are the chief item—they are so small that it did not seem remarkable for a young countryman present to eat eight of them—we sat for a while in the courtyard while our host got through the ordinary business with the *nazirs*, who govern under him his great estates. It is astonishing the number and variety of servants employed in administrative work on such estates in Egypt. And most of the staff, with many of the handicraftsmen, gather for service within the precincts of the castle.

The *katibs*, or clerks, are the largest class, as they are, in their own estimation, by far the most important. From the earliest historic empire of Egypt this class of men has taken a large part in the nation's work; for it has always been the habit in Egypt to write innumerable letters, the governing power seeming to find its chief expression in this way, and to this day the clerks in Egypt are nearly all Copts, whether the master be Moslem or Christian.

The head of the clerks is the overlord's confidential secretary, who takes part in all important deliberations. This too is a post which has been most often reserved for Copts, even in the counsels of the Khedive, where Copts have sometimes risen to be the virtual rulers of the country.

The work of the office is subdivided amongst the clerks, so that not only is each fellah employed on the estate known there by name, with a complete dossier of his history, but the animals are all recorded, even to the latest additions; it must have been in Egypt that "red tape" originated in the dawn of history, and its hold has never loosened.

The clerk is a being lowly towards his superiors, though filled with pride as he contemplates the untutored fellah beneath him; his mind for ever dwells ambitiously on the advancement which may come to him if he is faithful—he may rise to a place of confidence or (and this is the seventh heaven) he may be promoted to his master's estate office in Cairo.

How little do things change in the land of Egypt! It is recorded of a certain clerk in the XVIIIth dynasty, 1600 years before the Christian era, that in his ambitious dreams he saw himself "sailing up the Nile for Memphis," the Cairo of his day.

On one side of the courtyard the harness-makers are always busy, for the beasts of burden, the asses, the mules, the camels, are innumerable; it must be remembered that the distant railway counts for little on an estate like this, and the absence of roads means that almost everything that must be moved is put upon the animals' backs; and, where no one walks who has any right even to an ass, the wear of the saddles is great. The chief man in charge of the animals must be ready at all times to provide means of progression for his master, and all the family, and guests; to fetch parties of officials from the station, to send out pleasure excursions, and to equip men for all the innumerable business journeys to all parts of the estate.

In another workshop close by are the wheelwrights, whose work has changed no whit since the days of the Pharaohs; they are fashioning the *sakieh* (water-wheel), and the *shadoof*, the simple appliance by which the water is raised from the Nile level on to the higher land by the mere process of balancing the water vessel with a ball of mud of equal weight at the other end of a pole, which is worked on a swivel. They are making a chariot, too, for carrying heavy weights, chiefly sugar cane, and sometimes heavy stones for the making of canal banks—such a chariot as Egypt has known from its earliest civilisation. The wheels are rough solid discs, so that, drawn by the two slow and sure-footed *gamooses* (very like bulls), they can stand the jolting over the ill-formed tracts, or up and down across the channels of the dried-up canals.

I have often to repeat how the early life of the Bible is seen in every phase of Egyptian life as soon as one leaves the haunts of the tourist, or the *effendi*, those city gentlemen who love to mimic Europe in all their ways. From the time that "Jacob sent messengers before him to Esau" (Gen. xxxii. 3), and Joseph's brethren "sent a messenger" unto him (Gen. l. 16), this particular servant figures in most of the scenes of Egyptian life, as well as in many pictures of the *Iliad* and the *Odyssey*. And here to-day the man himself, true to every detail of those pictures, which so delighted our youthful imagination, stands before us. On every estate of any size the messenger is a trusted servant, waiting to bear for his master every word which it is necessary to send to men at a distance, and to loyally execute the commissions of those members of the household whose position entitles them to give them.

To have such a man in one's service makes life very easy; so that even the rich man living in retirement will never part with a faithful messenger. Who of us, having acquaintance with the East, does not know this quiet, alert, prudent, courteous, and dignified servant, a sort of second self, who takes the softly murmured orders of the Pasha, and carries them out as though but one will actuated himself and his master.

In a country where the hunger for *backsheesh* is declared to be universal, such a messenger, if one were so indiscreet as to offer it, would, with simple pride, look away from the offered coin, saying gently, "I have no need of it," in a tone which was final. If a meal at your expense (should you meet him in Cairo) is suggested, he says "No" with Oriental politeness—your words are all the nourishment he requires.

What he always claims is to receive audience of the

man to whom he is accredited, no matter what his position, or the business on which he is sent; he will brook no intermediary either then or on his return to his master. He always has the special gift of remembering the exact words, as well as the details, of the business on which he is sent, adding nothing and taking nothing away. These are the qualities which have given the messenger such an important place in the Orient, as in all the ancient civilisations.

CHAPTER III

Country Rambles and Chats with Bedouins and Fellaheen

AT last our host is free from the many claims upon him, and we are ready to start on a little tour of the domain. It is a delightful experience, on a glorious morning like this, to wander about such an estate, to be greeted, as I know we shall be everywhere, with signs of pleasure by the simple fellaheen.

To keep the whole estate in touch with the centre, a system of light railway has been built, which is lengthened as the level land is increased. At present it is about eight miles long, and we travel from point to point on the little open cars built for passengers. We are accompanied by the chief *nazir*, for I am particularly interested in seeing the reclamation of the sandy desert and of the salt land of the Delta, which has been going on.

The process of reclamation, briefly, is this — the desert sandhills, which were too high for irrigation, have been laboriously and slowly carried to the sour and water-logged swamp, over which the sea not very long since sluggishly found its way. By careful and scientific calculation as to levels, and the possibility of bringing the fresh water of the river to the new elevation, and by enriching the sand with chemical food, the country has seen miracles of fertility performed. The succession of three valuable crops are already gathered here in the year, including cotton and corn, in the place of one crop, and that a matter of uncertainty depending on the Nile floods.

Where such work has been skilfully and judiciously done it has brought wealth to the man who had the faith a few years since to give money for the apparently almost worthless swamp. This very land which was bought for a few pounds, is now worth from £150 to £250 an acre.

The process of reclamation is not, however, a matter so free from obstacles and difficulties as might be supposed from this description, and some men have, by miscalculation and bad management, poured fortunes into the desert sand, without winning the rosy smiles which they had anticipated.

But if this particular land is once properly reclaimed it is, as Pharaoh described it to Joseph, "the best of the land" of Egypt; for we are in the veritable land of Goshen, where Israel came to dwell, and had possessions therein, and grew and multiplied (Gen. xlvii. 27).

Papyri of that epoch, written by Egyptian officials, contain frequent mention, in enthusiastic terms, of the charms of the country—life here was "luscious" from the beauty and fertility of the land. In the days of the Exodus, as recent surveys have shown, it owed its fertility and beauty to a branch of the Nile which ran through it and discharged its waters into the Red Sea.

In these days Goshen depends on the fresh water canal running from the river to Suez. It is still one of the most beautiful parts of Egypt, with wide stretches of rich land, great herds of cattle, and luxuriant groves of palm, bearing the best dates in Egypt. Such fruit as this is never seen in England, unless one has a friend, like the Pasha, who is kind enough to favour one every autumn with a private supply by post—for they are never exported. Even the land in the palm gardens yields a rich harvest of corn. We are reminded of the time—up to the sixth century—when Egyptian corn ships sailed every year for England to trade for tin, and "corn in Egypt" was a Western proverb. The people in Goshen are again multiplying exceedingly, to occupy the new land brought into cultivation.

To any one even vaguely familiar with the story told in the early books of the Bible, the life which hourly unfolds itself before us, as well as every detail of its geographical setting, takes on a familiarity, and an intimate faithfulness, that almost suggest to one a reincarnation, so closely does everything accord with the traits of scriptural history, which has been so wonderfully corroborated by the history which can now be read in the hieroglyphics of the ancient monuments. Here is abundant evidence of the contemporary character of the narrative of Exodus and Numbers. It is easy to see that this valley was the only convenient entrance into Egypt for Jacob with his flocks and herds. Its separation from the rest of Egypt made it a most desirable spot for the settlement of a people devoted to a pastoral existence, and differing from the mode of life of the native Egyptians. It is only by realising the galling nature of the oppression, that one can understand how they were willing eventually to leave such a land, though for the desert.

During our walk we came upon two men making the mud bricks of which all the buildings are erected, as they have been for all time. The methods of brick-making used are exactly as of old, as the pictures on the monuments testify. It could not fail to recall the particular oppression—"There shall no straw be given you, yet shall ye deliver the tale of bricks" (Ex. v. 18). I have often examined the bricks, both ancient and modern, used in different parts of Egypt, to be puzzled by the fact that straw is so very rarely found in their composition.

Professor Flinders Petrie[1] has suggested the explanation from watching the work of such men as these. They constantly use finely chopped straw in which to dip their hands to prevent the mud sticking to them, also to dust over the place where the brick is to rest, and to coat each lump of mud before dropping it into the mould. It is obvious that the work would be infinitely prolonged and vexatious without a supply of this fine straw; so that the children of Israel might well consider themselves "in evil case," in having to minish nothing of their daily tale—the "bricks without straw" of the universal proverb.

Our host was very desirous that we should pay a call upon an ancient bedouin, who for countless years had been settled on his land, and who would soon reach his hundredth birthday.

It was a long walk for an Egyptian Pasha to the old man's tents, but I gathered he had an affection for him, and often paid him a visit.

Till this day I had never myself thought that to be a centenarian could have any attraction, but when we met this tall, upright, old man, his face beaming with happiness, and heard what he had to say of life, old age took on a new aspect.

We found him sitting in the sun on a rug in front of the tent he and his wife used in the daytime.

When he caught sight of the Pasha he got up with

[1] *Egypt and Israel*, p. 33.

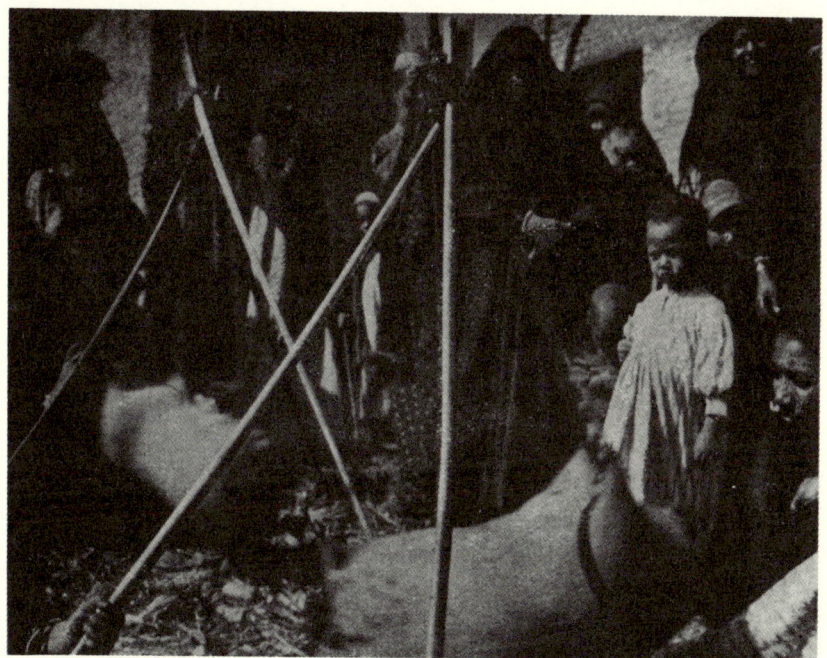

BUTTER CHURNING IN THE VILLAGE.
"Here some women are churning for butter, the milk being simply thrown from side to side in a goat's skin, suspended from a bamboo tripod."

THE OLD BEDOUIN, AGED OVER 100 YEARS, AND HIS WIFE.
The coffee beans were put into an iron ladle and roasted. They are sitting in the enclosure in front of their tent. The woman is wearing the string-woven veil of the Delta.

an ease possible only to such a spare figure, and gave us greeting with a grace which might have honoured a royal court.

With his own hands he spread more rugs for us, bidding us welcome as though to a palace. For the Frankish lady he took off his own outer burnous and spread it upon the ground, smiling the while and showing a set of regular white teeth untouched by age.

His wife was summoned, the only wife he had ever had, he told us. It was no part of her duty to share in the greetings and the entertainment, except to make the coffee, which signifies a ceremonial politeness no less in the tents of the desert than in the great houses of the plain.

The old woman, however, set about her task with greater pleasure because of the Pasha's polite recognition of her. She was closely veiled in the manner peculiar to the bedouin of the Delta, as shown in my photographs (in some parts of Africa the bedouins discard the veil), but her age (she thought she was about eighty-five) allowed more liberty than would be considered proper in a younger woman.

The two bedouin tents of the old man were merely square roofs of camels' hair stretched low over poles, open to the East, the three sides being of the same material as the roof. The second tent was for sleeping, and we could see the rolled-up rugs and blankets which made up its sole furnishing.

In front of the tent, where we sat, was an enclosure of about the same size, the three walls of which were made of the tall stalks of maize, giving a protection from the wind. Here the cooking was done, and here those guests who could not get into the small tent were quite cosily entertained. The fire for the coffee-making was made of bits of stalk and the husks of Indian corn laid upon the ground, and, owing to the peculiar gipsy skill of the old woman, was soon burning brightly.

The coffee beans were put into an iron ladle and roasted, for the bedouin would under no circumstances offer coffee to a guest which had not been made in every stage in his presence.

Quickly the beans are ground, under the pounding of a long stick, the while a jug of water, sitting on the now red-hot ashes, is brought to the boil.

The coffee is put into the jug, when a second boiling completes the process. Tiny cups are produced, and unshapely lumps of sugar are broken into pieces, of which we are offered a choice, as the half-filled cups are handed to us.

While we have had one eye upon this interesting process, we have had the other on the old man, engaged in animated talk with the Pasha. It has been upon the subject of his age; of reckoning by years he himself knows little. For one thing he is a Moslem, so that his year would be a lunar one, while the Coptic Pasha has a solar reckoning, and they calculate of course in widely differing eras. But the Pasha astutely leads him to speak of the chief doings of his youth, eventful from the fact that he served in the army of Mohammed Ali, and, here, from the safe ground of the historical dates of certain wars, the Pasha is able to estimate that the old man has possibly already passed the century of years.

Of course one always asks for the secret of unusual age, and, of course, it differs with every living soul. This cheery old man says it is the life of the tents, simple living, avoidance of wickedness, above all, his daily prayers and strict observance of the fast of

Ramadan, and those extra fasts which the old Moslem men like to observe.

"Are you tired of life?" I asked.

"No! no!" with a laugh that rings with truth. "I would like to live for five hundred years. The great God has been good to me all my days, and will always care for me. Why,"—with an air suggesting that of gratitude and pride he can say nothing beyond this,— "I have been to Mecca *twice*!"

The old nomad, I find, like all Egyptians who know the deserts, is an accomplished astronomer, with names for the constellations and ways of grouping the figures unlike those known to Englishmen.

Then we turned to less serious topics, and the Pasha chaffed the old man about a "nest egg" he must have saved—for he is a clever herdsman, his sole livelihood being derived from the flocks of sheep which he pastures by some easy arrangement with our host.

He laughingly evades the point, and replies that the Pasha has come from Cairo, and, for the first time for years, has brought him no present.

It is true, and he is asked if there is anything he particularly needs; replying that his fez is worn out.

He is promised a new fez if he will let me examine the one he is wearing.

I may here pause to remark on the difference in the clothing of the bedouins from that of the fellaheen. Many of the men still wear the raiment of camels' hair "with a girdle of skin about his loins" which John the Baptist doubtless copied from them when he sought the desert. No garment could be more suitable to that way of life.

In the heyday of life those nomads who are prosperous love to array themselves, for festivals and visits to the towns, in gay-coloured robes, winding round their heads bright-coloured turbans with tasselled ends hanging over their necks behind. An old man like our centenarian friend will dress in the white burnous; on his head he will wear a fez (over a white skull-cap), round which he will bind a white turban. The red tarbush, so familiar to the city Egyptian, is never seen in the desert.

It is apparent that a great joke lies behind this request for a new fez, and while the old man is chuckling, with feigned reluctance, the Pasha dexterously removes his outer head covering, and gleefully discovers a collection of treasures hidden in it which would have done credit to the pocket of an acquisitive schoolboy. There were several needles, with threads and wools of different sorts; a packet of cigarette papers, a number of neatly folded papers which represented all the business side of the old man's life—outside those things which with the bedouins are trusted solely to memory and to honour; the discharge of his indebtedness, and the proof of his comfortable savings. And then a long knitted purse, which was handed to the owner, who turned out its contents to prove that it held only a little silver; though the Pasha was not to be deceived, for, taking the purse again, he reversed it, when from a secret opening came tumbling three or four gold pieces. Never did two schoolboys enjoy a series of little jokes with greater gusto.

The old man, I noticed, had a good head of hair; not an encouraging fact to those who fondly imagine that by going bareheaded they will increase their locks, for the head of the Eastern man is never uncovered—day or night.

Soon we began to show signs of leaving, when the old man for the first time looked very serious, as he pressed us to stay for a meal. Did we see this fine turkey—it should be killed for us; or he would slay a lamb; he had rice and bread; and of course he had lentils—since Esau's day the favourite food of the bedouin. We should dishonour him to refuse.

We were warned, however, to be adamant, and when, after long parleying, we started forth, the graceful old man walked with us, protesting, literally with tears in his eyes, that our going in this way made him sad; and it was only a promise to repeat the visit that restored the smiles which made the old face look almost young again.

It is when one gets away from the talk and agitations, and the intriguing Press of the town, that one always finds how little division there is between the Copt and the Moslem. On this particular visit I never saw a sign of any sort of restraint or reserve in the intercourse; the Pasha indeed shows in many ways a deep interest in the religion of those of his people who are Moslems, and he discusses the details with them with a frankness only equalled by the way in which they respond. If it is suggested that this comes from his exalted position, I can say that I have stayed with a Moslem Pasha in exactly similar circumstances, and have found the same good feeling to exist between him and the men of different faith. My present host has built at his own expense a mosque; just as there are Moslem Pashas who have built Christian churches on their domains.

We next visited the two houses of prayer. This is not the place for a description of a Coptic church, which I will deal with under another heading. But I may remark, that in the church there are partitions, of *mushrabieh* work, behind which only men of the higher class are admitted for worship. In this part the floor is carpeted. In the division of the church just inside the door the lower classes assemble, the floor being bare. The women enter the church by a separate door, being closely veiled, and hide themselves behind the screens of the galleries.

In the mosque (and there is no exception to this plan from the time when the Prophet built the first House of Prayer) everything is arranged to put all men, from Pasha to serf, on terms of equality: the praying floor is open, free and undivided, and the passing beggar may, at the hour of prayer, take his place by the side of the Imam (or leader) in front of the Kiblah (the niche indicating the direction of Mecca, towards which all worshippers turn) without exciting one word of comment, much less rebuff.

On the way home we visited the powerful steam pump of which the estate is so proud, bought from a great firm in England, to supplement the canal irrigation by tapping an exhaustless well.

We called, too, at a humble dwelling by the side of a *sakieh*, where the whole family came out to greet us. One of them was a very pretty girl of fourteen, who looked demure when the Pasha asked her father if her marriage had been arranged yet; though she answered "Yes," without hesitation, to his question, "Did she want to be married?" He knew of a suitable youth who was seeking a bride, and he would see if the matter could be arranged.

We now turned to scenes of great activity in the fields; on the one side of us a large party of men were planting the cotton, for the most important crop of autumn, under the eye of an assistant *nazir*. Our party took a turn at dropping seeds into the holes made in the well-prepared earth, which only a year or two since had been yellow desert.

On the outskirts of the vast field a large gang of men were at work adding to the cultivatable area. They were steadily moving the little sandhills to the swamp level, to render desert and swamp alike fertile.

A fine, strong, handsome race are these patient toilers of the Delta, as little changed from the primitive people of Egypt as are the bedouins, the restless Semites of antiquity, who in considerable numbers have always wandered by the edge of the cultivated tracts, or on the shores of sea and lake where fish and fowl have offered good provision.

In speaking with my host about the hours of labour (which are very long) and the wages (which are very short) I caught a word which had obtruded itself with me since I had read of an early Egyptian monk who, in recounting his pious services, said, "I perform work with my hands each day to the value of two carats." I confess I did not know that in the East everything is measured by a standard of twenty-four carats (or *kîrâts*). People will even ask their doctor to tell them in carats how he regards the hope of recovery of a patient. The carat as a measure found its way to England, and survives in the use the jeweller makes of it in indicating the quality of gold.

As the men were at work in the fields in the glorious sunlight, I caught snatches of the songs which they sang; here and there a lad would so far forget Oriental custom as to raise his young voice to the very heavens in the joy of living. I give one or two of these songs of the fields, asking the reader to remember that they must lose a great deal of their primitive poetry in being turned from the Arabic, which is rich in the qualities needed for such songs.

The ploughman sings, first exclaiming a "good morning" for his lovers, in a sort of recitative :

O God, let their morning be good and princely; as that is of good men on horses' backs.
The cattle trader deserves an Indian cloak for the two oxen he has brought me.
With my head covered I follow the two, and fret the evil eye.
And with these eyes and tears of mine, I weep for loved ones who are absent, but alas! from whence can I bring them?

It is because the ploughman is so fond of his oxen that he fears the evil eye. The man who works the shadoof sings in a monotone :

Alas! they have taken my sweetheart, and left me an empty home.
How lovely are the maids of Lower Egypt when cutting the mallow.
O maid, I pray you unfold your hair
And let the wind set it awave.
Seven long years have I spent in vain, searching for long flowing tresses, and the glossy neck, and the sparkling eye.

When winnowing the wheat, the fellah relieves the monotony of the old-fashioned method of beating the straw and waiting for the wind to separate the chaff from the grain with this one curious line, which he chants again and again :

> My heart is longing for something delightful and new.
> It longs for the red mare, that has glittering stirrups.

The man who threshes the corn with the heavy ancient implement, on which he sits to drive the oxen who drag it, has quite another song :

Tell me, uncle, who are the haughty ones behind us?
Oh, these are the beautiful girls who take captive hearts.
How has Alia wept for Abou Zeid, and changed the garb of rejoicing for that of woe.

An Egyptian friend explains that Abou Zeid is a legendary character in Arabic poetry, something like

King Arthur. His story is like that of Troy. Alia was his wife.

Very beautiful was the palm grove, with its green corn beneath, into which we turned to rest awhile in the shade, before returning to the house. With great contentment we sat on the canal bank, one of our native friends remarking that it is an old saying that "to be happy, an Egyptian needs only the sight of water, of green crops, or a handsome face."

Our party was soon joined by passers-by, men and boys, who quietly sat near us, no doubt hoping to hear something interesting and amusing from people known to have come from the far-off city.

In the mysterious Eastern way, news of our presence spread at once in all directions, so that in a few minutes a bedouin woman, among many other folk, her veil heavily hung with coins, appeared from an invisible encampment, bringing with her all the necessary supplies and appliances for making coffee! She was known to the Pasha, "the good friend of all," and as, being a widow, she was in charge of the tents in the daytime while the men were away. She had come as the representative of the absent sheikh of the camp to offer this poor sign of hospitality. She had with her her only child, a sweet little girl of five years, who carried the fuel.

The little fire was lighted, the beans roasted, and all the ritual gone through exactly as before. A more charming Oriental tableau could not be imagined.

The Pasha is evidently a great matchmaker. I heard him quietly questioning this woman as to her circumstances. Well, it had been hard for her since her husband died; but, thank God, she had her darling child. Did she think of marrying again? She had till now always said "No" to the offers she had had. In every case she had thought of the happiness of her child; perhaps a stepfather would not understand.

By this time the coffee-making was ended, and the little one had nestled to her mother's bosom, covered by her black robe, to be crooned over with simple affection.

The Pasha mentioned the name of a worthy man engaged at his corn mill, a widower, of equal age with the woman, as a possible partner.

The pride of the answer lost nothing from the quiet tones of it: "I am a *bedouin*, and the bedouins never marry the fellaheen!" "We have Abraham to our father!" The Pasha had forgotten this universal rule; the bedouin, with his long descent, the story of which he learns from his fathers, and never forgets, regards himself as a prince compared with the people of the fellah class, who have little more concern with pedigree than have the animals which serve them.

I have mentioned the Pasha's corn mill. On visiting it, we found a well-equipped steam mill, with the most modern of machinery bearing the names of well-known British firms; the whole place humming with activity, under a native overseer.

We often say that the East never changes, and in nearly every aspect of life there seems to be no sign of deviation from the manners and customs recorded in earliest history. It is because of this that one is astonished at the one or two things in which change has been accepted with almost common consent by the Oriental.

I, for one, never see an Arab man of the remote oasis, for instance, working a sewing-machine of the latest model, without a shock of surprise. And yet a common load for the camel caravans, traversing the lonely tracts of the remoter deserts, are cases that bear the stamp of the firm of Singer, who possibly sell more expensive machines from their great Oriental agencies than in Western centres.

And here, in an out-of-the-way part of Egypt, we find that the women no longer sit in pairs "grinding at the mill," crushing the daily portion of corn between the grindstones. They come—from within a radius of several miles—to the modern mill, and in the hareem department provided for them (a convenient peep-hole gave me a sight of it) they sit and gossip, while the steam engine does their work.

It is a pretty sight to see the women set off for home, with their corn sacks upon their heads, and the merry children who accompany them everywhere, dancing by their sides. They carry the water in this way too, and a very upright carriage results. The women of the villages are as a rule very strong and healthy.

The woman's work in the Egyptian villages is never done—nor is the man's. They rise with the sun, only to rest when darkness overtakes them. The first call to prayer from the minaret, "before the sun has risen," is the signal for men and women, Moslem or Copt, to begin the day. The belief is universal that to allow the sun to rise above one's slumbering head is in a very positive way prejudicial to health.

The men go to the fields; for the women there is food to be cooked, water to be brought, fuel to be found (in a woodless and a coalless country this is no mean task), *doura*, or maize, to be picked from the husk, wheat to be sifted, the winding of thread, the churning of butter, indeed, a hundred tasks to keep her eternally occupied. Unlike her English sister, however, she has no beds to make, no plates and dishes to wash.

Her great day is that of bread-making. All the

women of a family are called to this task, for what with sifting the flour, mixing the leaven, and laboriously kneading the dough for the two to three hours which she thinks necessary, and then baking the many small loaves in her mud-oven, there is great activity. Such belief have the people in the medicinal virtues of helba, of which I shall speak elsewhere, that she adds to her labour by pounding the seeds of this plant to mix in the bread. I have in other parts of the country eaten cakes with the whole seeds of sesame sprinkled thickly on the top.

Delightful were these days that we spent in this village of the Delta. I think no one can claim to know anything of the people of Egypt who is not acquainted with the fellaheen. To visit with them familiarly in the remote villages is an experience of unfailing charm and interest.

The graceful courtesy of Egyptian manners is always a delight to the Western visitor, though I admit it may be because we are not engaged in any pressing business that the pleasant Oriental ways do not lose their charm. It is told of a missionary, that he wished to urge upon a native, who was a hearer of his message, that he should become also "a doer of the Word." He read the parable of the two sons in Matthew xxi., and then said, "Which son is to be commended?" The instant reply was, "The one who replied politely to his father, even though he did not go"!

If one is fortunate enough to gain the confidence of the country-folk so that they will accept trifling kindnesses and attentions, one is constantly finding how far astray are certain universally accepted formulæ by which the Western world has dismissed them, after a cursory consideration.

We are told, for instance, that gratitude is unknown to the poorer classes of the East; on no more just ground than that it is not customary to say the " Thank you " which in England formulates the first duty urged upon the lisping infant. The fact is that no people are quicker to appreciate love and kindness, or to give in return an unreasoning devotion. Their thanks they show by all sorts of little gifts and a touching solicitude about the health and affairs of their benefactor.

A certain English lady, who lived with these people for years, tells how the women came to her when they heard she was sick, and said, " May we not kiss thine hand to-day, because thou hast pain?" offering her a share of everything they possessed.

The truth is, that a widespread custom of the East would make of our formal words of thanks a discourtesy, suggesting that the giver was the sort of mean person who would not do a kind act as a matter of course. But, nevertheless, you may be sure of the grateful glance; and sometimes the thing given is kissed as a seal of deep appreciation. Is it not sufficient thanks to hear the murmured blessing, "The Lord preserve thee!"?

We speak so readily of religious fanaticism; how often have I heard the remark, " Every man who loves the poor will go to Paradise; Allah will ask of him nothing more." Everywhere in Egypt you will find the poorest people cheerfully offering a share of anything they may be eating and drinking to a friend; and possibly in no country is there so little actual personal want, notwithstanding the poverty of the fellah class.

In this sharing of food there is a common understanding that the recipient will, on another occasion, do the same thing. These hospitable customs induce a certain brotherliness, which is a marked feature of

Egyptian country life; and especially is this so amongst the men who live on the innumerable boats of the Nile. To have eaten salt or bread together is sufficient ground for avoiding or ending quarrels. No doubt the parasite is encouraged by this easy generosity, but if he meets with a certain amount of good-natured tolerance, the fellah is not deficient in the quiet wit which can often rout the shameless vagrant.

The mistake is so often made of comparing the poor fellaheen with the labouring classes of Europe—which, until education has advanced, and a higher standard of morality is carried to them, can never be just. With scarcely any means of self-cultivation, or any of the enlightenment of what we call social service from a class more advanced, there must still remain many traces of barbarism.

The poor folk of Egypt are still so deeply penetrated by superstition that they cannot be understood apart from it. In spite of this, however, there are virtues in which they excel that are only practised by Europeans of quite a different class, and then only after teaching and example.

They live lives of constant industry, of great patience, most regular and orderly; they turn to the great God, with devotion, in unfailing daily worship; and they are certainly the most courteous people in the world, with a mannerliness in their dealings with each other, and with strangers, which is looked for in Europe only in the people who claim to be "well-bred."

CHAPTER IV

Amongst the Country-Folk. Their Beliefs and Superstitions. The Interest and Humour of their Talk

THE men of the Delta are of fine build with well-developed heads—strong of limb, light of gait, cheerful of countenance, with intelligence and aptitude—altogether an admirable type. The family affections are strong, and the buoyancy of spirit of the fellah is almost invincible. He is easily made very happy. If by chance his temper is disturbed, it flares up with tremendous heat; and as suddenly subsides, when, with a shamefaced smile, he looks up, saying, "Our refuge is in Allah!"

There is a propensity to dispute for the love of it, with a half-humorous detachment from the matter discussed, that often reminds one of the Irish people; as their love of conversation does, their mirthfulness, and a whimsicality they show in the stories they tell, and the way they relate their ordinary doings. When the fellah is parting from any one he knows, he quite simply (apart from any sort of dispute) begs for forgiveness, lest inadvertently at any time he may have given his friend offence.

The Egyptians are very sensitive to the beauties of

nature; and they all revel in the delights of a garden, especially if it has in it the shade of trees and the sound of running water. They find such ecstasy in these things that one easily understands the old monk who wept with grief when taken to a garden, explaining that here was a thing that restored to him a love of life which he thought he had conquered. "Such joys are for Paradise alone."

When I meet a man in the village who invites me in gentle tones to "come and see my dates ripening," and I find him sensitive to the delicate colours of the fruit-laden palm tree against the blue sky, I wonder where one must look for the origin of such appreciation of natural things. His extreme satisfaction in the possession of a well of sweet water (most of the wells in Egypt are brackish and only fit for irrigation), and the poetic way in which he speaks of the salvation it is to the land, recalls all the poetic Bible expressions about "wells of water." It is only in the East that the disputes of Isaac and the Philistines for the possession of the wells are understandable.

In the hot days of summer the men and boys of the village gather round the *sakieh*, or primitive water-wheel, with a deep delight in the splash, splash, of the water from the pitchers, as they come up from the stream below, to empty themselves into the stone trough on the level of the thirsty land. Many a popular song tells of the refrain these imaginative folk hear in the creaking revolutions, and the steady tramp of the buffalo which works it—urged thereto by a small boy who sits, possibly quite naked, on the shaft.

They are deeply conscious of the exhilarating delights of the country air; and the common expression both in town or country on going out, either for a walk or a drive,

Photo: Dittrich, Cairo.
IN THE HOT DAYS OF SUMMER.
The men and boys of the village gather round the primitive water-wheel.

Photo. Lekegian, Cairo.
A VILLAGE SCENE IN EGYPT.
Threshing the corn as in the days of the Pharaohs.

Their Beliefs, Superstitions, and Humour 65

is, "I wish to breathe the air." The realistic representation of country scenes on the monuments of ancient Egypt, where every occupation of the fellaheen is shown, with all the domestic animals, and all the wild birds, suggest a primitive delight in nature which must have been handed down.

As an opening to conversation, the weather is a disappointment to the Englishman in Egypt, for weather varies so little as to make comment absurd. Where we speak of climatic changes, however, the Egyptian speaks of the state of the Nile; and if his greetings are settled for him by polite forms, in which weather has no word, this one unfailing topic of the river is sure to be reached sooner or later.

It might be thought that the river would be of deeper sentimental interest to the Copts than to the Moslems, if one did not know that all life in the Great Valley entirely depends upon it. The religious veneration the Christians have for the river comes to them from the Pharaonic race.

The mariner of the Nile of to-day has scarcely changed since his early forbears were represented on the monuments, although the boats used to-day are strangely unlike those of ancient Egypt. We may even recall, with a smile, that the contests of rich abuse which we often hear going on between the different crews of the boats, especially when they are in competition for an advantage of some sort, are very similar to those related of the ancient Egyptians, on the pilgrimage to Bubastis.

The sports, with which to-day the yearly rising of the Nile is celebrated, succeed the feasts of Hermes, or Thôth, in the days when the river was adored as a god. That the idea of sacredness lingers on in the Coptic mind is shown by the way the people rushed to the river to purify themselves in its waters, when a Christian visionary, in the year 1734, created a panic in the country by foretelling the immediate end of the world. As was to be expected, the Moslems were as ready to take alarm and to plunge into the river as the Christians. To this day the Abyssinians, who profess a crude form of Christianity, have wild scenes by the river bank at the season of the Epiphany; it is reported that they believe its waters will wash away their past sins. In Egypt still, at the same festival, a little water from the church is poured into the river at different spots, and the people plunge in.

The Coptic calendar is based upon the course of the Nile's mighty flood, and these dates still decide all the agricultural activities of the year, the shifting Moslem calendar, which is lunar, having never affected the arrangement. The day when the Nile is expected to be at its highest is the first day of the year—the 1st of the month Tut, falling on our 11th September. The days leading up to this date palpitate with the excitement of the great crisis. The people eagerly stop each other, asking, "How much has the Nile risen to-day?" Even the animals and the birds show signs of agitation.[1]

If the gods of the flood have been generous, then a joyous carnival reigns. Cairo has its own river festival, but there are still a few of the villages which keep revels entirely of their own for three days. The people first choose a ruler from their midst, whom they call *Abu Nerus*. He is clothed in a robe of brilliant colour, a towering fool's cap is set upon his head, with a long

---

[1] The world is becoming so unified that even the unlearned folk of England hear now of the Nile flood. This year (1914) I heard a poor woman lamenting the high price of onions. "They tell me," she said, "that it's because there was a low Nile last year"; which was quite true.

caricature of a beard of flax, and a sceptre in his hand; and, followed by a crowd of quaintly dressed attendants, some of them hangmen and scribes, he sets off direct to the hall of the chief magistrate. Here every one humorously bows to his rule; he takes the chair of authority, and proceeds to hold a stern assize, arraigning more particularly the magistrate himself and all his functionaries. The hangman is to be hanged, the jailor to be thrust into the lowest dungeon (in the old days the jailor whose duty was to whip the prisoners had an awful verdict of lashes given against him); on the rich, fabulous taxes are assessed. Everything is done with mock pomposity; and every judgment is punctiliously written out. The procession again sets out, to enforce its will; the only chance of pardon is to offer a few small coins in *backsheesh*. When the jest is exhausted, a bonfire is lighted, and a pretence is made of burning the tyrant himself. In these days it is only possible to meet *Abu Nerus* by travelling to the distant villages.

Many marriages take place at this time, as the fellah has more leisure at the period of high Nile than at any other part of the year, especially in those places where he must wait for the subsiding of the flood before he can till his soil; and, if there is now enough water in the river, he need scarcely anticipate a moment's misgiving or anxiety in the agricultural year, being spared the harassing trials of a variable climate.

The Nile gauge was always thought sacred, and when it was first moved from the Temple of Serapis into a Christian church, the pagans thought the god would avenge himself by averting the annual inundation. That year—390 A.D.—the flood was delayed, and the people—Christian as well as pagan—saw in this a fulfilment of the pagan prophecy; and the growing danger of riots was only turned aside by the late arrival of the truant waters. From this date the rising of the river was celebrated, with full approval of the people, by Christian clergy instead of the priests of the ancient temples.

Many indeed are the miracles of prayer, of which the common people still speak, that have been wrought in accelerating the floods of the river—when, terror-struck at the delay of the water, they thought of the famine, with all its suffering and ruin, before them and cried aloud to God. The memory of the starvation of many thousands which always attended the failure of the flood, in the days before the great irrigation schemes so successfully husbanded the country's chief resource, has still an hereditary keenness in the minds of the common people.

I have heard garbled stories given by quite illiterate folk of one of the great miracles of the Nile—an instance of the way history is handed down from father to son. In the year 751 the water was very low. On the 17th of Tut a great congregation of clergy and laity walked in procession, before sunrise, carrying the Gospels, and censers with incense, to the Church of St. Peter, which had its foundations in the river at Old Cairo. Here the Patriarch raised the cross, the Bishop of Memphis stood by him with the holy Gospel, and they went out, bearing other crosses and Gospels, and stood on the banks of the river. As the Patriarch and the Bishop prayed, the people kept up a continuous cry of "Kyrie Eleison!" until the third hour of the day; when the river rose one cubit, and every man gave thanks.

Then the Emir, not liking the credit to go to the Christians, ordered the Moslems to go in great pomp the next morning, and by their prayers ask for another cubit

Their Beliefs, Superstitions, and Humour 69

of water. But, says the story (as the Copts tell it), the waters fell so that the gain of the Coptic prayer was lost. This filled the Emir with such despair that he begged the Copts to hold another service of intercession; and then the river rose three cubits, and the fear of famine was past. Whatever we may think of the miracle, secular history does actually record at this date a short period of freedom of the Copts from oppression.

Hundreds of years later, a custom sprang up of taking a sacred relic from one of the Cairo churches, in the month Rejeb, when the Nile flood should begin to appear. This relic consisted of the fingers of a virgin martyr; and these were lowered into the river, in the belief that they would affect the rising. This was called the Festival of the Martyr. It is an instance of how Western writers have often founded misrepresentations of Egyptian life on nothing more than the turn of a word, that until quite recently they have believed that a living virgin has been sacrificed every year, by drowning in the Nile, at this festival.

As always happens in Egypt, a great common calamity never failed to unite the prayers of all the people. A low Nile oft-times led to great liturgical processions, made up of Christians and Moslems, who raised their mingled voices to heaven for the water without which the people must perish, the "Kyrie Eleison!" of the Copt being chanted in unison with the Moslem cry of "Allah! Allah! la illah il'allah!"

It is interesting to recall that almost the last time the Nile was as low as it was last year (1913), the same overmastering passion for prayer over a national need drew all men together. In the year 1808, the great mosque of Amr in Cairo witnessed a truly remarkable scene. All the chief Moslem sheikhs, the Coptic clergy, with those of other Eastern churches, and the Jewish rabbis, with one accord assembled in the magnificent courtyard of the mosque, to unite in supplication for the rise of the water.

Many country visitors go to the Church of St. Michael, in Old Cairo, where there is a large painting of the angel Michael, before which it is specially good to make intercession, more particularly for the rising of the Nile ; and great numbers of worshippers have tied to the grating of the shrine pieces of their clothing, and their silk bands and kerchiefs. Those who come to pray will sometimes bring oil for the church, or a gift of incense. When their prayers are answered they will return with other gifts.

Of nothing is the Egyptian so absolutely convinced, as that the waters of the Nile are heaven-sent for all human needs, not only in their health-giving qualities, but in the delicious refreshment they impart. After much experience I can say that I agree with the native estimate. It will take a great deal of modern science to affect a universal belief as deep rooted as this. Indeed, the scientist is obliged to confess that this instinct of the people is superior even to his diagnosis. Dr. Klunzinger, who was an official sanitary physician for some time in Egypt, when he first looked at the water, was sick with apprehension at the deleterious contributions it had gathered on its immense journey through Africa. He asked himself if he could venture to drink such a mixture. " We venture " ; he adds, " the Son of the Sun has done so before us, and all his sons continue to do so, and are quite healthy. And, indeed, it *is* pure nectar ; we quite agree with the natives of the country, especially those from the desert, who consider a draught of Nile water one of the greatest blessings the world can give."

Their Beliefs, Superstitions, and Humour 71

There is no wonder that in the old days Christian physicians, like the famous Ætius, recommended (as far back as the days of Athanasius) the Nile water for what, in these days of the revival in Europe of the medicinal spa, we should call a "treatment." He believed there was a touch of magic in it; but then he also thought that a green jasper set in a ring had qualities as a curative charm.

It is when chatting in the evening, in the *salemlik* (the great hall) of a country host, or returning visits with his neighbours, that all these subjects connected with the Nile inevitably crop up; the way in which the history of the river, and its fables, are interwoven in the conversation being quite fascinating.

The village folk, who always have the entrée to the great houses in Egypt, slip quietly in to these evening gatherings, and take the greatest interest in everything that is said. Through the host many questions are asked of the English visitor, as to his opinion of matters as modern as that of the doings of the suffragettes. I often turned the tables by returning question for question; sometimes being fortunate enough to surprise Oriental reserve out of some of the things it guards so well.

On one occasion, I set up a most amusing babel by asking if in Egypt the married men loved their mothers-in-law. It is a subject that makes the whole world kin; the funny stories of this lady, coming down to us mostly from primeval days, are almost the sole frail link which binds men of every race together. These Egyptian fellahs promptly told a story, which I had heard, in almost the same words, in Ireland. The house of an Egyptian being on fire, he went upstairs and tenderly brought down his mattress (in Ireland it was a feather bed), having in his excitement made the mistake of first throwing his mother-in-law out of the window. One man declared—and with eloquent approval—that when the women of the Ababdeh tribe, in Upper Egypt, marry, they must never see their mothers again. The bridegroom, immediately after marriage, always leaves the neighbourhood, for a place as far away as possible, chiefly in order to avoid his mother-in-law. An Arabic term gives her the same description as the German *tiger mutter;* while an Egyptian proverb declares that the devil is no match for her.

There is always a great deal of talk amongst the fellaheen on the subject of animals and birds; they tell many quaint stories of them, and one is always coming across fresh superstitions in which animals figure. I have spoken of the absence of any fear of mankind that the birds show in Egypt. From a good deal of questioning, in all parts of the country, I think this may be accounted for, first by a genuine belief that any senseless slaughter is a sin towards the Creator; even when the creature is repugnant, as the pig is to the Moslem, or the monkey and the dog to every Oriental.

The story of Macarius the monk has, I think, some bearing on this belief. As he sat in his cell he killed a mosquito that was stinging him; and straightway, being troubled that he had so avenged himself, he condemned himself to go to the inner desert, where there were many great mosquitoes, and there sit naked for six months. When he returned to his cell he was unrecognisable but for his voice. Certainly the aversion of the Egyptian to take life applies to the most insignificant creatures, to the tiny insects, and particularly to beetles. I have seen an hotel servant turn sorrowfully away from proffered *backsheesh* rather than kill a beetle that had been attracted into a room by the lights.

There is also a universal fear that a demon may dwell in certain animals or birds, or that the *ginn* may disguise themselves in their forms. As for the *ginn*, so particular is this belief, that I know quite well that not one of these village folk with whom I am talking will ever call any animal without beckoning very carefully to the one animal he is calling; a *ginn* might be in the neighbourhood, and mistake the sign, if the gesture did not make it clear, and in revenge do harm to the person beckoning him. The Oriental beckons in a way exactly opposite to the English way—by waving the hand just as we do when we wish a person to go away.

The serpent is a representative of the Evil One himself, as it was in ancient Egyptian mythology; to this day it is the most accursed of all created things in the East—to Christian and Moslem alike the agent of all evil.

Seeing how the West cherishes the stories of St. Francis and the animals and birds over which he had such power, it is interesting to find the opinion very generally held in the East, that any man of a pure life will find every living thing subject unto him. The Copts tell marvellous tales of the power of their sainted Fathers over even the dangerous beasts. Lions became tame and friendly before them; the beasts have been known to leave their own caves for the use of a homeless monk. Of one recluse the story goes that he went forth every night into the desert to mingle with the wild animals, without hurt. The gentle voice of a monk once sent away an angry hippopotamus—of course in the sacred name; another holy man was ferried across the Nile on the back of a friendly crocodile. Abba Macarius was visited one day in his cave by a panther, which took hold of the corner of his garment, and led him gently to its cave, where the animal went in and fetched her young, dropping them at the monk's feet. He found that they were blind, so he prayed and spat on their eyes, and they were opened straightway. On the day following the panther came again to the monk, bringing to him a sheepskin; and this skin the saint used to sleep on, till it was quite worn out.

Not one of these men with whom I chatted but believed that their domestic animals were especially susceptible to "the evil eye"; hence all the charms which the animals are made to wear. It is thought that the ornaments which Gideon took, that were on the camels' necks (Judg. viii. 21), were protective charms—crescent-shaped brasses, blue glass beads, or discs—exactly like those worn by the camels inside the courtyard of the house in which we are speaking. To the same pagan origin I suppose may be traced the brass ornaments which are attached to the harness of cart horses in England.

It is in Egypt that we should expect to find the most deeply rooted superstitions relating to animals, for their use as oracles is truly Egyptian, and goes back to very ancient times. When the bull Apis was consulted, the omen was good or bad according as the bull accepted or refused the food offered by the worshippers; or as Apis chose to go into one or other of two stalls. It is probable that this use of the sacred animals kept in the temples was solely the outcome of the superstitions of the people, and was not encouraged by the priests until after the classic period had passed. What happened in the case of Apis, recurred in the Temples of Ombos, where sacred crocodiles were kept; and in the case of the rams of Elephantine or of Mendes.

The reason for the general detestation of monkeys by Egyptians (nothing would ever induce certain of my

Their Beliefs, Superstitions, and Humour

friends to go near their cages in the Cairo Zoological Gardens) is that the ape is a metamorphosed man. The baboon represents that terrible scoundrel of a man who stole the Prophet's red shoes, and hid them under his coat. This the Prophet noticed, when he said, "Thief, may your form become a caricature of that of man, and may your body, at the place where my shoes are hanging, be coloured red like them for all time, in memory of your evil deed!" No one of the fellaheen is the less convinced of the truth of this story by the fact that the baboon is often represented on the ancient monuments. Not that they are ignorant of the sculptured records, for it is often mentioned in their conversation that many of them have wondered—as the Western scholars have—at the strange fact that neither the camel nor the buffalo is found on any of the monuments.

A funny, rambling story was told one evening of a rich owner of camels, who, when his time of departure from this life drew near, could not get the release he desired. Many friends tried to guess what the reason might be, but in vain, until at last one said he must have offended some animal, possibly a camel. So they sent for the chief camel, who, however, would not come until he had had a meeting of all the herd, to whom the master's plight was explained. The "resolution" of the meeting of camels, sent by their chief, was something like this: "Master, you may now be at rest; the camels now forgive you. But before you go, they would like you to know why they were so deeply offended. We could bear the heavy loads, as well as the lash of the drivers' whip. These were from Allah, and are in the day's work. What we found to be an insufferable insult was, that, when you had strung us together for the caravans, you put a puny ass at the head to lead us!"

A vile enchanter of olden times is represented to-day in the hyena; he was transformed by the anger of God. But by one of those almost savage contradictions, so often found in their superstitions, the people, instead of shrinking from such an accursed being, chose to put a high magic value on the hyena, and the teeth, hair, skin, and flesh of this animal are all much sought after as charms. If a Moslem is assured that a hyena has been slaughtered according to the orders of the Koran (this only rarely happens), he will readily eat its flesh, the sheikhs especially being fond of it; for they believe it will give masculine strength. If a man has pains in his back, the best cure is to lie on the skin of a hyena. If he is so lucky as to possess a skin, he has to keep it hidden, for every visitor who gets the chance will pluck from its mane a hair, in the belief that it will secure love and faithfulness, as well as the favour of those in high places. The teeth are highly esteemed as amulets.

Innumerable are the stories told of the cunning of the fox—though they all belong to the order of the humorous fable. The great joke in all of these tales is to represent Reynard as the village *kadi*, or judge. The story I heard most often was of the fox which met a man going to market with a basket of fowls. The fox naturally coveted the birds, and proceeded to play a trick upon the owner to get them. He crept on ahead and lay down in the road, pretending to be dead. The man glanced at him, but went his way; until he passed, farther on, two more foxes, also lying dead. He now began to think that three fox-skins would have a good value; so he put down his basket by the last fox, and went back to pick up the others. But he could find

Their Beliefs, Superstitions, and Humour 77

nothing; and when he went back for his basket it was empty.

I found everywhere in the country a very profound belief in the magic of stones—of quite ordinary sorts—which have been brought from holy places, such as Jerusalem, Mecca, Damascus, Medina, and other sacred spots. One of the men with whom I talked had a collection of such stones, which were regarded as a great treasure by the whole countryside; he was always being asked to lend them in cases of severe illness. A bowl of Nile water must be brought, and in this the stones are rubbed together, the water then being drunk by the patient. As the stones may come from both Christian and Moslem places, so the people of each faith are equally ready to use the same charm. For the infliction of gall-stones this cure is thought to be infallible.

A cure for jaundice was mentioned to me, our host sending for his "magic dish" as he called it. It was a round brass dish, rather deep, with an inscription in Arabic on it—in this case a Scripture text; those used by the Moslems have a verse from the Koran. This dish must be taken, in the evening, and filled with Nile water, into which must be dropped several filbert nuts. It is then placed out of doors, so that the dew of night may fall into it. In the morning the sick person must take the dish, and, standing with his back to the rising sun, eat the nuts, throwing the shells over his shoulders; when all the nuts are consumed he must drink all the water.

One morning we went to see a sacred tree, one of the few there are in Egypt. This tree was a very large *nubk*, and it was literally covered with shreds of the clothing of the people who had visited it. The custom of regarding certain trees as sacred is another of those brought into Christendom from the ancient practices of Egypt. I believe that holy trees are to be found in Ireland.

The Moslems have a great belief in certain trees being the abode of departed saints; they think that Paradise is surrounded by a hedge of the *nubk*, which is so sacred a tree that it always becomes the dwelling-place of a saint when it has reached the age of forty years.

On special days, all the village folk think their sacred tree is bright with the most delicate illumination, and soft voices are heard in its boughs; the Copts and the Moslems alike thinking that the saint is about the tree at that time—saints of the trees are called "the people of the blessing."

In Egypt there used to be a variety of tree called the *persea*, sacred to Our Lord, because this was the tree that Jesus and His parents rested under when they passed through Matarieh. Some time before the Arab invasion a law had been passed to preserve this kind of tree, a heavy fine being inflicted on any one cutting one down. Even this did not save the tree from extinction; for now no one knows what tree is meant by the name *persea*. The sacred tree now at Matarieh is a sycamore fig, which it is curious to find is not venerated by the Copts, but by the Latin Christians.

I have questioned the people who resort to these trees, not only in Egypt, but in different parts of North Africa, especially as to why they tie on to them pieces of their clothing, and so far as I can put their somewhat vague replies into the words of another language, I have found that it is always their hope that by so doing the saint, by a sort of clairvoyance, will be kept in touch with them, and will remember their needs before God; and God will hear their humble prayers because of the superior merits of the saint.

Their Beliefs, Superstitions, and Humour

Very amusing are the children of the village, whom we see playing together in groups in the fields. At the age of adolescence the country children of Egypt are beautiful; both the girls and the boys are well formed, and though spare, they are strong, and full of a graceful activity. The features are good, and the soft brown eyes and the white teeth (so carefully cleaned after each meal), with the warm brown skin, make the most pleasing pictures of youthful beauty.

The little processions of girls going every morning and evening between the village and the canal, carrying the water-pitchers on their heads, form one of the most charming sights in the Nile valley. The girls' feet are naked, and if her body is too much swathed in her draggling black robe, one still sees a beautifully moulded arm stretched out to hold the pitcher; and, as she does not aspire to the full veil of "the forbidden ones," as she calls the ladies of the cities, and only pulls her robe over part of her face (if there are no Egyptian men about she will not even do this) one often sees a face of delicate beauty. The small blue tattoo marks would spoil a face of paler complexion, but they seem to accord with the gilt ear-rings, the necklet of gold coins, and the cherry-red beads, which she so proudly wears.

The games played by the children are of the simplest order. A noisy group of boys are playing a game which seems to consist of two sides, who, hopping on one foot, try merely to bring each other to the dust. Further on we pass a quieter group, seated on the ground, on which they have drawn, in the dust, a sort of enlarged draught-board; the game they are playing with small stones has certain rapid moves which lead to a quick conclusion. It is strange to hear the "men" used by the two sides in this game called Moslem and

Christian; Moslem begins, and the names are called aloud at each move. I have seen boys in a desert oasis, thousands of miles from this spot, playing exactly the same game. A common game of the boys of Egypt is something like "rounders," a ball being driven by a club exactly as the pictures of ancient Egypt show it to have been; sometimes the boys play it mounted on each other's backs—so did their far-off forefathers.

Rural Egypt has few toys, but there is a primitive humming top that is often found. What I thought more remarkable was to find that the boys of the fellaheen sometimes were in possession of those annoying little crackers which are exploded in most English villages on the night of Guy Fawkes.

I have often come across a number of small children, in all parts of Egypt, solemnly engaged in a game of mimicry of the most weird description. The babes, generally from about four to seven years old, stand round in a circle, and, following the actions of the mock sheikh sitting in the centre, in sober unison sway from side to side, making agonised grimaces, as they chant over and over again in their sweet infant tones the "La illah il'allah, Mohammed rasul Allah!" After a time one of them will feign exhaustion, and fall to the ground, to be followed, one by one, by the others, until all have fallen, when the game is at an end. They have been playing at having a *zikr*, one of those religious exercises of the East in which the Moslem seeks to attain to spiritual ecstasy; and it is clear that no detail of the rite has escaped the childish observation. One thinks of the white tablecloth surplice, and the solemn preaching from behind the back of a high chair, in an English nursery; and the groups of children of a similar age in every English village, who often leave the real school only to

Photo: Lekegian, Cairo.

A HOLY TREE OF GREAT AGE.

The sacred trees are covered with shreds torn from the garments of those who visit them, by which they hope to establish a beneficent connection with the particular saints who visit and dwell in the branches. The author has also found these sacred trees in the deserts of the Saharah, of Nubia and the Sudan.

Their Beliefs, Superstitions, and Humour

engage in a very earnest imitation of "teacher," with no abatement of hard questions, and a sterner use of the cane than in reality would be allowed.

Sometimes we look in upon the poor in their huts while they are at meals. They all eat with their fingers, but I must say that generally their table manners will compare for daintiness and unselfish restraint with the peoples who use the knife and fork. They eat moderately and of the simplest diet, of which bread is the chief item.

The native bread is a flat round cake, of a dusky colour, very like a large stone: reminding us of Scripture again—"If a son shall ask bread . . . will ye give him a stone?" A piece of bread, with pickled turnip and a taste of salted curd, often makes a meal. I have sometimes seen the children eating this bread merely dipped in syrup, though vegetables are so cheap that it is rare not to be able to afford the relish of raw carrots, radishes, tomatoes, onions, and the tiny cucumber which is grown so abundantly in Egypt. In the hot weather every one eats the cucumber; indeed, without a dish of these cool and refreshing vegetables the people would often not eat at all.

The water melon, too, is so plentiful that all may enjoy it—it is food and drink in the sultry days of midsummer. We know that the men who built the Pyramids ate the same food as the fellaheen eat to-day, and they ate it in the same simple manner.

It is not good manners to watch the people at their food, so we turn aside again, after accepting a morsel in response to their eager offers. "The envious eye" is very active over food, and so we never betray any desire, even for the fruits which are so tempting.

CHAPTER V

Birth and its Attendant Celebrations

In writing these chapters dealing with Egyptian customs the author has been able to supplement his own personal observations by the invaluable notes of two Coptic gentlemen belonging to old conservative and orthodox families—Dr. Sobhy, and Marcus Simaika Pasha, of Cairo.

THE essential type of the Coptic Egyptian bears out the assertion that as a race the Nile dwellers are amongst the most conservative of mankind. In their physiognomy, and their peculiarity of manners and customs, there is a great deal of evidence on the ancient monuments, and in the literature of the Pharaonic period, to show that in many ways the people of to-day differ very little from their pre-Christian ancestors.

If there is any tendency to change, it is amongst the comparatively small class of the rich and highly educated, who have travelled largely in Europe, and are eager to adopt everything from the Western civilisation. The desire to live in the manner of the English and the French carries the people of this class so far away from the habits of even their last generation, that the casual observer might be led to imagine that a social revolution was rapidly changing an entire race. It only needs, however, a slight acquaintance to show that habits acquired in this way do not really displace the Oriental temperament, which, as the writer thinks, must still express itself in its own way in spite of any artificial restraints whatever.

In the great mass of the people there is no change at all. The spread of education may, perhaps, very slowly modify the barbaric excesses, especially of the women in times of grief, but it can never bring to an Eastern people the sustained restraint of the people of a different race, living in a colder clime.

The skill and science of the physician may gradually win the people from their belief in charms and incantations, though it is unlikely that the cherished superstitions of eighty centuries can be easily dispossessed from the wonder-world of the Orient, alive as it is with all the romantic possibilities of magic—a world in which every man has his guardian angel, and is familiar with the ways of the whole race of fairy and *ginn*. All these things have flourished for so long because they found root in the needs and the longings of the human soul.

It is for the same reasons that the ancient Church of these people has preserved its Oriental characteristics. Nothing illustrates this more clearly than the work which the Americans have done in Egypt in trying to convert the Copts from their orthodox faith. In many ways the American Mission has rendered a most excellent service to the Egyptian Christians; in their splendid schools and colleges, and in their hospitals, they, with wonderful ability and a lavish generosity, have benefited the whole of Egypt.

They have established numbers of mission halls, with all the Presbyterian bareness, and from their platforms they appeal to the people, not only to live the life of personal holiness, but to shun the errors of their ancient Church. Their adherents are numbered by tens of thousands; and I can speak of the zeal and the earnestness of these converts, including as they do many of the richest and most influential Copts in the country.

While I can go so far as to believe that the eventual outcome of this Mission may be nothing short of the reform of the Coptic Church, bringing back to it the spirituality it has lost, from what I have seen I cannot think the Oriental people can ever find any lasting satisfaction in a Presbyterian form of worship.

The converts are constantly longing for the glowing ritual of their old Church. How many of them even now, when they feel the need of the ancient sacraments, forget for the time their chapel missioner, and go to the priest and the sanctuary. If ever the Church is reformed, and becomes a living Church, I believe these converts will not be able to resist the natural instincts which all the time are calling them back to its fold. It is touching to hear the tones of intense affection with which they speak of the Mother Church, even when to all outward seeming they are in complete dissent.

The customs which surround the birth of a child have perhaps more than any others been handed down unchanged from the earliest days of Egypt's history. It is not possible in every case to trace the origin of each particular custom, and explain the meaning of many practices and observances of to-day, yet there is warrant for attributing their very obscurity and apparently meaningless character to the fact that they were a part of the primitive religion of the ancient Egyptians, and have only become inexplicable since the religion itself became obsolete.

In those houses in which the hareem system is preserved, and with the poor, the male physician is never consulted by the expectant mother, even though

Birth and its Attendant Celebrations 85

her peaceful course should be interrupted. If her life is very seriously threatened, the doctor may be called in, but this is a recent concession to those who like to take refuge in medical science as an extra precaution to the native antidotes. Otherwise, the entire responsibility is undertaken by the *quabilah*, or midwife, more colloquially called the *daiah*; if this woman is certificated she is called *hakeemah*.

It is interesting, in view of recent discussions on various subjects connected with eugenics in England, to find that the Egyptians have always held that very special care should be taken to influence the mother before the infant is born, as every effect made upon her nervous system will have its impression on the unborn child.

Readers may remember that in the life of the late Charles Kingsley it is especially commented on as a modern idea that his mother went away to Devonshire believing that all the impressions made on her mind then would be transmitted to her child. Years afterwards the Kingsley family were specially mentioned by Galton in his book on Hereditary Talent.

It has always been one of those deep beliefs in Egypt, which are too familiar to need comment, that not only the character and even health, but the appearance, of the coming offspring depend upon the objects with which the woman is brought into contact, especially in the first three months of the *enceinte* period.

The sight of a beautiful face, habitually looked at, goes far to ensure a comely child; any object for which the mother has shown a fondness may be reproduced in shape or form upon the child's body.

The story is commonly told of a woman who had a great longing for apples—a rare fruit in Egypt—which could not be gratified; and she gave birth to a child with a growth upon its body not unlike a red apple in colour and shape. In another case, a young woman who tamed an ape is believed to have had a child of an ape-like appearance.

I have heard a Copt, well versed in the Scriptures, declare that this principle was known, even as it applies to the animal world, from the days of Jacob's experiment with the flocks, by which he became rich.[1]

It certainly was the rule amongst the ancient Egyptians that in every case the woman who was to become a mother "should live comfortably and should have what she longs for,"[2] a rule carefully observed to this day.

Dr. Sobhy has known women who during the whole of their period have carried about with them the picture of a beautiful child, at which they constantly gazed, in the firm belief that this would ensure similar features to their own offspring.

On the other hand, it is highly injurious, in such a condition, to smell any pungent substance, such as lime in the process of slaking, carbolic acid, asafœtida, or garlic roasted in butter.

Everywhere in the East childlessness is looked upon as the worst misfortune that can belong to a woman, but it is never regarded as a mere physical defect. The doctor is never consulted, the remedy being sought in many of the directions which superstition has suggested. Certain kinds of coins, if worn on a visit to a friend in confinement, are considered to bring about this curse; and if the visitors should chance to see a funeral, or a dead body, on the way, this will

---

[1] Genesis xxx. (from verse 31 onwards).
[2] *Manners and Customs of the Ancient Egyptians*, Wilkinson.

Birth and its Attendant Celebrations 87

have the dreaded effect: such a condition is not, of course, to be treated by any human methods, but it must be assailed by remedies of the same order. Coins, similar to those that caused the mischief, must be soaked in water, and the infusion must be drunk by the patient, or used as a douche.

If the cause is the sight of a funeral, or a dead body, then a visit must be paid to a cemetery, or permission must be privately gained to step across a dead body; the proceeding being called *mesharah*.

There are wise old women, of great experience, who prescribe charms and amulets, which are accepted in earnest faith by those who consult them. These women also occasionally number amongst their patients those who, because of poverty, are satisfied with the number of their already large families.

The attentions of the midwife mostly consist of invocations of all the saints of which she knows, her chief cry being, "Ya sitti Kahla, enta'iana min di el wahla!" that is to say, "O Lady Kahla, deliver us from this our trouble!"; while she administers, if necessary, hot stimulant drugs, generally decoctions of either cinnamon or crocus.

On the morning of the second day of the child's life the midwife performs the operation of "benefiting the eyes," which consists of raising the infant's eyelids, and painting round the eyes with a solution of coal tar, and then sprinkling with *kohl*. This substance is made by burning incense and almonds, and collecting the soot thus formed. This soot, being very soft, is everywhere used by the women as an eye-paint, the constant use of which is supposed to colour the eye black. This also is a custom from ancient Egypt.

The mother is thought to need no attention yet; the

complete rest enjoined for the Western mother is not thought to be necessary—indeed, she now moves about at will. For a week, however, she is not allowed to do any work; if she is poor her relatives and her neighbours quite willingly come to her assistance in household matters, even till the fortieth day after the birth.

The only treatment is on the third day, when a douche is used, made of the leaves of bitter oranges, dried leaves of *shih*[1] (valuable for its alkaloid), myrrh, and the dried fruit of *quarad*,[2] which have all been boiled together.

It is in the matter of diet that the skill of the midwife is mostly exercised, as this is regarded of the utmost importance. However poor the woman may be, she has to be provided with one chicken at least for each of the first three days of her confinement; if means are plentiful, she is kept almost exclusively to a chicken diet during the first ten or twelve days.

It is deplorable that wine is given in nearly every case to Coptic women, in such excessive quantities that sometimes it leads to a certain hæmorrhage, which the doctors have traced to this cause. Another very important item of diet is a sort of pudding, made with bread and thoroughly soaked in treacle, with a great number of the seeds of the native helba.[3] The plant is held in the highest repute in Egypt as a general family medicine; it is universally considered an excellent nerve tonic, and being bitter it acts as a stomachic.

In country houses, especially, the last act of consideration of my host, at the end of the day, has often been to send to my bedroom a jugful of hot liquid made from helba, in the firm belief that it would

---

[1] *Artemisia maritima.*   [2] *Acacia nilotica.*
[3] *Trigonella fœnum Græcum.*

Birth and its Attendant Celebrations 89

ensure sleep at night and good health in the morning. The natives believe that the seeds of this plant, together with the bile of an ox, made into pills, are a sure remedy for diabetes.

Another most important drug, used by the midwife, is made from the powdered root of the plant known as *el mughat* (known to the French as "grenadier sauvage"); it is usually mixed with the powdered seeds of *nigella sativa* (called by the natives *habbet-el-baraka*), and sometimes with the dried and powdered fruit of the *ciratonia siliqua*, or kharoub. The mixture is called *mughat*, and is everywhere used by the people, who have the greatest faith in its efficacy.

Sometimes the midwife, being a woman of more than usual energy and skill, makes a still more elaborate decoction, called *mughat mihawik*, meaning literally woven *mughat*, having an addition of the familiar aromatic drugs, such as cinnamon, cloves, cardamoms, nutmeg, and many others, all pounded into a very fine powder.

The preparation is made in this way: a quantity of butter is first melted, and some crushed nuts and drugs cooked in it; ordinary *mughat* is then mixed with it, and the whole cooked again; lastly, water is added, sweetened with sugar, and the mixture is well stirred, and served in teacups. Sometimes it is made without butter, and then has the consistency of jelly, of a brownish yellow colour, with a delicious aromatic odour; it has decided tonic and stomachic properties. Not only are these decoctions taken by the patient, but they are offered to all her visitors. As a drink a hot preparation of caraway is taken.

A very special delicacy, made only for these occasions, is called *halawa-el-mefataqah*, or the composite sweets. It consists of the powdered extracts of forty kinds of odoriferous plants, mostly of the species of bitter stomachics. These are roasted in sesame oil, called *sirig*, and treacle or honey is liberally poured over the whole. Women of experience have to be called in to prepare this dish, as great skill is required to get the flavour which makes it so delicious. Of the forty substances used in its composition, the following are the most important: nuts of various kinds; of drugs, galbanum, powdered root of the camphor tree, cinnamon, nutmeg, extract of *nigella sativa*, rhubarb, cardamoms, cloves, cascarilla, sandal-wood, cubebs, *piper longum*, ginger salep, orange and lemon peel, quassia bark, tragacanth, liquorice, tamarind, fig, fennel, cinchona, camomile, taraxacum, with a suggestion of asafœtida. I have sipped it, but found it too rich and complicated for my taste.

This *halawa* is usually eaten with a specially made pastry called *kumaga*, which is made into little flat round loaves, ornamented at the edge, and having a layer of sesame and honey. The dough is kneaded with butter—or oil if the patient be a Copt and the season is one of the fasts. Chickens specially prepared with milk and flour are distributed with these delicacies to important visitors. The Egyptian chicken is always a small bird.

We now come to the momentous seventh day, the *lelet-el-suba*. Among the rich, especially those who have few children, this night is kept as a great festival—a splendid banquet is served, musicians are hired, and in every way the occasion resembles a wedding feast.

This seventh night is the first occasion on which the child is given a bath. The water in which the child is washed may not be thrown away, but is kept in a glazed earthenware pot, called the *magur akhdar*. In the

Birth and its Attendant Celebrations 91

centre of the pot is placed, if the infant is a boy, an *ibreek*, the big copper jug used for washing the hands, or a *gulah*, the ordinary small clay water-pot, if it is a girl.

In either case the vessel is decorated with the insignia of the respective sexes—the *ibreek* is adorned with a red tarbush, or head-dress, and a watch and chain; and the *gulah* with a handkerchief, ear-rings, and other feminine jewellery, according to the wealth of the parents.

Round the rim of the pot are stuck three candles (originally there were seven), which are lighted simultaneously. The parents and friends choose three names, applying one to each candle; the name of the candle that burns longest being the one chosen for the child.

This is a custom that almost certainly had its origin in the mythology of the ancient Egyptians, who believed in the presence of seven Hathors at the birth of every child, in whose hands his destiny lay. Lots were cast among them, and the one on whom the lot fell decided the name and fate of the child. To the same source may be traced the belief, which still survives all over Egypt, that every child is connected with the star under which it is born.

The names used by the Copts furnish traces of all the nations which have successively dominated Egypt, while a good number linger from the ancient race, such as Hur from Horus, Serapamoun from Serapis and Amon; there are Greek names, such as Theodorus (pronounced Tadrus), Philotheos (pronounced Faltaus); Roman names, such as Claudius (pronounced Ekladius); Persian names, such as Narouz; many French names, such as Louis and Alphonse; and now, English names. Many girls have been called Victoria and Alexandra, and Bible names in their English form are very popular; numbers of boys are called Cromer and Kitchener; Henry and Jeffrey are often met with. The old-fashioned Copt, who is in an overwhelming majority, scorns such importations, almost equally with the Moslem, and, with him, never uses anything but Arabic names.

The midwife is an important personage at this festival. She has provided herself with small quantities of cereals of every kind,—wheat, maize, peas, beans, lentils, and others,—and she places a portion of each, together with some nuts, in the pot. Taking another portion of the cereals, she stuffs a small pillow with them, and on this pillow the child must sleep until it has grown old enough to distinguish its own name. A third portion is tied up in a piece of cloth, and must be placed under the pillow on which the mother sleeps.

Towards morning the child is taken from his bed and placed in a large sieve (called *ghurbal*), and is shaken just as though wheat were being sifted. The midwife then takes a large brass pestle and mortar, and, going close to the child, she pounds as loudly as possible, saying in the ear of the child the while, "Hear thy father's speech," and with another vigorous pounding, "Follow thy mother's advice." Then the mother is directed to step three times over her child as it lies in the sieve.

The *ibreek* (or the *gulah*) is now taken out of the pot, and the water found in the latter is sprinkled over the threshold of the room. Each of the guests tries to snatch some of the nuts from the pot, putting money in their place as a gift for the midwife; the captured nuts the women guests place in their purses as charms against financial failure.

A very interesting procession is now formed. All

Birth and its Attendant Celebrations 93

the children in the house are gathered together, and are given long, lighted candles. As they start from the room where the birth took place they chant the nursery songs of the East. In most cases, the mother, dressed all in white, holding the child to her bosom, goes first; sometimes the midwife leads, holding the child; and in any case the latter always carries a quantity of the cereals and common salt held in a cloth, which she scatters on the way.

From time to time this rhyme is addressed to the infant, chanted by all the company: "With thy hands and thy feet, a golden ring in thine ears, mayest thou live and rear thine own offspring." When the procession has visited every room in the house, its mother and the child are escorted back to their chamber, where they are left to rest.

For this occasion the grandparents of the infant (on the mother's side) have also had made at their own home the sweets and cakes called *kumaga*, and they send a portion, with a quantity of nuts, such as almonds, walnuts, and cocoa-nuts, to each family connected with them.

The mother is not allowed to go out of doors until forty days have elapsed from the birth. She then visits the *hammam*, or bath, and after its elaborate and frolicsome ablutions, she is free from any further restrictions.

The love of children, shared equally between the father and the mother, shown by all Eastern people, can scarcely be exaggerated; it is one of the most charming features of Egyptian life. In this the Copt does not differ from the Moslem. A beautiful sign of this love for the little ones is shown by the fact that in the ordinary way no orphan children are to be found. There is always some family ready to take the poor mites whose parents die, and the adoption is a very real one. No such child is ever made conscious of being a "poor relation." Is not this another instance of the similarity, which strikes one at every turn, between the temperament of the Oriental and that of the generous-hearted Irish folk, who take unfortunate children into their homes in the same way?

This is what Job meant, literally, when he said, "Have I eaten my morsel alone, and the fatherless hath not eaten thereof? from my youth he was brought up with me" (xxxi. 17, 18).

As for the resemblance of Eastern folk to the Irish, it may be an interesting digression to mention the story of the cook in the desert monastery of Pachomius. He neglected his duly appointed work of cooking vegetables for the brethren, and devoted his time to plaiting mats. All he would say, in excuse, was that the brethren did not eat all the food he cooked; he worried himself about the forty flasks of oil which were mixed daily with the peas and vegetables. It is not related that a mat-making brother insisted on doing the cooking; but I expect it was so. Let any lady who has kept house in southern Ireland say if this does not remind her of her chief domestic trials. To "duly appoint" work to one of those lovable but vexatious creatures who serve in an Irish home, is to be sure that every device will be thought of to avoid it for other tasks not appointed. And who could be found to sadden those gay hearts with a punishment like that of the Abbot. Pachomius had the five hundred mats, made by the cook, brought to him, and he threw them into the fire!

CHAPTER VI

Baptism

IT is the rule of the Church that a male child should be baptized on the fortieth day, and a female on the eightieth day, and the baptism must always take place in a church, unless the child be dying, when it may be performed at home. In the case of sickness the need for baptism becomes very urgent, as the popular belief is that a child who dies unbaptized will be blind in Paradise—no mention is ever made of the soul of an infant being lost from heaven.

The rule of the fortieth or the eightieth day is not now strictly adhered to; indeed, two days of the year have come to be very largely chosen as most favourable to the rite—the last Sunday but one of Lent, and the day of the Feast of the Cross, in the second half of September, are called Days of Baptism. The season of Epiphany has from the earliest days of the Church been thought suitable; for special graces for all men are showered down at Epiphany. Before the rite both the priest and also the infant (or convert) must fast. In the case of a convert the vigil must be kept with reading and prayer.

The service of baptism is most curious evidence of the strict and unreasoning conservatism of the Eastern Church in the preservation of its ancient ritual.

The first part of the baptismal service must have been composed in the earliest days of missionary Christianity, for it is solely applicable to the case of adult converts from heathenism, who are to be admitted to a course of instruction in Christian doctrine, with a view to their subsequent baptism.

There is no doubt that originally the service for converts took place long before baptism, a course of instruction coming in between; for they were only allowed to attend part of the ordinary service of the church, a prayer still used marking their dismissal. And yet this service is to this day solemnly read over young infants, the children of Christian parents.

In this rite, as in all others, practices are preserved of the highest antiquity—the renunciation of Satan, for instance, by the catechumen, who turns to the west and raises his right hand; the wearing of a white robe and crown by the neophyte, the bestowal of the ring at betrothal, and the coronation at marriage.

The very language of the services shows this conservatism. At a very early period the Greek rites of Alexandria must have been translated into Coptic. But still whole phrases were preserved in Greek, and are so used to-day; later on, Coptic died out of use—as early as the beginning of the fifteenth century it must have been unintelligible in Lower Egypt—but the religious services are still recited in this dead language, only rendered partially intelligible by a faulty Arabic version written by the side of the Coptic in the Church books.

The baptistery is placed on the left side of the church, and is decorated with a picture of St. John baptizing the Lord Jesus Christ.

Every child must have a godfather or a godmother, who are so closely considered as parents that their

Baptism

children, being regarded as brothers and sisters of the godchildren, are not allowed to marry.

After the service of purification has been said over the mother, her forehead being anointed with oil, the first prayer asks that "all remains of the worship of idols may be cast out of their hearts."

The oil of thanksgiving is then blessed, "for the casting out of demons, and witchcraft, and magic, and all service of idols," and the priest anoints the breast, and hands, and back, of the infant, saying, "May this oil destroy all the enmity of the enemy."

The child is now unclothed, and is turned to the west; his right hand is raised and he renounces Satan and all his works and his evil angels; in the case of an infant the parent or sponsor orally renounces for him. Then turning to the east, the babe's arms raised to form a cross, a submission to Christ and all His saving laws and all His life-giving service and works is made.

After many prayers, the priest takes the second oil which he has blessed, the chrism, and anoints him that is to be baptized on the breast and arms, and from the front of the breast to the back, and on the middle of the hands, with the sign of the cross, "in defence against all the works of the enemy."

In the prayers it is asked that angels of light will guard the life of the baptized, defend them from all the darts of the enemy, and from evil assaults, and from the demon of noontide, from the arrow that flieth by day, and from the thing that walketh in the darkness, and from the imaginations of the night; casting out from their hearts all disturbing spirits.

The priest lays his hands on the infants in blessing; and then, prostrate before the font, prays for himself a very beautiful petition for power that he may not give absolution to others and himself be a castaway. Such a prayer, repeated in other services, must be remembered when an attempt is made to gauge the extent of priestly claims in the Coptic Church.

He then takes the first oil, and pours it into the font three times in the form of a cross, signing the water again four times with the sign of the cross with his finger, from east to west and from north to south.

He then consecrates the water, which must be "living," and cold,[1] to the burning of incense, praying that God will give the infant power that by this water all hostile forces may be destroyed; all evil spirits may be driven away; all witchcraft, magic, and the services of idols may be destroyed.

The priest then breathes upon the water three times in the form of a cross, with fresh invocations, that it may be a holy water, a water which washes away sin, a water of the laver of regeneration. "Grant to this water that no evil spirit may be within it, or descend into it with him that is to be baptized; neither a spirit of the day, nor a spirit of noontide, nor a spirit of evening, nor a spirit of night, nor a spirit of the air, nor a spirit of drowning—let them be crushed before the sign of Thy Cross, and before Thy Holy Name."

Then the priest takes the holy chrism and pours it into the font three times in the form of a cross. Disturbing the waters with his hand, he recites passages from the Psalms.

The priest, taking the naked child from the deacon, and raising him up, first breathes on his face in the form of the cross, and then baptizes him. Triple immersion is the only form recognised in the Coptic Church; aspersion is condemned, except in cases of extreme weakness.

[1] In extreme cases of weakness a little warmth is allowed.

Baptism

The priest lays his right hand upon the head of the child, and with the left performs the trinomial lifting and dipping. The first time the child, in the name of the Father, is dipped to the waist; the second time, in the name of the Son, to the neck; the third time, in the name of the Holy Ghost, over the head.

Immediately after the baptism the water must be absolved, or deconsecrated; the priest pouring some of the water upon his hands, upon the font and its surroundings, prays that it may be changed to its former nature, and may so return to the earth.

Taking the holy chrism, and praying over it on the altar, he now confirms the child. He anoints, with special invocations, the forehead and eyes, the nostrils and mouth, the ears and the hands on both sides, and the breast, the knees, and the instep of the feet, and the back and arms, saying, "Receive the Holy Ghost, and be a pure vessel, through Jesus Christ, our Lord." This is an act peculiar to the Coptic Church, and seems to indicate that the unction, to be effective, needs the insufflation of the priest; or, as one authority states it, the proper matter of confirmation in the Coptic Church is the breath of the priest, and its form the words, "Receive the Holy Ghost."

After the laying on of hands in blessing, the priest takes off the child's wrap, and clothes him in a white robe, tied with a holy girdle, or *zennan*, which is tri-coloured; the girdle being unique to the Coptic Church. He blesses a crown, and places it on the infant's head. These acts are symbolical of the putting off the old man and putting on the new, the loins girded to run the Christian race, and the crown promised to those who prove victorious.

The child is now brought to the altar, and the Mass

is celebrated and administered to the child, a drop of the wine, in which the bread has been soaked, alone being given in the case of infants; the priest dipping his finger in the chalice, and putting it on the tongue of the babe.

During all this long time, the sealed copy of the Gospel is resting on the Gospel-stand in the baptistery, with lighted tapers about it. As I often saw this in Cairo, a note may be permitted on the idea of the material notion of the sanctity of the Bible, which possibly had its birth in this very place. The Genizah, at Cairo, yielded a rich harvest of extremely valuable ancient copies of the Bible. Copies had been preserved in sacred burying-places through being sealed in their metal cases.

At first this notion of material sacredness was unknown to Christianity. But very early the people adopted it, and the Bible became tabu. This was especially the case with the Gospels, which, with the Host, and the likeness of Christ, came to be valued as the sign and assurance of the sacred presence and His miraculous power.

Here we see the place still assigned to it in the Coptic Church, keeping alive the decision of the early Councils that the Gospels, as representative of Christ, must have the place of honour. In the consecration of a bishop, the Gospels are laid upon his head as a means of communicating the Spirit and Christ's indwelling.

Now the child is carried in procession three times round the church by the clergy, dressed in their full canonicals, the acolytes following bearing candles, the cantors beating bells and triangles and clashing cymbals.

Children receive a second name at baptism, usually that of the saint of the day, unless the parents prefer

Baptism

the name of a favourite saint. For boys *Girgis* (George), and for girls *Maria* (Mary), or Miriam, are very common baptismal names.

On the eighth day after baptism the rite of loosing the girdle is observed in the baptistery of the church. A vessel of pure water is placed on the Gospel stand, with a cross lying on the rim, and lighted tapers around it. Incense is offered and the following portions of Scripture are repeated:

> Epistle of St. Paul (1 Cor. x. 1-4).
> The Trisagion.
> The prayer before the Gospel.
> Psalm cxiv. 3 and 5.
> Gospel (St. Matt. iii. 13-17).
> The Three Great Petitions and the Creed.

After a special prayer the water is signed thrice in the form of a cross by the priest, who then removes the girdle and washes the child and his clothes.

There is a Coptic story of the fourth century (which might have come from a village to-day) illustrating not only the importance attached to baptism, but also the infinite hope these Eastern people have in the mercy of God. A certain man living remote from the world had a little daughter, who died before she could be baptized. Her father distributed among the poor the portion that came to her; and he never ceased to make entreaty to God on behalf of his daughter because she had departed without being baptized. As he prayed one day, he heard a voice, which said, "Have no sorrow; I have baptized thy daughter"; but he lacked faith. And the voice spake again, saying, "Uncover her grave, and thou wilt find she is no longer there." And he did so, and he found her not, for she had departed, and had been laid with the believers.

The union of confirmation and baptism is peculiar to the Coptic Church, and so is the use of the holy chrism for confirmation, and also the fact that the priest has authority for confirmation as well as the bishop. It is maintained that here the Copts have retained the early teaching of the Catholic Church which has been abandoned by the Western branch.

Circumcision is generally practised in the country, but rarely in Cairo. The Church, for some strange reason, clearly prohibits its performance after baptism, even declaring the sacrament to be annulled by the operation; but the country people pay little heed to the rule, mostly conforming to the custom of the Moslem majority, which is to wait till the child is five or six years old, and then to have it done by the official village barber (who, however, slightly varies the nature of the operation in the case of the Copts), making a festival of it like their neighbours. September is the month usually chosen for these fêtes, for the fruit harvest has then brought wealth to the people after their labours.

Islam adopted this custom, for circumcision was an Egyptian rite as far back as two thousand years before Abraham. It is shown on the early monuments, and the mummies have shown clear evidence of the same fact. It is mentioned in the Book of Exodus, and it is interesting to recall that it was Ishmael, the son of the Egyptian Hagar, who was first circumcised by Abraham, long before Isaac was born.

The Copts firmly believe in it on health grounds; for one thing they believe it to be a preventive of cancer, or a cure if done later in life. The wound is treated with powdered pomegranate bark. With the Moslems a boy is made eligible only by this rite to pray in the mosque.

Baptism

It is the occasion of a great feast, beginning on the night before, when henna leaves are kneaded into a paste, which, especially in country places, is rolled into pieces, set on a tray, with a taper set on every piece. The boy who is the occasion of the festival walks behind the henna tray through the house, with all the women folk singing and *zagreeting* (a curious shrill bubbling cry) to show their joy. Before retiring to rest the boy has one of the lumps of henna paste bound into the palm of his hand, and the women do the same for themselves, the result being that the next morning they are stained a reddish brown.

On the day of circumcision, the boy is dressed in the finest clothes possible, taken from the treasures of the hareem, as a sign that up to this time he has belonged to the women. A gold embroidered cap such as the women wear is put on his head, and he proudly rides on horseback in a grand procession through the town or village, with music, and the firing of guns without which no *fantasia* is complete.

There is, of course, a bountiful feast, provided by the father; and the guests contribute to the fees of the barber, who is a properly appointed person in every community. It is a striking comment on the statements of those who seem to delight in fostering animosity between Moslem and Copt, that the same barber, irrespective of his religion, performs this ceremony for the whole community.

CHAPTER VII

How a Wife is Chosen

THE old traditional Coptic custom, that it is the duty of the parents to marry their children exactly as they think fit, without any reference to the children themselves, prevails to the present day, except in the cities, or in the highly educated families. In the country, where the old patriarchal customs remain unchanged, the young people still have no voice in the matter; in fact, marriages are sometimes arranged long before the children are of an age to contract matrimony.

In one thing there is a tendency towards a universal change: it is no longer thought suitable, as it was less than half a century ago, to marry boys of fifteen to girls of twelve years of age. The Church now insists that the man shall be twenty and the girl sixteen; and no priest may celebrate a wedding ceremony without a licence from the Patriarch or the bishop of the diocese.

Another advance has also been made by the Church, through the decree of the Patriarch. The sexes had been kept rigorously apart, so that no man ever saw any woman outside a close degree of relationship.

Many Copts profess to believe that this seclusion dates only from the Arab invasion (the scapegoat event especially of all those plausible men who strive to commend the Coptic race to the dominant English), but they are clearly mistaken, as the Scriptures alone might show them. It was one of their own early fathers, Abba Arsenius, who rebuked a certain noble lady who travelled from Rome to see him at Alexandria, "Didst thou not know that thou wast a woman, and that it was incumbent on thee not to go forth anywhere?" Like the veil, seclusion has always in the East been a matter of custom, and not of creed.

With the spread of education, and by contact in the cities with French and English civilisation, a relaxation of this rule gradually crept into certain restricted circles, with the result that young people met, and in some cases they declined to go on with an engagement already made for them. Or it was after marriage that they found a more congenial person than their mate. In the one case this led to great friction in families, for the insult of a broken engagement has always fomented the deadliest of feuds; in the other, immorality was the result.

Acting under wise advice, the Patriarch—and this should be remembered by those who declare that he is entirely reactionary—issued an instruction to all the clergy to the effect that, it not being contrary to the canons of the Church, young people engaged to marry should not only see each other, but should be brought together under proper conditions so as to know each other well. He further ordered that the priests were to undertake the duty of ascertaining that this rule was made effective, and that they were not to celebrate a marriage until they had an assurance from both parties that they freely consented to it.

A young man seeking marriage still acts through intermediaries, and does not propose directly to the girl; and it is almost, if not entirely unknown, for a girl to have married without the consent of her parents.

I can testify to the fact that there are many happy marriages amongst the Copts, though I cannot say they are confined to the younger generation; the evidence shows that generally the unions made under parental advice were successful.

It is not, I know, considered possible by Western people that a Darby and Joan romance can be looked for amongst Orientals. In this we have been entirely wrong. I know very many old couples in Egypt, Moslem as well as Copt, who were married as children, and have travelled happily side by side into a ripe old age, with an ever-increasing affection and respect—the old lady the sole ruler of the hareem, which the husband delights to enrich with costly and pleasing gifts, so that it is by far the most sumptuous part of the home. Here the one wife reigns supreme, and the hareem has become more and more, as years have gone by, the husband's favourite resort, as well as that of his grown-up sons, who treat their mother with every sign of loving veneration and respect.

In calling upon a certain aged Pasha in Cairo, a man of vast wealth, it became a sort of joke between myself and the confidential servant, that the master was always in the hareem; and as my wife had the entry to the reserved quarters of the palace, I heard much of the fine old wife, and the charming family life of which she was the one mistress. And this is only one case of many, contradicting the salacious notions about the hareem which I fear the West prefers to the sober truth.

I wish I could think that these changes in the Coptic marriage customs had made for an increase of morality. Unfortunately, the same Western civilisation which suggested them has brought in its wake social evils which were almost unknown before. Lord Cromer used to declare that a certain depraved quarter of Cairo was "the grave of Egypt's best treasure"; it is a grave dug almost entirely by Europeans, chiefly of the Levant.

As far as the Copts are affected, a great many misleading statements have been made. It is equally untrue to say, as Lane did in those cruel libels on the Copts which are the sole defect of a book which has so deservedly become a great classic,[1] that the Copts are "abandoned to indulgence in sensual pleasure"; as it is to make a statement so absurd as that of a recent writer, who, quoting it as something she had heard, says: "It should not be forgotten that there is not a Coptic woman of public bad character in all Egypt. . . . A fallen woman hides her shame by becoming a Moslem."[2]

This absurdly untruthful statement has been quoted by every subsequent writer, especially those with a Christian bias, regardless of the fact that for years the most scandalous of the public singing women in Cairo bears a name which she has made so famous that I have never met an intelligent person anywhere in Lower Egypt who was not most familiar with it—*Shafika el Coptieh*, or Shafika the Copt. And one remembers in this connection the story of Thais the Harlot, and the Coptic life of her times. What a terrible indictment that was, of a recent critic, that large sums of the revenue of the Coptic Church are derived from property in the immoral quarter of Cairo.[3]

My own observation has shown me the truth of the mature judgment of Lord Cromer, as applied to this

---

[1] *The Modern Egyptians*, E. W. Lane (written in 1833-35).
[2] *Things seen in Egypt*, E. L. Butcher.
[3] *Egyptian Gazette*, Dec. 2, 1913.

particular matter, that the Copts are on about the same level as the rest of the Egyptians.

I believe, however, that if the hopes of reviving the spiritual life of the Church are in any degree realised, a very great change will take place in the moral life of these people. No one who has seen the zeal and piety of some of the young men who have come under the reforming movement, can doubt that they are the true descendants of the men and women whose passion for godliness in the early days of Christianity led to one of the most remarkable spiritual movements the world has ever seen, the development of monasticism. If a prophet should arise in the Church itself—and in the East there is always an atmosphere of the expectancy of this—there would be a rich moral and spiritual harvest. The Oriental, of whatever religion, does not temporise if a clear call to the æsthetic life makes itself heard in his very soul ; he will leave all to follow.

As for the uplifting of women, in which we look to the Copts to lead the way, let me tell the beautiful story, as a parable, of a Coptic woman saint, of the nunnery founded by the blessed Pachomius in Egypt.

In the nunnery was a certain sister who was a virgin, and she made herself an object of contempt; the other sisters used to treat her so slightingly that they would not even allow her to eat with them. And the woman was so well content with this treatment, that she would wait upon every one in the refectory. So she became " the broom of the whole nunnery."

Over her head this sister used to throw a rough piece of cloth, whilst the other nuns wore the veils of their rule, well cut and well made. She ate apart, and none of them looked at her, and she never touched a whole loaf of bread, but ate the broken bits and crusts that fell from the table, and she drank the dregs from the basins of the other nuns.

And although the other women constantly reviled her, and struck her, and threw rinsings of the vessels over her, and thrust her away with harsh and insulting words, she neither reviled any one of them, nor murmured, nor uttered any superfluous words.

Now at this time there was a great saint, "a man of wonder," named Piterius, in Egypt, and an angel appeared to him, and said, "If thou wouldst see a saint who is more excellent than thou, go to the nunnery in Tabenna, and behold thou shalt find one who is far superior to thee." And he went quickly, and besought the Superior to let him see the nuns. Knowing that Piterius was a blessed man, these came asking for his blessing; but she who made herself a mere broom did not show herself.

And Piterius said, "There is one missing"; but they replied that there was only one other, and she was of no account. So they sought her in the refectory, but she declined to go, so that, with their usual treatment of her, they dragged her.

And when Mar Piterius saw her, he bowed down before her, and said, "Bless me, mother!" But she fell at his feet, crying, "Bless thou me, master!" And the nuns were struck with wonder, and begged him not to demean himself—this was a creature below contempt. Then Piterius said, "Ye yourselves are creatures of contempt; but this woman is your Mother, and mine, and I entreat God that He will give unto me a portion with her in the day of judgment."

I commend this story to the Coptic people, to whose early Church such a lovely saint belonged. The suggestion of it in connection with the woman question is too clear—to Oriental minds especially—to need a word of comment.

As soon as the consent of two families has been obtained for an engagement, the young man sends to the maiden, by a priest, a gold ring, possibly set with diamonds, which is called *el-shabka*, the engagement ring, and an early day is fixed for the formal betrothal. This ceremony is called *Jepeniot*, which is the Coptic for the "Oh, our Father" of the Lord's Prayer. In the evening of the day fixed, the groom, accompanied by a number of his relatives and friends, go with a priest to the bride's house, where her relatives are assembled to receive them.

The priest opens the proceedings with the Lord's Prayer, which is still used on all occasions somewhat as the *talisma* of the early Christians, all present joining. The priest then makes a little formal speech, referring to the antiquity of the ceremony, and alluding to the betrothal of Rebecca to Isaac.

The marriage contract is drawn up; the dowry mentioned in it must now be paid, and the date of the wedding is made part of the contract. The priest, and other important people present, sign the document, which is afterwards registered at the bishop's office, and placed in the archives of the diocese, a marriage licence being issued in exchange.

The dowry ranges from £10 to £200 (it must not exceed the latter sum), according to the wealth of the bridegroom. The bride's father generally contributes the same sum—sometimes he will double it—and the whole amount is spent on buying the beautiful jewels which most Egyptian women possess, or on the more personal trousseau. It is only in Upper Egypt that the bride supplies all the furniture.

Refreshments, supplied by the groom, are now served, and the company becomes very joyous; congratulations and compliments are offered, in the poetic language of the East.

In the interval before the marriage, which is not often prolonged beyond a week or two, the young man is expected to send to his bride-elect daily gifts of flowers and fruit. If festivals such as Christmas or Easter intervene, he generally sends her a robe, and some of the cakes and sweets which are eaten only at such times.

CHAPTER VIII

The Coptic Wedding

WEDDINGS are, as a rule, celebrated on the night of Saturday and Sunday. They are never celebrated during Lent or any of the fasts kept by the Coptic Church, except under very exceptional circumstances. Although very few people now keep the long fasts, these still preclude marriage for more than one-third of the year.

It is through the weekly fasts, too, that Sunday has been chosen for marriage, Wednesdays and Fridays being regular fast-days; and as three days are necessary for the proper solemnisation, Saturday, Sunday, and Monday alone are possible. As marriage is one of the seven Holy Sacraments, it is thought doubly fitting to choose the Holy Day. Tuesday is made impossible for any wedding ceremony by universal superstition as to ill luck.

The first night is called the bride's night, and is celebrated at her parents' house; it is sometimes spoken of as the night of *henna*, because before she goes to bed the bride applies henna to the palms of her hands and the soles of her feet, so that the red stain it leaves may be fresh the next day. In some way this is regarded as a sign of her virginity.

In the course of that day the bride, with her girl

THE SCENE AT THE FARM IN THE DELTA.
The girl whose marriage the Pasha offered to arrange with her father. The young brother was leading the buffalo which worked the primitive water-wheel.

THE DISTANT VILLAGE IN UPPER EGYPT FROM WHICH IT IS SAID THE MAGICIANS CAME WHO PITTED THEIR ARTS AGAINST THOSE OF MOSES AND AARON.
The author happened to be passing this village when on a country journey and native friends with him spoke of the tradition as though it belonged to almost recent times.

friends and her female relatives, have been to one of the public baths, which has been specially reserved for the party; here a great frolic is held, and the prettiest compliments are paid the girl by the older women, to the special gratification of the bride's mother.

At night she is adorned with all the splendour possible—girls of even moderate wealth will wear a valuable diamond tiara on such an occasion—and she holds a reception, to which all relatives and friends are bidden. All the guests stay to dinner, and spend a great part of the night listening to music and singing.

The house is gorgeously decorated with flowers and bunting, and at night the illuminations are brilliant, many sparkling lustre chandeliers being hired for the occasion. The women occupy the upper stories, the ground floor being reserved for the men. In most cases one of the beautiful pavilions, elaborately decorated in applique designs of many colours, and hung with countless lustre chandeliers for the candles, is erected in the courtyard or garden, or even in the street, for the use of the men, the whole house then being left for the women.

The food is prepared by special cooks engaged for the occasion. I have already described an Eastern feast, as it is served on the round metal trays placed on stools, when the guests eat with their fingers. Such Oriental feasts are often made on great ceremonial occasions, even when the hosts ordinarily eat in the French way. When a priest is present, as on this occasion, he takes precedence over all other people, whatever may be their rank. He begins by saying grace, then, taking a loaf, he blesses, then breaks it, and gives a small piece to each person present.

The groom does not put in an appearance at the bride's house on this night, but he sends a small deputation of his nearest relatives, and along with them a bouquet, and a wax candle that must be as long as the bride is tall. This candle remains lighted in her chamber during the whole night, and is also regarded as a symbol of the bride's virginity.

On the morning of Sunday, the bride and the bridegroom should, after confession, have attended the Mass, afterwards spending the time in quiet reflection, but this is only done by the pious.

In the afternoon—called the bridegroom's night—the *shebeen*, or best man, accompanied by two or three of the nearest relatives of the groom, goes to fetch the bride. The *shebeen* always pays for the carriages hired for this procession, and he tips the servants. The bride's father presents him with a gold or silver cigarette case; which accounts for the fact that every man of any position in Egypt seems to possess a valuable article of this sort; sometimes this is put down by travellers to an inordinate love of display.

The bride now leaves the home of her parents, and goes in state to the house prepared by the bridegroom, preceded by a band of musicians. Some years since these processions only moved at night, and they were very effective. First came the bearers of the great torches; then the band, followed by men each carrying a candle appearing out of the centre of a bouquet; then pages, walking backwards so as to face the bride, carrying incense burners and perfume bottles, with which they sprinkled the onlookers; then the bride, leaning on the arm of the best man, followed by the ladies, with family servants in the rear.

Such wedding processions may still sometimes be seen, but now they are generally Moslem; and of course the bride is then hidden, either in a closed carriage, or

The Coptic Wedding

in a palanquin, sometimes fixed, as I have often seen it in the country, on the back of a camel.

It is usual with the Copts of to-day, in the cities, for the bride and the ladies to be conveyed to the bridegroom's house in closed carriages, escorted only by the best man and their few male relations.

On arriving at the house, the old custom is, however, still observed of killing a calf or a sheep at the bride's feet in such a way that its blood shall flow on the threshold over which she must step. The flesh is given to the poor. The bride is carried or helped up to the ladies' quarters by the best man.

As the procession leaves the bride's maiden home, and as it enters the groom's house, it is sprinkled with salt, and sometimes with rose leaves, to avert the effects of "the envious eye."

Priests and acolytes and cantors, and the whole host of ecclesiastics, now arrive at the house to prepare for the religious ceremony.

After resting a little and partaking of slight refreshment, the wedding or "crowning" ceremony is begun. It is general for it to take place in the house; though there is no rule against its being celebrated in the church.

A table has been placed in the middle of one of the largest halls in the house, and on this a copy of the Holy Gospel is placed, in its sealed silver case, surrounded by six silver crosses, to each of which three wax candles are fixed. This symbol of the Holy Trinity is used in many of the Coptic services. A golden cross and the golden wedding ring are also placed upon the table.

Two arm-chairs are placed in front of the table for the use of the couple to be married.

In another room the groom is robed in a richly

embroidered cope, and then conducted in a procession, preceded by the choir, to the hall. He takes the left-hand chair—as one would expect, seeing that in the West he would take the right-hand—for East and West are always opposite.

The clergy and choir then go to bring the bride, who is dressed in white, adorned with orange blossoms, her face being covered with a thin veil. She wears diamond and gold ornaments. The deacons carry candles and bells, and the cantors clash the cymbals, all singing, "Blessed is he that cometh in the name of the Lord," and, "O King of Peace, give us Thy peace."

In the old days the robing of both the man and the woman was part of the service, the priest blessing the garments and vesting the bride and the bridegroom at the table.

The priest begins the service by saying three times, "We are assembled to solemnise the union of *N*. and *M*.," repeating after each announcement the Lord's Prayer, in which all present should join inaudibly.

The priest then says the Thanksgiving, and offers incense. Then several chapters from the Old and New Testament are read, referring to marriage. There are three beautiful Prayers of Betrothal, and a Thanksgiving for the Betrothal.

There is a prayer over the oil with which the couple are anointed, and then comes the Rite of Coronation. Two crowns of gold are placed upon the foreheads of the pair, and they are made to exchange rings and to join hands. Their heads are drawn close together and are both covered with a single embroidered sash. The couple are also bound together with a ribbon, as a symbol of the indissoluble character of marriage, and that they are no longer two, but one.

The Coptic Wedding

At the close of the service the priest lays the cross upon their heads as he pronounces the benediction. The crowns, as well as the wedding robes and the sash, are the property of the church.

In the exhortation at the end of the service (which takes three hours for its proper celebration), the priest, first addressing the groom, says, "I deliver to you your bride *N.*, who is now your wife. You have now more authority over her than her parents. You must always treat her with love and kindness, and never neglect any of her wants," and so on.

Turning to the bride he says to her, "You have heard, according to the Scriptures, that your husband is your head, as Christ is the head of the Church. That means that you must obey and respect him, as Sarah obeyed Abraham and always addressed him as 'my master.' You must keep his house well, and make his home always cheerful," and so on.

Finally, speaking to both, he says, "If you obey what you have heard, God will bless you as He blessed Abraham and Sarah, Isaac and Rebecca."

The service is concluded by the singing of hymns in Coptic and Arabic, and the women, who are never able to contain themselves, accompany the hymns by their peculiar *zagreet*, the sort of yodelling cry they use to express either joy or sorrow as the occasion may demand.

After the ceremony the bride goes to the hareem, and the bridegroom to the men's apartments, to take dinner and to receive the congratulations of friends, amidst great rejoicing. About an hour before midnight the bride and bridegroom retire, but the music goes on during the greater part of the night.

On Monday the nearest relatives of both sides spend the day at the groom's house. The bride waits on them herself, and every guest presents her with a gift according to means. These gifts may be a diamond or a gold ornament, or a sum of money, £1 to £10; every one receiving in return a handkerchief embroidered by the bride.

On the occasion of a wedding it is the custom of all intimate friends to help by contributing something towards the coming fête—one will send a sheep, another fowls, others rice, sugar, coffee, candles, and so on.

The recipient generally makes a list of all the things received, and on a similar occasion returns something of the same value if he be of the same means, or of more or less value, as he is a richer or poorer man.

In spite of this custom, however, the temptation to the Egyptian seems irresistible to spend far too much on display, and it is no uncommon thing for families to cripple their resources in this way. I have been to many weddings, on the festivities of which sums ranging from £1000 to £10,000 have been spent, and in nearly every case it was out of proportion to the means of the families concerned.

Divorce is not very common amongst the Copts. Remarriage is not greatly favoured, and it may only take place by the innocent party applying to the Patriarch for permission. No person can be crowned in marriage a second time.

One of the most gorgeous weddings of recent years, unequalled in Oriental magnificence, it is said, since the spacious days of Ismail, took place at Assiout, between two of my acquaintances, shortly after I had left Egypt after my last visit, in 1913. Miss Esther Fanous, the bride, had read to me some of her charming poems, written in English, and I had often had the pleasure of hearing her speak of her deep joy in the beauties of her beloved country, and of its magnificent, time-old history; and I had also seen her, type of the new Egyptian womanhood, using her gifts to uplift the poor fellaheen by her eloquent pleading in the name of the Cross. I had also met Mr. Wissa, the bridegroom, a graduate of Cambridge, and a member of one of the great Coptic families of Upper Egypt.

I give a short account of this wedding, for which I am indebted to a Coptic friend who was present, because it illustrates several things to which reference has been made, and especially shows how the native customs assert themselves on such occasions, in spite of the use that is made of some of the Western modes of life.

"Nothing had been spared to make the ceremony the complete success it proved to be. Eastern beauty and Western science blended harmoniously in the gorgeous marquee (*suvan*) with the myriads of ancient oil lamps and the gorgeous modern electric chandeliers. In this pavilion no fewer than 8000 guests were entertained on one night. Khedivial banners and a magnificent triumphal arch adorned the streets leading to the bridegroom's house. The preparations are said to have cost £20,000.

"The entertainment lasted for three days continuously, and the guests, who came from all over the country, included native Pashas, Beys, Omdehs, sheikhs, and other notables, besides European Government officials and a host of minor folk.

"On the first day eight hundred village notables were entertained to lunch and dinner, *à la Turque*, by the parents of the bride; and in the evening, Abdulhalim Effendi Nahas, the renowned singer, and Sami Effendi Shawas, the violinist, displayed their talents to the delight of a select audience, being accompanied on the mandolin (*kanoun*) by Mohammed Effendi Omar, most of the pieces being rapturously and repeatedly encored.

"On another day the guests from Cairo and Alexandria, and many from Assiout, including native and foreign officials, distinguished residents and their families, were entertained to lunch at the Wissa mansion, and in the evening they attended a special reception given by the bride's mother, Mme. Akhnoukh Fanous, whose house was beautifully decorated with flowers and coloured lights. At 8 p.m. the guests began to arrive, being greeted by the band of the Wissa school with Arabic and European airs; and at nine o'clock Fethy Pasha, the Mudir of Assiout, led the way to supper. After this, the toasts and speech-making ended, the male guests proceeded to the Wissa mansion to hear Arabic songs by Mohammed Effendi el Saba, accompanied by Mohammed Effendi Omar's orchestra.

"Another day was devoted to the entertainment of the native ladies, who lunched with the bride's family, and took part in the procession to the bridegroom's house, the Wissas meantime entertaining hundreds of native villagers, Moslem and Christian, to a Turkish luncheon.

"On the afternoon of each of the three days, splendid displays of horsemanship were given in front of the bride's house by members of leading local families on richly caparisoned steeds, each performance ending with a procession round the house, the horsemen beating drums and shouting such phrases as, 'Amar ya bib Fanous!'—'May the house of Fanous flourish for ever!'

"An interesting incident took place when the leading horseman, noting Dr. Fanous (who is an invalid) on the balcony, rode his horse up the great flight of steps to salute him, the doctor rising to his feet to grasp the

The Coptic Wedding

hand of the cavalier, who then rode down again, amid the frenzied shouts and cheers of the vast crowd below.

"At 8 p.m. on the evening of the wedding itself, the procession, preceded by the band and torch-bearers, and a contingent of mounted police, and composed of over a hundred carriages, proceeded to the large marquee. Here it was met by Coptic choristers, chanting a hymn of welcome, who accompanied the bride and her party to the dais, where the wedding ceremony was performed by the Coptic bishops and clergy. The officiating clergy included Orthodox and Protestant representatives, the Patriarch having delegated two bishops to represent him, writing at the same time his great regret that age and infirmity prevented his personal attendance. There were also present the Bishops of Assiout, Khartoum, and Kena, the latter being accompanied by the full choir of his church.

"The five prelates, and the Reverend Mouawad Hanna, united the bridal pair with full Orthodox and Protestant rites, according to the desire of the Patriarch, the Coptic Orthodox and Protestant choirs chanting sacred verses and selected psalms. Both bride and bridegroom belong to the Protestant Church, Dr. Akhnoukh Fanous being President of the Church Council, the Megliss el Milli.

"After the ceremony, which lasted an hour, Khalil Moutran, the native poet, and others, recited beautiful epithalamia in prose and verse.

"At 11 p.m. a sumptuous supper was first served to three hundred guests, and afterwards to several thousands of the poorer people, the feasting going on until 2 a.m. The Moslem and Christian ladies were privately entertained meantime in the house. The festivities were not over until 5 a.m., when they ended in singing and dancing."

CHAPTER IX

The Oriental in Grief; and the Coptic Burial Customs

OF all the customs consecrated by long usage, none are more sacred or more passionately cherished by the Copts, especially the women, than the many observances connected with death. Time has done less to eradicate some of the ancient superstitions in this matter than in any other, and customs survive from the old religion which the lapse of centuries, and the hopes inspired by Christianity, seem to have been almost powerless to supplant.

When a person is thought to be dying, the relatives and friends crowd into the house, and even throng the sick chamber.

The administration of the Holy Eucharist is performed, if the patient is able to swallow. As the sacrament must not be reserved, the priest must consecrate the elements afresh in the church, and then go in procession to the house; and the sick person must make a confession.

The early Oriental Christians placed the Host in the mouth of the dead; and it became the custom to enclose some of the elements in the coffin. At a Synod held at Hippo, in 393, at which St. Augustine was present, this custom was strongly condemned.

The Oriental in Grief

As soon as the end has come, there is a terrible outburst of abandoned grief, the wails and exclamations and shrieks of the women stopping short of nothing that can make the scene harrowing to an inconceivable degree.

As the women dance frantically about the bedside, in a way suggestive of utter despair, they strike their faces, calling upon the dead to arise to see the grief his departure has caused.

A wife cries, "Oh, my husband; oh, my sorrow, my death; oh, despair!" appealing to her husband as her "lion and protector," as the "camel who bore all her burdens" (the camel being the symbol of strength and support), as the "beloved father of her children." A daughter bewails her mother as her "darling protector and the sharer of her secrets." In the case of a young friend of ours who died just after her marriage had been arranged, I heard the constant cry from the hareem, "The bride is dead! the bride is dead!" Indeed, nothing that the Oriental imagination can suggest, that can harrow the feelings, is left unsaid.

Even the men, at other times apparently so undemonstrative, weep loudly, and give themselves up to grief, the while they say to consoling friends the word so often used by the Oriental, "Ma'leesh"—"Do not mind." "Life is so; thank God *you* are still alive to us" is a usual greeting to the chief mourner.

As Marcus Simaika Pasha, himself a Copt, has remarked: "When one thinks of the resignation and fortitude, amounting almost to apathy, which the Copts, in common with most Orientals, show when any other calamity befalls them, such as the loss of their eyesight, or a limb, or their fortune, one wonders that they give way to such despair on the loss of a near relative."

This wonder increases when you happen to know that during his lifetime the deceased was not the object of any special affection on the part of the disconsolate mourners; sometimes quite the reverse.

My own belief is that the panic that seizes the Oriental in the presence of death is something apart altogether from the qualities of the deceased. The horror of death comes with great force to a people who do not ordinarily allow their happy moments to be clouded by reflection or apprehension. They are creatures of the day, never anticipating or morbidly dwelling upon life's ills.

In the minor trials of life the first instinct of the Oriental is to turn aside from any consideration that would rob him of the happiness still possible to him; and this instinct, combined with a genuine faith in God, leads him to a peaceful submission to what he believes to be His will.

It is easy to call this fatalism, either in the Moslem or the Copt; for they are both equally Oriental. In the history of the one race, as much as the other, *kismet* has had its influence. It was a Coptic monk—Abba Sisoes—who, long before the Moslem Arabs rose to power, said, "In the road in which a man advanceth he goeth, whether it be to life or death."

It is only in the presence of that supreme calamity and terror of Death, the consideration of which cannot be easily put aside, that these surprising manifestations occur.

After the first outburst of grief, the body is washed, always by a person of the same sex; while, in pious families, the priests come to chant the Psalms. Then the body is dressed, in new underclothes, if possible of pure flax that has been steeped in the river Jordan; over

and the Coptic Burial Customs 125

this is placed the richest costume the man possessed. The hands are laid across the breast, and over the body is thrown a sheet of cloth, silk or cashmere; or, by the poor, a red shawl.

By this time the men have withdrawn to the downstairs apartments, and the whole of the upper part of the house is given over to the women, to become again the scene of indescribable excitement. They have put on, in the most careless manner, the dirtiest dark blue coverings they can find; have loosened their hair; and sometimes they smear themselves with indigo, and pluck out their hair, and injure their flesh, in the frenzy that is generated.

Like all bad news, that concerning a death spreads with rapidity, and soon all the friends and acquaintances of the family, women especially, flock from all parts of Egypt. The telegraph, the telephone, and the express train nowadays add even more largely to these gatherings.

The men, as they arrive, just touch the hands of the chief men mourners, and then quietly occupy the rows of seats provided in the *salemlik*, or great hall, or, failing that, the great tent which has immediately been erected; here they sit all through that first "night of loneliness," hardly speaking a word, smoking the unfailing cigarette, and occasionally sipping the coffee (now without sugar) which is brought to them in the special black cups only used on such occasions.

Very different are the women when they arrive. On reaching the door of the house they raise their voices in the piercing *zagreet* of lamentation, and are answered by renewed outbursts from the women above.

The whole interior of the house is now covered in black; all bedsteads or sofas are removed; the carpets are reversed, and the mirrors and pictures turned with their faces to the walls, when they are not smashed to atoms. Any ornamental furniture, such as cabinets and sideboards, is turned out of the house. Not so long ago, all the china and glass, often of great value, would be broken and swept into heaps in the corners of the room.

A friend in Cairo has shown me one or two pieces of valuable china from his late father's collection, which he rescued from the débris made of it by the women of the family on his parents' death.

Many enlightened families, however, especially in the cities to-day, moderate such excesses, and the use of drums and funerary dances has ceased with them. In several towns there are branches of a Coptic Women's Society for the enlightening of their sex. I have attended their meetings, and in answer to my inquiries I have found that one of their first duties they consider to be to attempt to overcome extravagant expressions of mourning, although they admit it seems to be the last thing the ordinary Egyptian woman will give up.

The professional wailing women never fail to come, uninvited, to add another wild note to the scene which is being enacted around the corpse, now laid on a mattress on the floor. They bring with them the little drums on which they beat an exciting tattoo, while by word and gesture they further provoke the unhappy women until they are quite beside themselves.

These hired women have a great and varied store of phrases about the qualities of the dead, which, as they sit on the floor, in the midst of the gathering, they chant to weird tunes—telling of his qualities, real or imaginary ; of prowess, and kindness, and gentleness, and courtesy, in exaggerated terms. Any lady who may be particularly touched by any sort of personal application she may see in one of these sentences, again bursts out into shrieks.

A curious thing is that any guest present seems to have the right to ask the hired mourners to chant special verses referring to her own private griefs, in return for a small fee, without reference to the lady of the house.

In the case of the death of a young person an additional type of professional mourner presents herself. These women bring large tambourines which they strike to a still weirder chanting. They do not sit, as the others do, but stand, the ladies standing closely round them; and they start every now and then a funerary dance of a wild order. It is hoped, however, that at least this feature will soon die out.

Like mad creatures, these women beat their faces and breasts again and again, tear their hair, and do not cease dancing and shrieking until they fall from sheer exhaustion; to begin again as soon as they recover. From time to time all the women join in a tremendous cry.

This is kept up until the corpse is removed, the law fortunately only allowing twenty-four hours for this to be done; until then, no one thinks of taking any food, the only respite between early morning and sunset being a short interval now and then, when the women smoke cigarettes.

In all this, the customs of ancient Egypt, and also of the Jews, are being followed—the loud lamentations, the smearing, the professional mourning women. When our Lord was called to the house of mourning at the death of Jairus' daughter, He suppressed "the minstrels and the people making a noise" (Matt. ix. 23). It is not according to the teaching of Christianity, and Mohammed strictly forbade it, but the women of neither creed will take heed.

The Church, and even the Government, have interfered to stop the professional wailing, and the shrieking of women mourners in public; but almost in vain. After many efforts, all that has been accomplished is that the women no longer blacken their faces and hands to accompany the funeral to the cemetery, so that the terrible scenes they created there have been stopped.

When the body, now placed in a coffin strewn with flowers,—rose water and other perfumes having been sprinkled over it,[1]—is removed for burial, the climax of the storm of the women's grief is reached.

The priests accompany the body downstairs, and the long procession starts at once for the church. The order of those who take part is as follows—in the case of families who are not too poor to conform to it. First there walk a number of the hired *shaushîya* (or policemen), then priests with black stoles, chanting the Three Holies, and the "Remember me, O Lord, when Thou hast come to Thy Kingdom," followed by deacons and acolytes in white, carrying banners. Then comes the "carpet of mercy," a large black cloth, with white crosses appliqued on it, held at the corners by four of the most distinguished friends of the deceased. Then follows the bier. Of recent years funeral carriages have come into use; previously the coffin was carried in turn by the nearest friends.

It has always been considered a meritorious act in the East to assist in burying the dead; although the Coptic Tewfic Society was started to initiate reform, one

[1] In Lower Egypt a few favourite jewels only are placed in the coffin; in Upper Egypt, always more conservative, it is still the custom to bury with the dead all their ornaments and clothes.

of the first duties it imposed upon itself was to help the people in this matter of burial.

Then follow all the relatives and friends, who must walk to the church; a string of empty carriages following, to take the relatives and intimate friends on to the cemetery.

In the church the coffin is placed on a bier in front of the door of the sanctuary, and the Service for the Dead is recited. It consists of the thanksgiving prayer and the prayer for the dead, chanted in Coptic, readings in Arabic from the Gospels and the Epistles, and especially prepared readings called "Tark."

At the end of the service the lid of the coffin, which has attached to it a large cross, is removed (it is never sealed until the ceremonies are concluded), and the chief priest scatters dust upon the body, saying, "From dust, and unto dust shalt thou return."

Then the coffin is carried three times round the church, the choir chanting the Three Holies. The funeral services of the Copts are according to the liturgy of St. Mark—a special service being used during Easter.

Every member of the congregation now touches the hands of the chief mourners, and those who are not going to the cemetery depart. At the cemetery, if the family is of any wealth at all, there is a family vault, and in this the coffin is deposited. The vault will have a courtyard, and a small house with two or three rooms, fitted with bedding and cooking apparatus, for the use of the family when they go "to visit the dead."

Returning to the house the mourners partake of food for the first time since the death took place, and for two days this food is supplied to them by relatives. One reason for this is that household servants expect to indulge their grief equally with their masters, and all work in the house, not connected with the mourning ceremonies, is thus at a standstill.

Till the third day the women continue the scenes described, receiving all their friends who join them in their frantic abandonment. Downstairs the men still sit silent, as friends come in to sit with them a while to show their quiet sympathy.

It is on the afternoon of the third day that relief comes, and the soothing consolations of religion, by the arrival of the priests to perform the service of "sending the soul away." This is based on an interesting and persistent belief from Pharaonic times, that the soul of the departed haunts his earthly home until certain offerings are made to it which give repose. The Church has adapted the belief, and given it a Christian meaning. The fact that part of the service of the priests is to bless the table from which the inmates of the house will afterwards eat, points to an origin connected with the offerings of food.

The priests now bless certain food which is to be given as funeral alms to the poor, and all the rooms are sprinkled with holy water, while many comforting and beautiful prayers are recited. The effect of this service is always to heal to some extent the torn nerves, and to calm the minds of the sufferers, after the awful ordeal through which they have passed.

In the evening of this day all visitors to the house depart; the Mass is read in the church, but it is not a Mass for the dead, as that is unknown to the Coptic Church.

Now, for the first time, the mourners may look forward to a night of peace. Many of my Coptic friends in middle life remember the time when the excitement was kept up for forty days, and in extreme cases the mourning customs were sustained almost without cessation for a whole year.

On the seventh day the peace is broken again by a day of mourning, and at intervals of a few days the women meet again to express sorrow, that is now more restrained—through forty days, during which they may not leave the house. Often one hears, in passing along the native streets, in town and village, echoing from the house of mourning, the sounds of the slow, sorrowful, monotonous songs of lament for the dead, uttered in low tones by the women gathered within, and mingled with weeping and sobbing. I know of nothing more painfully thrilling than this. Where the sorrow is a very real one, a mother or a wife will for years seek relief for her wounded heart in this way. Among the ancient Egyptians similar mourning hymns were sung during the period of the seventy days when the body was being embalmed.

The custom of commemorating the dead after forty days is a very old one, and is common to Moslems as well as Copts, although it was a long-established practice before the Arab conquest. In the case of a man of any note who has died, his acquaintances nowadays will meet together to listen to an oration in his honour, while the women gather in private, and harass themselves again with grief.

The time of mourning with the Copts is a year, and on every great festival during that time the women meet to wail and cry. They are not supposed to leave the house at all on feast-days, for a year, except to go to the cemetery, and they may not even go to church on those days. They must dress in black, and lay aside all their jewellery.

These customs are very hard on the women; and

the men, who may go about their usual avocations after the first three days of seclusion, should remember this when they are disposed to judge them harshly. One particularly trying custom insists that when the woman first goes out of the house of mourning, after the forty days, her first visit must be to another house where a death has taken place.

On feast-days, and at Pentecost, the family meet together in the cemetery, and spend the night there, the women in the upper rooms of the tomb-houses, and the men below; and there they distribute alms and food, this being another ancient custom. An ox or a sheep is killed for the poor, a custom lingering from the pre-Christian times, when the relatives of the dead made periodical visits to the tombs, taking food offerings for the *Ka* of the deceased, to refresh him in the underworld.

The Copts believe that the soul is weighed by the archangel Michael, who takes the place of the pre-Christian Thoth. All but those of modern education believe that the souls are let loose during the forty days succeeding Easter, from the place where they are confined, awaiting the day of general judgment.

On Whit-Sunday prayers are offered for the dead in all the churches, and it is considered specially meritorious to feed the poor on that day. In the week preceding Whitsuntide the members of every family meet at a funeral meal called *Sagda*.

When the ancient beliefs and customs concerning death are considered, it is not surprising that so many of them have survived in the Coptic Church. To the Egyptian, Christianity must have presented itself in a different light from that to which it appeared to other people. From the dawn of history the Egyptians had believed in a continuation of life after death. It is more than five thousand years since, in the valley of the Nile, the hymn began to the unity of God and the immortality of the soul. Their God of the dead was a God who had once lived an earthly life, who had been slain by the power of evil, and who had come to life again to rule as King of the underworld. It was in Osiris that their hope of living again rested.

It must have sounded strangely familiar to them when the Christian missionaries came with the message of a resurrection, and that the dead in Christ should live in Christ. It is not surprising, then, that when they accepted Christianity the people continued to practise the ancient funeral rites in ways only slightly modified to adapt them to the demands of the new religion.

The mummification of the dead, even, was practised till the beginning of the fifth century, when St. Anthony, whose preaching was that only by a supreme scorn of the body could the way to the great reward be found, vehemently opposed any sort of preservation of the body after death.

From his day the open desert became the burying-place of the monks, whither they were taken wrapped only in a winding-sheet, all trace of them to be soon lost. Only those of peculiar sanctity were buried in the churches, and holy relics were thus preserved.

But still the other funeral customs lingered on, especially those connected with the offerings of food. In the Christian cemetery of the oasis of el-Khargeh, the tombs follow the ancient design, the body being laid at the end of a long shaft, at the opening of which is a chamber containing the usual niches for offerings. Wine jars and baskets for food have been found buried with the Christian dead.

A great variety of food remains were found in the

Roman tomb-chapels at Hawara, seeming to show that the feasts at the tombs of the ancient Egyptians were kept up there. Festivals were held in honour of saints and martyrs at their graves, the Egyptian custom seeming to have been adopted by the Church.

As an instance of the way in which ancient charms were adapted to Christian uses, and the pagan uses were forgotten, it may be mentioned that ornaments such as a scarabæus, or a Medusa's head, are often found in old Christian graves.

Before the monks taught that the dead should be left to oblivion, the custom of the ancients of recording the life of the defunct on the *stele*, or tombstone, was continued by the early Christians. They gradually gave less detail, however, and then ceased altogether to sing the praises of the dead, giving at last only the name and the date at which the deceased "fell asleep" or "entered into rest," with a short prayer for the repose of the soul, with sometimes a Scripture text.

The pagan spirit breaks out sometimes on these tombstones in that Eastern expression (which I have seen on modern Moslem tombstones in North Africa), "Grieve not, no one is immortal." In the British Museum is a Coptic tombstone which reads like the wail of a hired mourner: "Oh, how dreadful is this separation! O departure to the strange land which removes one for all time! O condition of Hades, how do we come to thy gate? O death, name bitter in the mouth! . . . Let all who love to weep for their dead come to this place and mourn greatly."

Very rarely indeed are the Copts buried in their churches, though an exception has often been made in the case of the Patriarch and the bishops. The present Bishop of Assiout has shown me the tomb he has prepared for himself in the foundations under the chief altar of the new cathedral he is slowly building there. Very trifling clues are left as to who the men are who are so buried: in the case of some of the Patriarchs, tradition alone tells of their interment in certain churches.

CHAPTER X

The Marvels of the Saints' Tombs, and their Birthday Fairs

THE Copts love to worship at the tombs of saints, and, like the Moslems, they hold great *moolids*, or fairs, about the tombs of the men and women who are specially venerated. The feeling they have about this worship is the same to-day as that expressed by one of the early fathers, speaking of the tomb of the blessed Ammonius: "Many helpful acts took place at his grave on behalf of those who were worthy of help." They do not worship the saints, but pray near their resting-places, as they think, with the Moslems, that the spirit may sometimes hover there. They believe that God, because of the merit of the Saint, who is nearer to the Throne of Grace than they are, may be willing to bless them.

One of the most curious things about the devotion to the saints in Egypt is that it is shared equally by Copt and Moslem, for they each venerate the saints of the other religion as deeply as their own. Lady Duff Gordon, on her first visit to Egypt, on passing through the village of Bibeh, went to the Coptic church there, and found a mason at work on repairs. He told her with pride that he was a faithful Moslem, of Cairo, where for three nights running he had been visited by the saint buried in the Bibeh church, who ordered him to leave his work and go to the far-off village to restore his church. The mason told how he obeyed, offering to do the work without pay if the Copts would find the materials. He spoke with evident pride as one who had received a divine command, and the Copts all confirmed the story, being deeply gratified with the miracle. It throws a flood of light on the fanatic character so usually attributed to both Moslem and Copt that no one thought it at all incredible that this mason, known to be full of work, should receive and obey in all simplicity this command—while for years the priest had tried, without success, to get a builder even amongst the Copts.

There is, near Helowan, a church in the Monastery of Barsoum the Nude, to which great crowds resort every year on the day of the *moolid*. The saint who is buried there was one of the first of the Christian hermits: most of his life he passed in the underground cell which visitors to this day can see in the Church of Abu Sifain, in Old Cairo. There is a high dome over the nave of the church where he is buried, and here the crowds gather on the first Sunday of the second half of Lent, the people shouting the names of the saint, in the hope of seeing his shadow pass across the wall of the dome.

A very earnest young Copt of my acquaintance in Cairo, the son of a cleric, and himself of considerable education, as will be seen, and a keen advocate of reform, wrote for me an account of his own belief in the matter of such manifestations. I give this account word for word, as of psychical interest to English readers; after reading it, it will easily be understood how fervently the Coptic pilgrims to Jerusalem believe in the Holy Fire which appears on Easter Eve.

"I am going to mention all that I know, and have personally seen, about the church of Erian, near Helowan.

"To go to this church from Cairo, one must take the Helowan Railway as far as Maasara Station. The church is situated half-way between that station and the river Nile. It is about twenty minutes' walk from the station. The church itself is very beautiful, and surrounded from all directions by gardens, palm trees, farms, etc.

"I quote the following passage from the book *Al Mawalz wa el-etebar*, by Makrizi, who is a celebrated author on Egyptian antiquity. This author is a Mohammedan, and the book is written in Arabic.

"'The Convent of Shaaran (Shaaran is the village in which the church lies) is on the boundaries of Toura. It is built of stones and bricks. There are palm trees in it, and a large number of monks. Shaaran was a Christian philosopher, and it has been related that his was the name of a king. In ancient times this convent was called after the name of Marcorius, who was an officer and was killed by Diocletian. When Barsoum ibn el-Tabban settled in this convent it was called after his name till the present day.'"

My young friend continues:

"In the same passage it is mentioned that Shaaran is the place where Moses was born, and it was from this same place that his mother put him into the water.

"The Christian name of 'el-Erian' is Barsoum ibn el-Tabban, and he was a monk and hermit. He was called 'Erian' (or nude), as he chose to live naked; he was persecuted, and died in the name of Jesus Christ. There are no more monks in this convent at present, as they were all killed by the Arabs after they conquered Egypt. The church only remains untouched.

"An annual celebration is held in this church on the fifth Sunday of Lent. A very large number of Copts go there, and the day is considered as a general feast. They go on Saturday evening, and remain there till late on Sunday.

"They go out in the gardens, round the farms and palm groves,—men, women, boys, girls,—filled with joy and pleasure to roam about the place, without any conversation besides the sacredness of the place, and the vision which appears in the dome of the church during the Mass service or a little before it.

"I think I must be allowed to say, with confidence and assurance, that this vision *appears actually* in the dome of the church.

"I thought at first that this tale of the vision was a mere superstition, and that there was no truth at all about it. On this belief I went to the church on the Erian day, together with seven friends of mine, who had the same opinion as myself.

"We did not care about taking walks there, as we went for one purpose only—the vision.

"On Sunday, early in the morning, we all went upstairs and arranged with the servants to leave us alone and not to allow anybody else to go upstairs. We blocked the window of the dome, then four of us, including myself, went downstairs into the church, and the four others remained upstairs to watch the dome.

"I suggested to my friends that it would be as well if one of us go to each corner of the church and watch a certain part, as somebody may have a magic-lantern or some such apparatus which reflects the portrait up to the dome. But there was no such thing at all in the church.

"The Patriarch was present on that day, and he

was to perform the Mass service. Exactly at the beginning of the part of the Mass concerning the saints, the vision appeared right through the middle of the dome.

"Perhaps I was the first one who saw the vision. It is very much like the portrait of St. George on the English sovereign. The Patriarch stopped for a few moments, and all the people who were in the church bowed humbly to the vision, raising their hands and uttering solemnly their wishes and prayers.

"The Patriarch was praying with deep earnestness, and I was thrilled by his words.

"I sent for my friends, who were upstairs, and they came down immediately and saw the vision, which was as clear as the sun.

"I am obliged to say that their belief that the vision was a mere superstition has been shaken since then.

"My mother did the same thing twenty years ago. She did not believe that the vision was a true and a miraculous thing.

"She therefore took a sleeping garment of mine and put it up over the dome window, so as to prevent any light going through the dome, and she remained upstairs the whole time. But just at the beginning of the Mass service, which was also performed by the Patriarch himself on that day, the garment was seen burning immediately after the vision had appeared.

"There was a confusion in the church, and my mother immediately put out the fire in the garment. She was then taken to the Patriarch, when she told all her story.

"Some of the distinguished people who were present took pieces from the garment, and they are kept with them till the present day. The remainder of the garment is, I think, kept in the Patriarchate till now.

"After all, I do not know how to believe in this vision, and I cannot find an explanation to it. But I saw the thing, and I was convinced that it was not represented by a human hand.

"So, sir, take it whatever you will, and judge for yourself.

"Now let me tell you something else about another church, to which people possessed of evil spirits go every now and then to procure recovery from their illness. This church is called after the name of St. George. It is in the village of Mit Damsis, which belongs to the Mit Samanud District, of the Dakahlia Province, Lower Egypt.

"The St. George Day in this church is celebrated in the month of August every year, and on that particular day persons, of all religions, who are possessed of evil spirits go there dressed in white robes. After the service, they lie prostrated at the temple, and then the priests come and pray for an hour or two, when very loud cries are heard, from all the sick people, who gradually rise up one by one.

"You can then see at the bottom of each white robe of the prostrate ones a red stain of blood, having the shape of a cross—sometimes the cross is quite clear and distinct.

"This I saw myself, and I have no doubt that there is something holy about it."

The most important of all the saints' *moolids* celebrated by the Copts, is that of Sitt Dimiana, for it draws many thousands of people, who make a huge encampment round the church in the desert. Here again I think it best to let an educated Copt, of the orthodox faith, describe this wonderful festival. Mr. Farid Kamel, who wrote the following account for me, is a relative of the priest in charge of the church of Dimiana, and is himself very intimate with the *moolid* celebrations there.

"Reliable histories agree that St. Dimiana (or Sitt Dimiana) was a martyr of the terrible persecution raised by the Emperor Diocletian against the Christians, at the end of the third century and the beginning of the fourth century, when it is calculated that about 840,000 Copts perished.

"The father of Sitt Dimiana, whose name was Marcus, was a Government official—an administrator of a province called Berrelluo, in the north of the Delta. When she was fifteen years old, Dimiana expressed to her father a desire to give herself entirely to the worship of God, in solitude. Perhaps she meant by this to follow the new principle of the hermit life.

"Her father granted her desire and ordered a lonely house to be built for her in a place called Zafarana—about twelve kilometres from the north of Belkas.

"As she was the daughter of a governor of a province, the news of her action soon became known, and she was followed by about forty young ladies of the neighbourhood, whom she accepted to live with her the life of prayer in the same house.

"It happened that the Emperor now issued orders compelling his subjects to worship idols. The Government officials obeyed him, Marcus included.

"As soon as the news reached his daughter, she was very grieved, and wrote to her father. It is also stated that she went to him, and rebuked him for the weakness of his faith, and encouraged him to disobey the imperial orders. He listened to her and declared his intention to disobey the Emperor; and he suffered death.

"Having heard that his daughter was the cause of

Marcus' firmness, the Emperor sent some of his courtiers, bidding her to subscribe to the worship of the gods. She refused, so he ordered her to be subjected to every kind of torture then used in the persecution of Christians, But Dimiana never denied her Christian belief, and at last her head was cut off, and the heads of all her followers.

"When the Egyptian Church had rested after these terrible persecutions, it began to collect the accounts of its martyrs, and to treasure their histories as a witness to the value of the bloodshed to preserve Christianity in Egypt. Some of those recognised as Christian martyrs at that time are, St. George, St. Barsoum the Nude, St. Mena, St. Dimiana, and many others.

"The Church thought good, in memory of Sitt Dimiana, to build a church in her name on the spot where she suffered. When this church was consecrated, in the year 350 A.D., it was decided that the date should be an annual feast, to fall on the 20th May.

"This church has been destroyed and rebuilt several times. It was restored as it now stands by Amba Basileus, Coptic Metropolitan of Jerusalem, who died 26th March 1899. The buildings now consist of a monastery, including four churches, one of which is supposed to be over the tomb of Sitt Dimiana, a house for the Metropolitan to stay in, and several rooms for visitors.

"The *moolid* is still attended every year, between 5th and 20th May, by some 4000 to 6000 pilgrims coming from all parts of Egypt. They usually pitch tents round the monastery, and live there for a period of not less than eight, and not more than fifteen days, ending with the actual day of the festival.

"Numbers of merchants usually go and hold a bazaar, in which they sell food, drink, sometimes clothing, ornaments, perfumes, rings, handkerchiefs, sticks, etc., and especially wooden and brass crosses imported from Jerusalem to be sold there. Visitors buy these things and take them to their native villages, believing that they convey a 'blessing from Sitt Dimiana.'

"The Copts believe that as the saints allowed their blood to be shed for the love of Jesus Christ, they have a merit before Him, and that He will accept their intercession. And so if a man worship God, and prays to Him in the name of one of the saints, his prayer will be acceptable.

"They refer to St. George, for example, for the power to cast out evil spirits; they refer to Sitt Dimiana for the ability to give fruitfulness to women, or long life to the children of a woman who has lost many in infancy. Therefore, many gifts of money, jewels, and church plate in silver and gold are presented to her church.

"The people mention many wonders and miracles of Sitt Dimiana. Some say they were eye-witnesses of these miracles, while others claim to have heard them from authoritative sources. One of these received miracles is that Sitt Dimiana can prevent thieves from stealing, or from escaping with what they have stolen. So she is always referred to as the means of discovering stolen property, and of restoring it to its rightful owner.

"This belief is so strong that there is hardly any crime during the anniversary festival, a force of the police always stationed there having little to do.

"Another belief is, that if a man here looks upon a woman with evil intent, he will receive an injury to his eyes, or to some part of his body; and owing to this

Photo: Dittrich, Cairo.
Where the ceremonial candles may be bought which play such an important part in the social functions of native life, as well as in the services of the church.

Photo: Dittrich, Cairo.
IN THE BAZAAR OF THE CAULDRON SELLERS.
Here all the utensils for the kitchen may be purchased.

belief, women can mix freely among the men on this occasion, and there will be no painful incident.

"Some visitors go on to state that Sitt Dimiana used to appear in years past in a small window in an old dome which still remains, and is believed to be the dome of the first church consecrated in the name of Sitt Dimiana. It is said that she appeared after prayer and praise had been offered for several hours. But those who have inquired into this matter say that this might be only the reflection of some people passing along the roof, beside the dome.

"In short, Moslems, as well as Copts, living in that part, respect this saint considerably, and believe that she is the means of granting them most important benefits, when they address themselves to her. Moslems are usually heard singing to her name, calling her *Ya Sitt ya bint el wali*—'You the lady of the Viceroy.'

"The first object of keeping these anniversaries in the memory of saints was to urge the people to follow their example and their strong faith. The days of the festival used to be spent in worship, prayer, and religious conversations, and in some innocent amusements. But, since the clouds of ignorance darkened the sky of the Coptic Church, these beautiful ceremonies were turned to a considerable extent into play and mere enjoyment. In these days there is an increase of singing, games, drinking, and in the use of words sometimes not very polite. The numbers who attend the services in the churches are not so great, though there are usually a great many people attending the last day's prayer. In my opinion, some of those who attend the festival offer an insult rather than an honour to the saint. The heads of the church are to be blamed, to a great extent, for this state of affairs."

CHAPTER XI

Oriental Shopkeepers and Handicraftsmen

WHEN Napoleon said that the Egyptians are capable of making a pair of pantaloons but never of sewing on the last button, he was expressing a truth which applies only to the larger concerns of life. They are capable of great conceptions, but they weary before their ideas are completely realised, whether it is to build a barrage, to dig a great canal, or to make for themselves an extensive mansion, or a country garden. They will finish the house, perhaps, but never clear from the courtyard the builders' rubble; they will build a church, and leave it isolated for the want of a few yards of passable roadway leading to its main entrance.

This was not quite the case in the days of slavery; immense works of ancient Egypt were carried out with forced labour; and even down to the days when Lord Cromer abolished the whip, the rulers of the country were quite capable of ordering such undertakings as appealed to their imagination, and of using, with a total disregard of human life, all the power that reposed in them to get them carried out. It was in this way that Ismail caused the road to the Pyramids, and an hotel at the end of it, and the great Opera-House of Cairo, to be completed in three or four weeks from the start of them.

I have no doubt that if Napoleon had succeeded in getting the despotic power of which he dreamed, the pressure he would have exerted would have ensured the completion, even by Orientals, of all his schemes.

As to the actual making of pantaloons, no one will excel the Egyptian in the small task which can be undertaken and finished right away; or in such elaborate work as the engraving of brass, the making of the *mushrabieh*, or lacelike wooden screens (through which the ladies of the hareem peep, themselves unseen, upon the life of the streets), or in the exquisite inlaid work which adorns the mosques and churches. The Eastern mind is not overtaxed by such work as this. The enthusiasm which starts the Oriental on big schemes is exhausted by the strain of completing the irksome details, which need sustained alertness and the faculty to meet new difficulties as they arise.

But when the task is clear before him, the Oriental brings to his work an unexampled patience. He is as industrious as any man, if he may work according to his own will; he will work as long hours as any, if he may choose them; he is artistic and skilful beyond other men, in certain fields of industry; and he is painstaking and exact in the things he understands. But he will not be punctual, or care for promises or contracts. Indeed, it is only a European who would ever dream of pressing such considerations upon the Eastern craftsman; for to do so is to vex his temper to no useful purpose, and to put oneself outside the range of such interest and sympathy as might serve to get from him the best work of which he is capable.

A great deal of the finest craftsmanship of Egypt was developed by the descendants of the ancient race whose beautiful work is the admiration of the modern world, which has despoiled the tombs of their frescoes and their sculpture, and robbed the mummies of their coffins, and their jewels, and the very wrappings of the dead.

All the world knows of the skill of the ancient Egyptians in making all kinds of jewellery, and in working gems and stones. In the Bible there is constant mention of these handicrafts, which must have been learned from Egypt. There is a picture in Isaiah which might have been drawn to-day. "The carpenter encouraged the goldsmith, and he that smootheth with the hammer him that smote the anvil, saying, It is ready for the sodering" (xli. 7). There is little question that these arts had attained great development in Egypt before the time of Abraham, who is the first recorded Hebrew visitor to Egypt, and who must have taken back with him to Canaan some specimens of the country's artistic skill, amongst the valuables in gold and silver which it is recorded he acquired there.

This particular form of artistic skill still survives in the workers in the Egyptian bazaars, who show wonderful dexterity in the making, with primitive tools, beautiful objects in the precious metals. It is probable that for thousands of years men have worked in just such bazaars, in the same sort of tiny shops, clothed in the same way, and earning the same mean pittance providing them with the same varieties of food which we see them eating to-day.

As early as the second century, a letter, said to have been written by Hadrian, speaks of the Copts as "a body, wealthy and prosperous, of whom nobody lives in idleness. Some blow glass, some make paper, and others linen; there is work even for the lame and the blind." And in another paragraph he remarks that all the leading men, whether Jews, Samaritans, or Christians, are mathematicians, augurs, and soothsayers.

When the Arabs conquered Egypt they used the skill which they admired in the Coptic industries to enrich the mosques and palaces and tombs which they built; and it was only when the Turks gained the lordship over Egypt, and shipped off all the most finished workmen to beautify Constantinople, that Egypt lost her splendid pre-eminence in architecture and the decorative arts.

The skill of the Egyptian in inlay work and mosaic will be found exemplified first in many of the ancient churches, and then in the mosques. The use of variegated marble for wall decoration and paving can be seen in the churches at Al'Adra in Cairo, and in the mosques of Kait Bey and Al Ashraf, and in the tombs of the Caliphs.

In many churches and monasteries examples of another form of Coptic art will be found—the beautiful mosaics, made of minute pieces of coloured marble and porphyries, with an admixture of mother-of-pearl. This exquisite work is lavished on the places of honour, chiefly in the niches in the eastern wall, found without exception in all Coptic chapels, and in the tribune, with its throne for the Patriarch or bishop, and seats for the twelve presbyters or elders of the church. The tiny baptistery of the little church at Al Mu'allakah is thought to show the best early example. At Abu Sifain the *ambon* (or pulpit) contains a most intricate mosaic design. As for the way in which the Arabs adapted this work, the mosques of Al Ghuri and Al Hakim in Cairo are gorgeous with it, as are some of the tomb mosques.

It has been said that the beauty of the screen of the Church of Abu Sifain, in Old Cairo, of ivory inlaid on ebony, makes it alone worth a journey to Egypt to see.

In the new Coptic Cathedral in Cairo the only thing worthy of the attention of those who seek for art and beauty is the ivory inlaid lectern, which was brought to that undistinguished building from one of the ancient churches.

The Coptic Church is at last becoming alive to its treasures, and the work of Marcus Simaika Pasha, in forming the interesting Museum at Old Cairo, should do much to educate both the priests and the laity in the true value of many of their possessions, which they have so carelessly regarded in the past. It should soon become impossible, for instance, for a most precious illuminated book to be left in the care of an ignorant attendant, who knows so little of its worth that he showed it to me with a candle dropping grease upon its pages, and this in Cairo itself; or for a guide to take a knife to detach a piece of mother-of-pearl from a priceless church screen, thinking to please the English tourist by giving him a memento of his visit.

The origin of many of the handicrafts which are practised in Egypt to-day is clearly described in the pictures and hieroglyphics of the ancient Egyptians; the articles there shown in general use are still so dear to the Egyptian that he cannot be persuaded to set them aside. When the digging of the Suez Canal was started, a great number of wheelbarrows were brought from France for the work; not a single Egyptian labourer would use one of them for their proper purpose. They made shelters and huts of them, but all the thousands of tons of earth were carried in their familiar baskets made of soft palm leaf, on the head or shoulders, exactly as may be seen pictured on the walls of the ancient tombs and monuments.

The making of these baskets of palm leaves is

perhaps the oldest, as it is the most universal of occupations in Egypt. When the early Christians thought their only chance of salvation was to retire to the desert, and live a life of bodily hardship, founded on the literal interpretation of the teaching of the New Testament, men denuded themselves of all earthly possessions, and worked with their hands, for the bare subsistence which sufficed them. It was in making baskets and mats that the majority of the monks and recluses found a way of getting bread, and at the same time of punishing themselves for the soft life they had led in the world, by having to lacerate their hands in the work.

The story is told of a third-century monk in Egypt, "a brother of blessed memory." He had a cell apart from the brethren, he lived upon bread and salt only, and he used to make one mat of plaited palm leaves each day; and it would happen often, when he was plaiting the ropes of which the mats were made, that his hands would become covered with blood, and they were so full of wounds caused by the rough strands that the very mats as he made them were wetted with blood. But he never spared himself, or rested in the daytime, or missed a service in the church, either by day or at midnight. On one occasion a brother went to him, and seeing his bleeding hands, pleaded with him to let the brethren minister to his wants, as their duty was to care for the strangers and the poor. But he only replied that he must go on with his work. Then, "If it pleaseth thee to act thus, at least anoint thine hands with oil at eventide." He did this; but because his hands were tender, and possibly softened by the oil, they were still grievously chafed and cut and torn by the sharp palm leaves. Then the Abbot himself paid him a visit, and with that perversion of moral instruction so continually found in these

Egyptian monasteries, he reproved the poor monk in this fashion: "Thinkest thou, O Theodore, that the oil had any beneficial effect upon thee? Who forced thee to work? Didst thou not place thy hope of being healed rather upon the operation of the oil than upon God? Peradventure was not thy God able to heal thee? Yet when He saw that thou wast ordering for thyself, He left thee to this pain." The way the poor monk bore this stern reproof—to our minds as cruel as it was unjust—gives a true picture of the chastened spirits of most of these early Christians who took to the desert. "O father, I have sinned against God, and I acknowledge my sin, and I beseech that God may forgive me." And he passed a full year in mourning for this act of folly in oiling his poor hands, eating only once every two days.

The monks and nuns carried on all the ancient trades and occupations from pre-Christian Egypt. There were those who worked in isolated cells, and in the monasteries; and there were secular brothers who travelled the country as pedlars to sell the products of this labour. Not only did they make baskets and mats, but ropes, sieves, nets, sandals, shoes, and the work of their looms. A Patriarch of the Church had himself once worked as a needle-maker.

The monks sold cakes, and wine, and the flax which they had woven. They were public scribes, and workers in orchard gardens; in blacksmiths', fullers', bakers', and carpenters' shops. If they had no trade they gave service in attending the sick. Their industry was amazing, and one can only imagine that the consequent flooding of the market must have lowered the price of all the commodities of life, and fallen very hard on the laymen.

A story of a monk who sold the shoes made at his

monastery illustrates the economic principles which guided the Abbots. This brother, who travelled to sell shoes, was a clever man of business and anxious for the prosperity of his community. But his Abbot's ideas of integrity hindered him in the exercise of his gifts. In the time of famine which visited Egypt in the days of Pachomius, this man first exercised his commercial gifts by finding a man "exceedingly reverent and a fearer of God," who as governor of a city had a great store of wheat, part of which he was willing to sell at a low price to the monastery. "If thou wilt take the wheat thou wilt do me an act of grace, only pray for me." The traveller set off with his boatload of wheat. But news of his wonderful bargain had, of course, gone on before, and the boat was met by a messenger from the Abbot, with a terrible reproof. Not a grain of the wheat should enter the monastery, nor should the traveller enter the Abbot's presence until he had returned it. His sin was that he had become inflamed by a love of gain!

In the matter of selling the shoes, the brother was sent out with instructions as to the price he was to ask for his wares, evidently a contemptible one. "If these things had been stolen they would be worth a far higher price," said certain buyers. And the man, feeling ashamed, said they had not been stolen, and would they give him the price they wished to give. He never counted the money, but took it to the Abbot. But business was *not* business in those days, and smartness had no reward. "Thou hast sinned greatly in loving excess, O my son," was the Abbot's comment. "Run quickly and give back the excess, and come and repent. Sit in the monastery, henceforth, and work with thy hands, for it is not good that thou shouldst do again work of this kind."

It is told of the gardener to one of the monasteries that he passed eighty-five strenuous years in that one employment. He planted all the fruit trees that were in the monastery garden, and until the day of his death he never tasted any of the fruit whatsoever. What rest of body was, he knew not, because of the press of his labours, for with a ready mind he toiled always; he never ate any cooked food, but lived all the years of his life on plantains only, which he ate with vinegar. He never lay upon his back, even when at last he could not stand, nor ever had a cushion, nor anything soft to ease him. When it was dark he still worked, plaiting ropes without any light, while he recited Scripture. He had only one garment of linen, which he put on when he went to church to partake of the holy mysteries; he then took it off, and by this care it lasted him for eighty-five years!

And the nuns were equally strenuous. The virgin Taor, who would wear nothing but rags, declining even to wear a veil, sat at her work at all hours. By these means, relates Palladius, she acquired such a sagacious, wise, and ready appearance, that every man who was wont to abhor the sight of women would have been nigh to being snared and falling at the sight of her, had it not been that shamefacedness, which is the guardian of chastity, was ever with her, and that she ordered her gaze in a chaste manner by means of shame and fear.

To this day there has been no change in the innumerable articles of daily use made of the leaves of the palm. In all the industries of the East the artisan performs marvels of skill with very primitive tools. The palm, or *cafas*, worker needs only a billhook and a mallet for tools, and he will turn out a multitude of cheap articles in basket work, such as chairs, bedsteads, benches, brooms, cages, coops, and crates.

The carpenter, who is seen at work in the bazaars, has no bench, vice, or drill. In place of a rule, he will use a cord or palm twig; but he has the advantage over the Western worker, with a whole bagful of costly tools, in being able to work with his toes as well as his fingers, as the ancient Egyptian did, frequently using his teeth as well.

His principal tool is a small axe, and for boring he uses an iron spike fixed in a circular piece of wood, which he turns with a sort of fiddle-bow; which also dates from ancient Egyptian times. The manipulation of it looks to the European a very easy matter, though a trial of it is well suited to diminish self-confidence.

One of the most primitive implements used in the bazaars is the bellows of the silversmith, the lockmaker, and the worker in tin. A small mound of clay is made on the workshop floor, which has running through it a metal tube, generally an old gun-barrel. Attached to one end of the tube is a goatskin, which the apprentice opens at one end to admit air, and then depresses to send the air through the pipe, into the middle of the fire burning at the other end; the little heap of coals being kept together by loose stones.

Amongst the living artisans and dealers of the bazaars, then, many interesting survivals of the life and habits of pre-Christian Egypt are to be found, and certainly it is here that the vivid pictures drawn for us in the stories of the *Thousand and One Nights* live again with scarcely any change. As the Egypt of the Pharaoh merged naturally into that of the Christian ruler, so later on it passed, with little outer change, into that of Caliph or Sultan; the people themselves differ no more in dress than in the ways of life from their ancestors.

The modern ethnologist, visiting one of the shops in the bazaars of any Egyptian town (with the exception perhaps of the cosmopolitan ports), is convinced that if you pick at random a man belonging to the common people, and divest him of his more modern outer dress of loose shirt and turban, take from him his pipe and his coffee, shave his beard, make some little allowance on account of his Christian or his Moslem faith, you will have standing before you a genuine native of Kemi.

He will be sure to exhibit the same slim, yet strong limbs, the broad chest, the same type of face, with its broad cheeks, projecting lips, wide nostrils, and almond eyes; also the same solid shaven head, and, in spite of all the buffets of fate, at bottom the same inherited nature.

It is largely the same with the natural products of the country here offered for sale. Most of the fruits and vegetables are exactly the same as those found on the ancient monuments. The lotus, being no longer a sacred plant, has lost its proud place in the esteem of the people, although it is a mistake to say that it is quite extinct in Egypt; as for the ancient papyrus, the use for it has passed away; the sugar-cane, which every one in the bazaar is munching, is an introduction of modern times—the Caliphs brought it; and rice, indigo, and maize, forming so large a part of the stock of the chandler of to-day, are a later importation.

In one thing modern Egypt differs entirely from that of the Pharaohs. With the ancients different trades were rigidly confined to members of their own guilds; heavy punishment awaited those who left their own calling to encroach on that of other men; the son always followed that of his father. To-day every man is free to work as he pleases.

The street cries of the itinerant merchants of the bazaars deserve a note to themselves. Here is a man, with his goods thrown across his shoulder, proclaiming that he has " India muslin, and fine English muslin, O girls!" in a sonorous chant. He is rich in the eloquence of puffing advertisement when the women stop him with inquiries.

A comical old negro comes along with a tray on his head, singing with a sort of rhythm, "*Mulabeseeyeh! Homaseeyeh!*" He finds a ready sale for the sugar-plums, and sweetmeats made of parched peas and sugar.

Cries another, "Figs, the food of Sultans!" and a man with a great bottle attracts attention by clapping together his cups as he sings, "Oh, here is the refresher of the body, O men!" All these cries have a charm which cannot be retained in translation.

Often the terms in which a man vaunts his goods are so vaguely poetical that it is impossible to guess what he is selling. It seems with some street merchants to be the right thing to name something quite different, and much more attractive, than the wares he is actually offering. "Honey and sugar! Oh, honey!" repeats one old man, when he is carrying nothing but carrots! In the prettiest way a girl is calling, "White honey! pure honey and grapes!" when she is offering the *gemazy*, a very cheap fruit with little flavour. "Scents of Paradise!" calls another girl who is selling flowers. A proverb, often heard in Cairo, says, "Not every one who carries a tray has sweets to sell."

"The gift of God!" chants the water-carrier; sometimes, "May God recompense me!" and sugar-canes are offered "in the name of the Prophet." A lupine seller passes, with perhaps the most poetic of all the cries, "Help! O Embabeh, help! The lupines of Embabeh are better than almonds; oh, how sweet is this little son of the river!"

An Egyptian is always reminded of the various festivals of the year by the wares which are being cried by the sweetmeat vendors. Certain choice confections only appear at the festival with which they are always associated, and nothing will induce the vendors to produce them at any other time.

We pass now an archway, through which we can see the picturesque corn dealer's store, with a small crowd of countrymen doing their business. Not so long ago a traveller saw at the entrance to one of these stores, in one of the bazaars, two chairs of handsomely carved woodwork, evidently of considerable antiquity, and exactly similar in form to those seen with Egyptian antiquities in the museums. It was remarked that probably Joseph sat on such a chair when superintending the selling of corn, while the sons of Jacob stood beside their asses waiting for their sacks to be filled, as these men wait to-day.

A peasant whom we see passing through the bazaar carrying a pair of geese by the wings, in the fashion peculiar to Egypt, might have stepped straight down from a painting in one of the old tombs, for the picture he makes is photographically exact in every detail.

This old sheikh hobbling past us is supporting himself with a stick peculiar to the dervishes—it is always cut from an almond tree, with a peculiar crotch; exactly such a stave often appears in the hands of the deities represented by the ancient Egyptians.

The blacksmith, who is here at work, is an exact picture of a primeval artisan, and he is making implements, which, like the man who will use them, belong to the period of the Book of Genesis. He is bare to the thighs, and as he wields his hammer—a knotty branch of wood, just as it grew—and compresses his crude bellows, he might well stand for a picture of the first craftsman. The plough which he is making will find its way to the country, to be worked by a fellah, who at his labour in the fields will most possibly discard almost all his clothes, making a companion picture, which might be that of the first labourer in agriculture. The plough is certainly exactly the same as that used by the ancient Egyptians, and so are the pick and the hoe.

At the end of one of the many streets of the bazaar you will come across some very busy workshops, where, from the rough timber which lies at the entrance, brawny men are fashioning the great poles of the *shadoof*, the implement by which, at a thousand points on the Nile, the water is being continually raised to the level of the land which it is to fertilise.

The *shadoof* is, perforce, familiar to all travellers on the great river, and the principle of it is as simple as it is labour-saving. The raising of a bucket of water by an equal weight of clay at the other end of the balanced pole is one of the earliest inventions of man to save exertion by mechanical means.

In the same workshops men are also making the water-wheel, for raising water by the labour of the patient *gamoose*, or ox—a later invention, though not unknown in the days of the last of the Pharaohs.

The further back one's knowledge of the social history of Egypt goes, the more one is convinced that what changes have taken place in the people are more those of character than of custom and habit.

There were days when the people of Egypt were strenuous, in science and literature, and in the arts of progressive and defensive war, and in the support of the causes they held dear. Times, later, when they were so deeply stirred by their religion, that they were capable of enduring the most merciless self-inflicted suffering and denial, sustained through long lives, for the sake of Christ, in whose name they literally left all that they possessed.

Later, when the followers of the Prophet took possession of the land, there were many fresh examples of nobility of character, amongst Copts and Moslems alike; and when the persecutions set in, the Christian character was found to be ripe for a glorious era of martyrdom.

The supineness of modern days, the love of ease, the evasion of responsibility, the deliberate choice, by men with ability, to rise by means of cunning and flattery, and to intrigue themselves with any rulers who can advance them; having little or no concern for the good of their country, and a cynical disregard of the claims of truth and decency: these are changes of character that are deplorable. It is, however, the very indolence, outcome of their degeneration, that has preserved the social customs of the people of Egypt from those changes of habit which progression must always bring.

It is curious to read in an old document of the monkish days, long before the Arab invasion of Egypt, a description by one of the religious recluses, of the "Street of Cafés," possibly in Cairo, which he uses as an illustration to his teaching to those who visit him in his cave in the desert. "Against the thought of fornication be thou like unto a man who passeth through a street of

Photo: Lekegian, Cairo.
THE HARNESS-MAKER AND THE WORKER IN PALM-FIBRE.

Photo: Dittrich, Cairo.
A FRUIT SHOP IN THE WATER-MELON SEASON.

tavern-keepers, and who smelleth the odour of boiling meats, or the scent of something that is being roasted; he who wisheth, entereth one of them and eateth, another smelleth the meats as he passeth by, and goeth on. Drive away from thee then the alluring smell of evil thoughts, and stand up and pray, saying, 'O Son of God, help me!' The same is also to be said about other thoughts, for we are not the roots of the thoughts, but are those who strive against them."

One sees here at once the native café of to-day, where, so utterly unlike the eating-places of the West, the cooking is done by the entrance, so that all the odours of it are wafted into the street; the excellent purpose of this custom being that the customer may see not only every single item of food he chooses to eat before it is cooked, but may judge, before entering the place, of the skill of the cook and of the state of his utensils.

One of the most interesting shops in the bazaars is that of the candle-maker. The use of candles in religious services goes back to remote times. It seems to be established that for the first three centuries after the introduction of Christianity the candle was not used in the Christian services in Egypt, but after that the mention of its use is continuous.

Throughout the East, Jerome says, candles were lit at the reading of the Gospel, not on account of the darkness, but as a token of joy. Light is always a sign of joy in the East; no sort of festivity is possible in Egypt without the most brilliant of illumination. At a religious ceremony, whether Jewish, Christian, or Moslem, the church, or the richly decorated pavilion, will be dazzlingly lighted, and although electricity is now available in the cities, the splendid candelabra of days only just passing are too valuable to be discarded, and so they are still set ablaze with myriads of candles.

It is the same at all secular festivities, especially at weddings; and in the tents of mourning religious works are read to the light of innumerable candles, the while friends gather to show sympathy with the bereaved. If the Oriental has no place in which to forgather after sunset where there are bright lights, he will always take refuge in sleep from the genii of the night.

But it is only the very poor who will even sleep without a light; and scarcely any one will be left alone at night. If the husband is away from home the wife will go to relatives or neighbours. At the candle-maker's shop will be found the wax lights for burning in the bedrooms during the night, when small oil lamps are not used.

I have never heard of any trouble, of those which fall to the lot of man, spoken of with such commiseration as that of a fellah who was obliged, at a certain season, to be out all night alone to protect his crops. Moving about in the dark, the Egyptian continually murmurs, "With your permission, ye blessed ones," as a warning to the *ginn* to stand out of his path, so fearful is he that he might strike and injure one of them, and thus bring revenge upon himself. The Oriental seldom or never whistles; for one thing, it is a breach of good manners to create such a noise; but more than that, the *ginn* are attracted by whistling, especially at night.

No woman will sit on a doorstep, or stand by a threshold, at night; in the village especially one sees groups of them gossiping in the twilight, always well away from the entrance to any building; they would be more likely to be in the way of the *ginn* there. On

Fridays, especially, such places are particularly dangerous at such an hour.

Darkness is horrible to Oriental men and to the women a torture. To do any work in the house by candlelight, especially such as to sweep a floor, would be to run the risk of injuring the *ginn*; even to move about then is dangerous; it is not surprising that the poor go to bed almost invariably at sunset.

For religious use, it was enjoined that candles should be of wax alone, and not of tallow and other substances —"the fragrant wax, the labour of the bee, which dies when its labour is accomplished," has mystic significance. It is drawn from the nectar of the flowers, and has always been thought to have the highest natural worth as a material for offerings.

In one of the old Coptic stories it is related, as a superlative deceit of the devil, that in tempting one Valens, a monk, he "went and made himself into a form in which he resembled our Redeemer, and he came to Valens by night, together with phantoms of angels, in great numbers, who marched along bearing lamps and wax candles."

In the records of funerals of the monks and nuns of the fourth century candles are always mentioned. At a nunnery in the Thebaid, on the banks of the Nile, under the rule of Pachomius, when one of the sisters died, the other women would bring her and lay her at the riverside, and go away. Then certain brethren would cross over in a boat, and row her back, with the singing of psalms and with lighted candles, to lay her in their cemetery with great ceremony and honour.

Another quaint story tells of a certain rich and wicked man who was buried with lights and great honour. At the same time a monk was found dead, mutilated by panthers. A poor man who saw this craved an explanation of the Lord, and an angel came to him and said, "That wicked man did one good work, and he was rewarded here with lights and ceremony; but this holy man, because he was a man who was adorned with divine virtues, will receive these things in the world to come."

At weddings and other celebrations candles are used for purposes other than to give light, especially by the women. The Coptic bridegroom, as I have related, sends to his bride, on the night before she leaves her father's home, a present of a bouquet and a wax candle, which must be as long as the height of the bride, to burn in the bride's chamber during the whole night. These huge candles, here on sale, are for this purpose.

At Moslem bridal ceremonies the same candles are used in a fearsome manner, being carried in the processions in the hareem by the girl attendants on the bride, with an apparent disregard of the danger of their veils and robes catching fire, which makes the Western onlooker shudder. A lighted candle is given to every one of the guests on entering the bride's room.

Shopping in the East is known to be an occupation requiring great patience and endless leisure. It is needless to remark on the Oriental bargaining system, except to remind those who are most vexed by it, that it is not so very long ago—as time goes—that it was the general mode of trading in England and throughout Europe. It was to the Society of Friends that the introduction of the fixed price was due; their example quickly spread throughout England, and thence to many parts of the Continent.

And if the vexed traveller should think the trader in Egypt is entirely avaricious, I would recall the many occasions when I have found that a man had closed his shop so that he might join a friend for a chat, or go to pay his condolences in a mourning tent, or to perform his many prayers in church or in the mosque. The Oriental, whatever casual observers may be led to think of his character, is really the last man to sacrifice everything in life to gain.

The Arabic signs over the little shops are mostly texts. "O God! Thou who openest the source of profit"; "O Allah! who art our help." As he takes down his shutters, the shopkeeper will mutter these and similar verses. Such signs will turn aside "the evil eye"; that stuffed crocodile, that dried bone of a camel, or the aloe plant, fixed above the entrance, serving the same purpose.

The ancient Egyptians used inscriptions and symbols of good omen in the same way. Here in a street just off one of the bazaars is a doorway, with crude paintings all round it representing a camel, a locomotive, a ship, the means of progression by which the man living there has visited Mecca. I think it very probable that the Copt represented his pilgrimage to Jerusalem in the same way in the days before persecution made it advisable for him to obliterate all traces of his habitation. Among the Egyptians of the Pharaohs it was customary to paint a record of religious pilgrimages on the houses just in the way the modern Moslem does it.

Book II

CHAPTER I

The Oriental Christian in his Church

THE CHURCH ITSELF

THE traveller who finds himself on a Sunday morning in the Cathedral of St. Mary at Cairo, while the Holy Eucharist is being celebrated, will, if he knows anything at all of the history of Egypt and of the origin of the Coptic people, witness one of the most illuminating historical sights in a country so teeming with historical interest that it can draw both the learned and the curious from all parts of the world.

He will find a great crowd of men and boys, with earnest faces turned towards the great sanctuary screen, within which the Liturgy of St. Basil is being said by the *Abunah*. Many of these faces he will find are such as might have been copied by the sculptors who decorated the ancient tombs.

At a certain point in the service the choir will pass from the almost hidden sanctuary into the church, where they will make the responses; their appearance in their high scarlet helmets, recalling the head-dress of pre-Christian Egypt, and their white robes with the cross bands, also of scarlet (embroidered with crosses), seems to bring to life again some of the statues of the Pharaohs,

This helmet-like cap is not unlike the high round crown worn by the early kings; and worn by these lads, as the king's crown was, slightly tilted back, it accentuates the regular features and the rather prominent straight nose, with full and finely moulded nostrils, the full lips, and especially the Eastern setting of the eyes. I have seen young men in these birettas who might have been the sons of Rameses II., the king whose features are advertised to posterity as no others have ever been.

As the men of the congregation first enter the church, most of them make a deep sign of reverence towards the sanctuary—or haikal—and they then go and kiss the curtain hanging over the sanctuary door, or prostrate themselves so as to kiss the haikal threshold. In the old days every man took off his shoes on entering the church, and the Oriental custom still obtains in country places. No one ever in any church enters the haikal with shod feet.

Of this large congregation the spoken language is Arabic, but the liturgy is still spoken in Coptic, the language which grew naturally out of the speech of the Pharaohs and the hieroglyphics of their records.

And as the service goes on, and one notes the significance of many of its observances, and the use of its sacred vessels and appliances, it seems that Coptic Christianity itself might almost be a relic of ancient Egypt. That it still represents the life of the early days, when Egypt had become entirely Christian, there is no doubt at all. The only thing lacking is the spiritual fervour and the living inspiration which marked the days of the first converts to the faith of Christ. For it is certain that nowhere did that faith take root so quickly or so deeply as in what proved to be the congenial soil of Egypt. In this marvellous country, as in no other, the

The Oriental Christian in his Church 171

book of history is continuous, and page follows page, in almost perfect order.

We shall understand this service the more easily if we study for a moment the plan on which most of the Coptic churches are built. Roughly they may be termed half Basilican and half Byzantine. The entrance is always in the western end, the altars being in the eastern. Where exceptions existed to this rule they have of recent years been corrected.

On entering the church we first find ourselves in a compartment screened off from the nave; this is of interest, for the narthex, as it is called, was originally used by the heathen converts or catechumens, who might not approach nearer to the altar until they had been taught the rudiments of religion and had been confirmed. At a certain part of the service they had to depart, and the prayer for their withdrawal is still retained. In some churches the women now occupy the narthex, but it is considered too public a place for them; they are generally hidden in the galleries behind *mushrabieh* screens.

As for the children, there is nothing so curious in the Coptic church as the way the infants run about where they please during the service, as though they were at home in a nursery. Churchgoing has no fears for them, in spite of the length of the services, for they have privileges denied to their parents. They mostly gather about the sanctuary screen, where they sit on the floor, or climb the choir railings, as they please. They even invade the sanctuary itself, and it is a very pretty sight to see the toddling mites tiptoeing at the altar, looking on with wide-open eyes at all the mysterious doings of the priests. I have seen two babes, whose curiosity had tired them out, sitting blissfully asleep in the sanctuary while the Holy Eucharist was going on, no one thinking to disturb them. Our Lord said: "Suffer the little children to come unto Me!" This is how the Copts obey the command.

There will be two aisles and a nave. The men and boys of the congregation gather in the nave. The aisles are generally separated from the nave by pillars, many of them taken from the older temples. Every stage in the history of architecture speaks of new religions adapting the pillars of the older churches: in Egypt too much has been said by English writers in their bias against Islam of the use made by the Moslems, when their time came, of Coptic church pillars, in the building of their mosques.

I have seen an ancient church in the country divided into triforia in the style of the vaulted halls of the temple of Seti I. of Abydos, and with the two colonnaded halls just as the temple is. These halls were separated from each other by a wooden screen of the open *mushrabieh* work with doors in it, just as the colonnaded halls of the temple of Abydos were separated by a wall having as many doors as there were vaulted rooms in the sanctuary. Only the most distinguished members of this particular country congregation were admitted to the second hall, the floor being covered with mats. In the outer hall, where the floor was bare, the worshippers of the lower orders were assembled. One could but reflect on the fact that the builders of the mosques had as their aim from the very first, that every man who desired to worship should do so with absolute equality—the Sultan and the serf should stand side by side in prayer.

The sanctuary of the Coptic church is always entirely screened from the congregation in the nave, even the entrance being hung with a curtain, which at certain times in the service of the Holy Eucharist is closely drawn, so that the "mysteries" are completely veiled from the people. The haikal screen is always the most splendid feature of the church; sometimes its inlay of ivory is of the most exquisite and beautiful workmanship; even in the poorer churches the aim of those who built the church was to make this screen a masterpiece. It is always made of solid woodwork, of ebony or cedar, very richly inlaid with intricate geometrical patterns in ivory and mother-of-pearl, with the design of the cross in ivory generally dominating the whole pattern.

There are two lecterns, if we may so call the Eastern reading-desks, one on the north side of the nave and the other on the south. The reader, in using these, faces to the east, with his back to the congregation. Marvellous again is the ivory inlay work which has been lavished on these lecterns; one of the most beautiful is to be found in the Cairo Cathedral, and some excellent specimens are being placed in the new Coptic Museum.

It is a sad reflection on the condition of the country clergy that they part with such treasures very easily; one of them I heard of was only concerned—in letting a fine specimen leave his church—that the cheap modern desk promised to take its place should have a cupboard, as the old one had, in which he could keep the church books. There is little wonder that tourists in the recent past have, by comparatively trivial bribes, been able to take away with them even parts of the church screens.

I wish I could say that the Patriarch himself had anything like a proper appreciation of the treasures still left to his sadly depleted church.

In the richer churches tall candelabra stand near the lecterns, sometimes of great artistic merit. Candles must always burn during the reading of the Scriptures;

sometimes they are placed in simple holders fixed to the sides of the lectern.

The pulpit, which is called the *ambon*, always stands on the north-east side of the nave; the modern pulpits are generally of wood, but the early specimens are of stone, often lavishly decorated, sometimes being a credit to Coptic art, as exhibited in mosaic and marquetry and inlaid panels of mother-of-pearl, some of the supporting pillars also being particularly good.

Of course the pulpit will follow the rule of being exactly opposite from that known to us in the West. For one thing, it will invariably extend lengthwise from east to west and not across the church; this being the more marked because it has a long balcony as well as the preaching end. Occasionally the pulpit is reached by a flight of steps; often it is mounted by means of a portable wooden ladder. I wonder that the preacher always considers himself secure from any temptation on the part of the congregation to leave him stranded in the pulpit, by taking away the ladder, when he has overstrained their patience.

Before the sanctuary there always hangs a series of lamps, which should be of silver, and whose flame should never be allowed to die. In almost every church, ostrich eggs will be found suspended with the lamps; it is an ornament common also to the Greeks and the Moslems. The ancient Egyptians hung ostrich eggs in their temples and sanctuaries. It is difficult to discover the explanation of the custom; even a young Coptic friend, who had himself brought, with great pains, ostrich eggs all the way from Abyssinia to decorate his parish church in Cairo, could not explain to me exactly why he did it. I believe, however, that there is a vague idea that the ostrich egg is a symbol of the unceasing care of God for

His children. This bird is thought to be vigilant above all other creatures; it is generally believed that the eggs may not be left for a single instant, if the process by which the young are brought to life is not to be stopped.

Behind the great screen there are three chapels, each with an altar, the middle one being the haikal, or sanctuary, and containing the high altar. It is a curious requirement of the Coptic Church that the very altar itself must only be used in the celebration of the Holy Eucharist "fasting"; on no one altar may the holy mysteries be celebrated twice in one day, and this applies to all vessels and vestments. Bishops even have been excommunicated for violating this rule.

Fasting for the Holy Eucharist begins from vespers of the preceding day. The great monks said: "You shall not give food to your body until you have given spiritual sustenance to your soul." Apart from this rule it is forbidden to eat anything before reciting the Psalms appointed for the morning services. The chapels are dedicated to saints, and on the saint's day the Holy Eucharist is always celebrated at their altars.

The haikal is always in the form of an apse, and in the middle wall there is always a decorated niche; beautiful mosaics are used in the adornment of some of the niches, others are painted with the image of our Lord in benediction, or with that of the Virgin and Child.

The evidence is clear that the Arabs adapted the Coptic niche to their use, for there are examples in Cairo mosques of the *mihrab*, the niche showing the direction of Mecca, which, but for the symbol of the Holy Spirit in the form of the dove, are exactly like many of the niches in the Coptic churches.

Round the end of the haikal wall steps are built leading to seats and to a throne in the centre. This is the ancient tribune, which is such a feature in Coptic churches. The throne is for the Patriarch, or archbishop, who sits surrounded by the twelve presbyters, with their backs to the eastern wall, watching the celebration of the Holy Eucharist. In the niche above the tribune, a lamp, often of beautiful design, is always kept burning. In the best days of Coptic art much exquisite work was done to adorn the chapels, both in mosaics and inlay.

The high altar always stands in the centre of the sanctuary. It must be built of stone, and is not raised on any platform, but stands on the floor. It always has a wooden dome, or baldaquin, supported by four wooden pillars. The under surface of this canopy is always painted with the image of our Lord in benediction, and the four apocryphal beasts at the four corners of it. At one time a still deeper air of mystery attended the celebration of Holy Eucharist, for the baldaquin had curtains which were drawn to entirely hide the priest himself at certain parts of the service. The altar should be covered with rich silk, embroidered in silver and gold.

Every altar has on the left side, level with the floor, a small open doorway showing a large interior cavity. There is little doubt that this cavity has symbolical reference to the Revelation of St. John: "I saw under the altar the souls of them that were slain for the word of God." In the early ages it was usual to bury the bodies of great dignitaries and especially of martyrs beneath the floor of the sanctuary, or even in the altar itself.

The body of St. Mark was laid under the altar of the ancient church at Alexandria; the sacred remains were forcibly removed by the Venetians, and the high altar at St. Mark's in Venice now encloses the remains.

The chief use made of the altar cavity by the Copts

THE SCREEN DIVISIONS IN THE COPTIC CHURCH OF ABU SERGEH, OLD CAIRO.
In this church, according to tradition, the Virgin and Child took refuge on their flight into Egypt.

Photos: Dittrich, Cairo.
THE PULPIT AND MIDDLE SCREEN OF THE CHURCH OF ABU SERGEH.
Showing many of the other interesting details referred to in the text.

The Oriental Christian in his Church 177

to-day is on Good Friday, when a picture of the cross is buried within it in rose leaves, being recovered on Easter morning. (I describe this ceremony in some notes at the end of the volume.)

The altar furnishings are of deep interest and significance. In the centre stands the tabernacle or ark of the chalice. It consists of a box made of wood about a foot high, having a circular opening in which the chalice fits so that it is completely hidden. The four sides of the ark are painted with different sacred scenes.

The chalice itself is generally made of massive silver, but there are specimens of gold and also of glass. It has a somewhat conical bowl, long stem, and always a circular foot.

In front of the tabernacle, lying on the altar, is the paten, a flat circular dish with a raised lip all round, of gold or silver, or enamelled glass. Its dome consists of two half-loops of silver crossed at right angles. At the celebration of the Holy Eucharist the dome is placed over the consecrated bread which lies on the paten; and over the dome is spread the small square of silk with a cross in the centre, called the corporal, so that it does not touch the bread. There are two other veils, one for the chalice, and one, called the prospharin, to cover both paten and chalice.

Here is the spoon, having a deep bowl, with which the sacred elements are administered to the communicants. Behind the ark is laid the case in which the four Gospels in Coptic are enclosed and sealed. These textus cases are generally of silver or silver-gilt, though some are of iron; they are sometimes decorated with precious stones. They are exclusively Coptic, not being found even in the churches of the other Melkite

Egyptians. There are some very beautiful examples in the new Coptic Museum at Cairo. Many are enriched with interlacing work, with crosses and inscriptions in Coptic and Arabic in relief.

The significance of these textus cases, most of which have never been opened since they were first fused, some of them as long ago as between four and five hundred years, might of itself lead to a most interesting chapter in Coptic history, as it is intimately connected with the wide subject of Biblical formulæ, which in the early centuries affected the whole Christian Church. The last sign of it in Britain is the taking of the oath on the New Testament, and the lingering belief amongst Christian people in "dipping" into the Scriptures which was once universal.

In my own experience I have come across many instances in England—not confined to country-folk—where it was sought to find out what the Lord's will was in certain emergencies by "dipping" or putting the thumb into the Bible. I know a woman, of a leading position in society, and of great possessions, who regularly resorts to "dipping."

The late Dr. Parker relates in *Tyne Child*, his book of reminiscences, how his mother always practised this.

In Egypt these beliefs have not yet been disturbed, among the great mass of the people; the Christian Church itself fosters them. In the Coptic Church service "dipping" is regularly resorted to.

The belief underlying the monastic legend, that a monk who was sorely beset with fleshly lust was enabled to resist temptation by having the Gospels hung upon his neck by a cord, is never doubted. The Bible is still a marvellous talisman against pain and disaster. The Lord's Prayer is used on all occasions, secular as well

The Oriental Christian in his Church

as religious, by the priests and dignitaries of the Church in a way that I thought suggested the old idea of the magic spell.

And here in the textus case we see the most highly venerated token of these beliefs; these Gospels are the very representative of Christ, sign of His presence, symbol of His miraculous power. In all the important services the textus case is carried in procession round the church, with censers, tapers, and crosses.

On the Thursday in Holy Week the textus case is covered with a high mound of rose leaves on the altar.

On every altar is laid the little flat hand-cross, also characteristic solely of the Coptic Church, and speaking so eloquently of the way in which it has conserved the very early practices of Christendom. The Copts are ignorant of the crucifix, for the simple reason that this form of the cross was unknown until the seventh century, by which time the Western Church was developing many inventions of which the Coptic Christians knew nothing, and did not want to know—for of all hatreds that of the Pope of Rome and all his ways was the bitterest, and is to this day.

The hand-cross has always been laid flat upon the altar since the year A.D. 855, when the Moslem Governor forbade the Copts to show a cross in their public services. These crosses, which are about nine inches in length, generally bear an inscription.

The Coptic cross is always equilateral; it would be quite enough when Rome adopted the cross with unequal limbs for the Coptic Church to use only the present form; for at first both churches used the two forms indiscriminately. The hand-cross is not known at all to Western Christendom.

It is always used to give the benediction, and in all

ceremonies it has a place. To the common people this cross has magic powers, used in exorcism, and at the anointing and blessing of the sick it is looked upon as an essential part of the cure. I know that the sainted bishop of the Fayoum, whom I visited, himself thought that power passed through the particular cross he had always used. He told how on one occasion when he sought to exorcise an evil spirit which showed great obstinacy, he found that by a mistake he was holding the cross of one of his clergy; when his own cross was restored to him the exorcism was complete. Every church has its processional crosses, generally of silver.

A belief in "the Symbol of Merit," as the Sign of the Cross is called, has always been very deep rooted in the mind of the Eastern Christian, especially so in Egypt, as the cross very naturally took the place of the magic *ankh* of the ancient religion. "Where the seal of the cross is, the wickedness of Satan hath no power to do harm," said one of the early fathers. When Anthony made the sign, it was said the devil trembled. One of the monks of that day always made the sign over his food in the place of oil; another opened the door of a cell, by the sign, without a key.

It is still the sure protection for the Christian against the phantoms and the genii, of whom all Eastern people go in terror; where the Moslem names the name of God, the Christian makes the sign of the cross. It is effective over polluted water, and used three times it is powerful to heal disease; nothing else can so surely counteract the mischief of "the envious eye."

It is in this significance that one must look for the explanation of the cross which Coptic parents are so careful to have tattooed on the wrist of every child; although the credit should be given them that in the

The Oriental Christian in his Church 181

days of persecution they were brave enough to desire also by this means to make it impossible both for themselves and their children to deny the Cross of Christ. Every monk and every priest wears next his skin an arrangement of fourteen crosses, woven in leather cords, in such a way that a cross protects him at every vital part of his body. This girdle is put on secretly at his ordination, and is never removed. I have never seen any mention of this fact by a Western writer; I only discovered it by an accident on an unexpected visit to the nunnery where this leather brachium is made. Before I realised its sacred meaning, I had, with the Western importunity which always overbears Oriental courtesy, possessed myself of one of them, and had exposed the secret of its use; and by the time reflection had shamed me, it was too late to withdraw from my prying, or to restore the sacred symbol.

At the four corners of the altar, standing upon the floor, are four great candlesticks, sometimes of silver, as in the cathedral, but often of wood, which must bear lights during the service. Two candles, and no more, are allowed upon the altar itself, though any number of candles or lamps may be lighted round it. The acolytes stand close round the altar with lighted tapers in their hands at different parts of the Holy Eucharist; they move round the altar again and again with the lights, and often hold them over the altar.

There are three small round straw mats woven with silk on the altar, called the *hasirah*, or eucharistic mats, unique to the Coptic ritual. Early in the celebration these mats are held on high by a priest, apparently in consecration for their subsequent use in the service.

The priest during the commemoration of "the Redemption" takes a red mat in his right hand and a green one in his left, and holds them with outspread arms. He signs the congregation with the cross with one of the eucharistic mats in his hand.

On these mats the cross is laid and the three small loaves which are used. As the Host is never reserved in the Coptic Church, no provision is made for it in the form of any sort of pyx.

Always on the altar there is a fan, or *flabellum*, the use of which dates from remotest antiquity. Some of these fans are made of repoussé silver, a disc attached to a handle; others are of peacock's feathers, vellum, or linen, and doubtless the original use, made necessary in the sultry East, was, as the Liturgy of St. Clement directs, "to drive away flies or gnats, lest they fall into the chalice." The holy elements are still ceremonially fanned at certain moments in the service, but the fan is generally regarded now as an ornament. When the textus case is taken into the choir the fan is in some cases taken too, and when the handle is of wood it is pushed into one of the candle prickets, and a taper is rudely stuck with its own wax upon it.

Every altar must have its incense box, of silver; and the censer, of silver repoussé and open work, swinging by chains, often with little bells attached.

At the north side of the altar is a low wooden stand on which rests a basin, for the priest to wash his hands. If the basin and ewer were once made of precious metals, the early examples have been lost. Very common tin bowls are in use now, and the ordinary clay *gulah* suffices for a ewer. It is said there is a silver ewer at the Cairo Cathedral, but I saw only a common *gulah*.

CHAPTER II

The People at Worship

WITH these explanations we may now return to the cathedral congregation, with a possibility of understanding in some measure the service in which it is taking part. One thing we may notice is that they have no printed book of any sort with them;[1] the whole service is recited from inscribed books.

Another remarkable feature is, that notwithstanding the great length of service (which on Sunday morning includes the long service of the offering of the Morning Incense, previous to the Holy Eucharist), lasting about four hours, there is no provision for the men to sit down. Though perhaps not one of these men intend to partake of the sacrament they will all have to come fasting, arriving at the church between seven and eight o'clock in the morning, and knowing that the service will not finish until between eleven and twelve. Moreover, most of the long prayers will be in Coptic, a language in no way understood of the people; indeed, it is doubtful if many of the priests understand more than the rote of the Coptic parts of the service, which they are obliged to learn.

---

[1] The Church is now giving some attention to the printing of books of the service, but they are as yet little used. A copy of the Bible in Coptic still costs as much as £40.

It is extraordinary how persistent all through the history of the Coptic Church has been a belief in the merit of standing before God. Standing up, said one of the old monks, is a sign of the humility of the primitive man. So great a merit did standing become in the days when the body was utterly contemned, that competition in spiritual excellence went so far as to lead certain brethren to stand for whole nights in prayer, only to be eclipsed by others who continued praying for forty nights without bending the knees. Then others went further still, and took covenants with God never at any time to sit or lie down, thus seeking to win approval of Him, and renown for their own monastery. For forty years certain brethren in one monastery neither leaned upon anything nor lay down.

In this way standing at prayer became a holy way of life, which the Council of Nicæa (A.D. 325) made into a rule of the Church, by decreeing that "everywhere prayers be offered to God in a standing posture."

Of late years a few benches have been introduced, but they are not favoured by the old-fashioned men of pious habits. Only the very aged or the ailing are supposed to take advantage of them, though I have seen a tendency on the part of the men of Western education to sit down during some of the many Scripture readings in the services.

The crutch which is so often seen in Coptic churches may be said to punctuate another page of the Church's history. When the pains of the body were no longer compensated by the deep religious fervour which had courted them, and men grew slack towards God, they thought they might by subterfuge escape suffering and yet retain their credit with Him. They had not the courage to decline the fatigues of the church by sitting down; if they only rested upon a crutch "how should God know" that they were not still standing?

The office generally used for the Holy Eucharist is the Liturgy of St. Basil of Cæsarea in Cappadocia, though it has suffered severely as time has gone on at the hands of translators and compilers. The Coptic copies differ from each other, and from the Liturgy of St. Basil used by the Greeks. The Liturgy of St. Gregory is used on the feasts of the Saviour and other solemn festivals; while during Lent (and in the month *Kihak*) the Liturgy of St. Mark is used.

The liturgy is full of beauty, the prayers being marked by grandeur of expression and a spiritual earnestness of tone. Dean Stanley considered that "a high theological view of the Trinity was shown," going on to point out an absence of any precision of statement in regard to mediation or redemption. On this opinion of the Dean's, stated in terms less fluid than the facts may demand, judgments of growing exaggeration have been based by Western writers. It is true that the ancient Egyptian seems never to have expressed anything of the sense of the guiltiness of sin, and the deep contrition, which are the characteristic of the Hebrew or of the Christian religion. But if they did not confess sin, they always fully repudiated it. On the monuments they repudiate on behalf of the deceased every sin of which they were conscious—"No little child have I injured; no widow have I oppressed," are words found on a tomb of the XIIth dynasty at Beni Hassan, and they are characteristic. Especially heinous to the ancient Egyptian were such sins as the dishonest appropriation of irrigation water, and the inscriptions very often repudiate this offence on behalf of the deceased. So frequent and so widespread are these repudiations that it is impossible to believe that the subjects could have been so guiltless as they or their relatives wished posterity to think.

It is astonishing how often this trait, which seems to be deep in the Oriental mind, appears in the Egyptian —whether Copt or Moslem—of the present day. Speaking generally, one may be quite sure the modern Egyptian will under all circumstances rely on justifying himself that he has not done wrong, no matter what the evidence may be.

As for the sort of childish conceit of the people of the East, it is not confined to any one of the Oriental nations, just as religion has nothing to do with it. "Ye are the best people," says the Koran, and the Moslem believes it. "I possess all the virtues," declares a monk of pre-Moslem days when, as an authority has said, the Christian brethren "loved to make a record in austerities, and they would freely boast of their achievements and were filled with a spirit of rivalry in asceticism."

The desire for approbation is found in the tiniest children. Miss Whately, when teaching one day, tried to check it, with amusing results. Taking the parable of the Pharisee and Publican, she set out to show the little ones the sin of pride and boasting, saying that God did not like people who praised themselves, but that the Publican was right because he was humble. Next morning two or three children began as usual to vaunt themselves for their supposed merits, when a little Copt girl, in many respects a very good child, but particularly addicted to this habit, said to her, "Sitti! I am very *bad*!" (in a tone of triumph and exultation). "I am good for nothing! I am a *pig*!" At which climax the teacher's dignity gave way, and she burst out laughing. With the "pride that apes humility" the child went on to declare: "I am not a Pharisee; I am good for nothing; I am a pig!"

There certainly is no word in the hieroglyphic texts standing for "repentance," and, when the Coptic version of the New Testament was made, the translators were obliged to take a Greek word for it. But at the same time there is plenty of evidence to show that early Christianity really did to a large extent gradually overcome this inherited habit of mind.

The most pious of the monks constantly wept for their sins and prayed for forgiveness; some spent many suffering years in atonement and sorrow, though the counsel to stop short of despair was never absent. But as spirituality died in the Church the old natural instincts reasserted themselves. In the monks the one idea that early possessed them all was to save their own souls; which had been the one desire of their pre-Christian forefathers.

But still I think the idea of repentance, and of redemption, is more deeply rooted in the ritual than Stanley suggests. All through the history of this Church it will be found that when a truly spiritual call has penetrated the degraded life of the people, sunk in a utilitarian conception of morality and a reliance on external rites, men have come to true repentance, and cried for grace; and the teaching of Christianity has again been proved to have the power to change not only the heart, but the mind, so easily warped with long inherited instinct, through the teaching of their Church. And I am confident the same thing will happen again, when the Prophet of the New Day shall appear.

The chief priest opens the service of the Morning Incense by standing bareheaded opposite the door of the sanctuary with his back to the congregation, and saying, "We worship Thee, O Christ, with Thy good Father, and the Holy Ghost. Thou hast come, Thou hast saved us. Amen. Alleluia. Kyrie Eleison! Lord have mercy! Lord have mercy!"—signing himself with the cross in the name of the Father and the Son and the Holy Ghost; then signing the people with his right hand in the same way.

The vestments of this officiating priest are of interest, and like nearly everything else in the Coptic Church carry us back to ancient Egypt. This is particularly the case with the staff on which the bishop, who is present, is leaning. The Arabic term in which it is referred to calls it "the staff of authority"; it has no crook, and no idea of pastoral care is attached to it. At the end it has two short branches in the form of the head and neck of serpents, with a small round boss in the middle surmounted by a cross. There is evidence that this staff is the immediate successor of the snake-headed wand used in remote Pharaonic times, in the mystic cults, the serpent having a place in the symbolism of some of the ancient sects.

The surplice as worn by all the Catholic Church is the white linen garment of the priests of Isis; and it was from the old Egyptian priesthood that the tonsure was taken.

This priest of to-day, wearing the vestments additional to the original surplice, is really a well-dressed Oriental of two thousand years ago, whose garments have been enriched by embroidery for the special service of the Church. As Dr. Butler has remarked, the Eastern dress has been very little changed, and an Arab of the better class from the bazaars of Cairo is a truer illustration of the origin of Christian vestments than all the sculptures of Athens and Rome.

The white embroidered tunic, with sleeves, worn by the Coptic priests, is exactly the same garment which Rome gave up fifteen centuries ago.

Those priests who enter the sanctuary must wear a loose silk covering to the head, now called the amice; in which they look still more like the well-to-do Arab, who protects his head and neck by such a garment—the difference being that the priests' head-dress is richly embroidered with crosses. In the same way the outer robe which the priest wears is the burnous, or voluminous cloak of the Arab, not of Egypt alone, but especially of North Africa. The priests wear a stole, varying both in shape and the mode of wearing it, with the different orders. If the Patriarch is present at this service and takes part, he must wear vestments of green.

A word of reference may be allowed to the famous Coptic girdle, although it is not worn in the celebration of the Holy Eucharist. It comes from remotest antiquity, and to the Christians of Egypt must always have a special meaning. When the early Moslem Caliphs sought to humiliate the Copts, they ordered that every man of them should wear a girdle to distinguish him from his conquerors. Later the Western people, led by the marauding Venetians, always referred to the Copts as "the Christians of the Girdle." I may mention here perhaps that the ordinary out-of-door dress of the Coptic priest is the black robe and black turban of the days of the persecution, when all Christians in Egypt were forbidden to wear bright colours. Before the Arab conquest, judging from the icons and pictures, the priests seem to have dressed for out of doors in white robes, much like the priests of the ancient temples, though colours were not excluded.

In the course of the service of the Morning Incense

there is a hymn to the Virgin, "the fair dove, who hath borne for us God the Word," and to "the ecstatic Apostle Mark," and the apostles, saints, and martyrs, and the holy fathers.

At this point the priest, after kissing the threshold, and putting off his shoes,[1] enters the sanctuary, and going up to the altar kisses it. He then, with signs of the cross, and prayers and blessings, consecrates the incense. He then censes the altar again and again at each point, going round it three times, kissing it at each corner.

Descending from the sanctuary (he walks away from the altar with his face towards it) he censes the people three times, and then turns to the picture of the Blessed Virgin three times, giving her salutation with the angel Gabriel, the other pictures being censed only once. Accompanied by the people, who show such anxiety to be censed as might almost suggest that the belief in the magic use of incense is still alive, the priests and deacons—the deacons being little boys dressed in white ungirded albs—make a procession through the church, returning to the sanctuary doors.

Here is offered a beautiful litany, of which I give some of the passages, omitting the continual cry of the people—"Kyrie Eleison!"

We pray and entreat Thy goodness, O Thou lover of man,
Take away from those who are afflicted all sickness and all disease;
   drive away the spirit of sickness—
Them that have long lain in sickness do Thou raise up and strengthen.
Them that are in prisons or in dungeons or in exile or in slavery.
The Hope of the hopeless.

---

[1] This is based on the instruction to Moses when God appeared to him in the burning bush.

The Help of the helpless.
The Comforter of the weak-hearted.
The Harbour of the storm-tossed.
Every afflicted soul, and them that are bound,
Grant them mercy, grant them rest, grant them refreshment, grant them help.
And as for us, even for us only, O Lord, who are sick in our souls, do Thou heal them; and cure our bodies.
O Thou true Physician of our souls and of our bodies, the Shepherd (or Bishop) of all flesh, visit us with Thy salvation.

Going now to the altar, the incense is replenished and offered, and prayer is said for those "who provided the sacrifices, the oblations, the wine, the oil, the frankincense, the vessels of the altar, that Christ our God may repay them in the Heavenly Jerusalem," with many other supplications and hymns, leading to the recital of the Nicene Creed.

While the Creed is being recited the priest stands at the door and holds a cross in his hands, on which are fixed three lighted candles, and with this he crosses the people. Still with the cross of lighted candles in his right hand the priest turns to the east, and with both hands extended offers a prayer, chanted to a very slow measure, to God the Father, the cantor responding with the cymbals. After further prayers, and much censing of the altar, and signing of the cross over the people, the bishop takes the Gospel and leaves the sanctuary. The open book is censed, he then kisses it, saying, "Kiss the Gospel of Jesus Christ, the Son of the living God; the glory be unto Him for ever"; offering it to all the priests to kiss in the same manner. As the priests leave the sanctuary with the Gospel the deacon shouts in a loud voice, "Stand ye with the fear of God, for the hearing of the Holy Gospel."

The bishop reads the Gospel, as this is always the

duty of the chief person officiating. As the reading is in Arabic (after a first reading in Coptic), the congregation show every sign of deep attention; all the people of the East love to hear reading, and, like children, never tire of the repetition of the things they appreciate.

No one who has not heard the Scriptures well read in this wonderful language can have any idea of the power they have to impress and deeply move a congregation. Very often the reader, almost unconsciously I should imagine, is himself stirred, and the feeling is conveyed through the language so capable of exciting every human emotion.

I have spoken to young Copts who were showing by their lives that they had realised a call to a spiritual life, and they have told me that it was the reading of the Holy Gospels that had roused them from a state of indifference to a sacred enthusiasm, while the sermon had never touched them, and the sacraments had been to them mere formalism.

And so in Egyptian Christian history one finds that most of the great conversions have come from this reading of the Scriptures in the language of the people, which is such a great feature in the Coptic services.

The great and noble Origen, first of the splendid saints of Christian Egypt, when the temptations of youth urged themselves upon him, strove to adopt in their literal meaning the precepts of the Gospel. He refused himself two garments, went always barefoot, ate only bread and the uncooked green food of the fellaheen. Then one day he heard certain words in the nineteenth chapter of St. Matthew's Gospel which he thought gave him hope of conquest over the body; and he straightway put them into execution. In him denial was first carried to such lengths that he withdrew himself from literary

Photographed specially for this work.

The Portico and the Interior of a Coptic Church, showing the magnificently inlaid sanctuary screen, and the beautiful ancient pulpit. This church El Moalláka is built in one of the towers of the Roman gateway in Babylon, Old Cairo. The name of the Church means "The Suspended."

studies, because it was in this he found delight; as other holy men a little later ceased to wash themselves because of the pleasure there is, especially in such a hot climate, in the use of water.

St. Anthony, the first of the desert monks of Egypt, received his call to his great work, the influence of which is vital to this day, through his reading of the Scriptures. He was in church, meditating on certain things, when his attention was arrested by the words of the Gospel: "If thou wouldst be perfect, go and sell everything which thou hast and give to the poor, and take thy cross and come after Me, and there shall be unto thee treasure in heaven." It came like a direct message from the Lord to himself; and when Anthony hesitated in fear, for he had great possessions, again the clear call came to him from the Gospel reading in church: "Take no thought for the morrow." And in that hour Monasticism, with all its teaching of the utter abandonment of the world, and its bodily suffering and privation, was born.

And many are the stories of worldly-minded monks being roused from their errors by these same readings; even the heart of the harlot was opened when she heard Abba Serapion repeating "verses from the books of the Apostles."

It is not surprising that when monkish inspiration began to decline, Scripture reading became a fetish, and men came to think that there was merit in mere repetition. It was then the monks engaged in competitions in reciting, as feats of endurance. "I can repeat fourteen books of the Bible," boasted one, "but if I hear one little word outside it will make useless my service to me."

To return to the cathedral service. The Gospel is again censed and given to all the priests to kiss, when the bishop kisses it himself. When the bishop is not present the priest sometimes delegates a distinguished layman to read the Gospel, and I can testify that nothing is lost in the dramatic power with which the Arabic periods are then delivered.

Another deeply impressive feature of the Coptic services is the reading of the lives of the saints in Arabic, according to a very ancient custom sanctioned in the fourth century. This I know is most interesting to some of the young men, especially arresting their attention at the hour when the service must begin to be monotonous. The stories are recorded in a book which is only found in the churches; as one would expect in such early records, they keep alive the miraculous traditions which the Coptic people still cherish with undoubted reverence.

In the prayers that follow, it is very Eastern to plead for deliverance from oppression by savages, and from the sword of the stranger, and from the uprising of heretics, that the worship of idols may be uprooted out of the world, and for the atmospheric changes of the air, and the fruits of the earth. From June to October the prayers include one for the inundation of the Nile. Another prayer is that the people may be blessed a thousand-thousand-fold and ten-thousand-ten-thousand-fold. The Oriental always loves the effect on the imagination of piling up words and calculations in this way. One of the prayers in this same service (translated for me direct from the Coptic) shows this characteristic in another form:

"O Master and Lord, God Almighty, Father of our Lord and God and Saviour Jesus Christ: we thank Thee, upon all conditions, and for all conditions, and in all conditions, for that Thou hast protected us . . . and brought us to this hour."

Another prayer has these words:

"Also, the Lord, the Lord, who hath given unto us power to tread upon serpents and scorpions, and upon all the power of the enemy, break Thou his heads under our feet speedily, and scatter for us all the difficulties of the evil power of the enemy."

The Prayer of Absolution by the bishop, said inaudibly, with the sign of the cross, on himself, over the priests, and over the people, brings to a close the prayer of the Morning Incense, leading to the Holy Eucharist. There is a prayer of Evening Incense, which differs very little from the morning prayer.

The first prayer of the Holy Eucharist is that of the Preparation of the Altar, during which the chalice is uncovered, and the paten and the spoon, the veils and mats, are arranged. Then the Psalms are recited.

The very position now taken up by the deacon at the altar is a reminder of past history. He stands, not as one would suppose he ought, by the side of the officiating priest (who, at the west end of the altar, stands with his back to the congregation), but on the eastern side so that he can see down the whole length of the church to the western door. The early doctrinal feuds between the two sections of the Coptic Church became so deadly that it was no uncommon thing for the Melkite mob to rush into the church where the Jacobites were at worship, slay the priest at the altar, and scatter the sacred elements. The deacon was therefore placed so that he could see to the door and give warning to the priest; and his position remains the same, though it is twelve hundred years since the necessity for it passed away.

The deacon brings to the priest on one of the altar mats three of the small loaves, which I shall describe later, as they make a curious appearance amongst the congregation itself towards the close of the service. He chooses one of these loaves and holds it in his hand, kisses it, and lays it upon the altar. Then he examines the wine, smells it, or even causes it to be tasted, in order to be sure of its fitness.

Now the basin and ewer are brought, and he washes his hands three times, saying, with other sentences, "I will wash my hands in innocency, and will go round about Thy altar, O Lord." Having recited the 25th Psalm, he dries his hands slightly, and then rubs the bread above and below, referring to the baptism of our Lord.

Taking the bread in a silken veil, he walks round the altar with it held on his head, preceded by one of the deacons carrying the vessel of wine, also held on the head, and another with a lighted candle, the choir singing.

There is something weird, if not almost barbaric, in the performances of the Coptic choir. The lads seem to be chosen for nothing but a faculty for learning the hymns and responses, mostly in a language they do not understand, and not for any vocal qualities or attainments. Some of them are children with unbroken voices, others are in the intermediate stage when the voice is neither soprano nor bass, others growl with the deep ungoverned notes of the late teens. The only point on which they are agreed is that their duty is to make a loud noise; their grimaces show their enjoyment of their part in the service. The responses of the congregation are always led by the cantor, who is almost always a blind man.

Of course if the music were anything more than the Eastern monotone, or the accompaniment anything more refined than the clashing of cymbals, and the beating of triangles and bells,[1] it might be painful, but the general effect, which is truly Oriental, seems suitable to the setting; and there is something wildly impressive and exciting in the great shout of praise and supplication which goes up.

The cymbal seems to be another relic of pagan tradition; it is of Eastern origin, and suggests the orgies accompanying the ancient rites of the temples. The Copts claim scriptural warrant to "praise God with the loud cymbal"; and one of their fables tells that it was Noah who made the first bell, or gong, such as they use.

The priest, having finished the circuit, stops at the front of the altar, with his back to the people, and holds the bread in one hand close to the vessel of wine, still held by the deacon. Bowing to the other priests, he says, "Do ye bless?" and they answering "Do thou bless?" he signs the bread and wine with the cross three times.

The bread being put upon the paten, and the wine in the chalice, with a little water added, there follow various prayers and responses, the people, and the altar, being signed with the cross, in every direction.

After the choir have cried "Saved indeed! and with Thy Spirit," the Prayer of Oblation is reached, from which I quote, as it is evidence of the Coptic belief in the Real Presence in its most physical literalness.

"We pray and beseech Thy goodness, O Thou lover of men! [he points to the bread] cause Thy face to shine upon this bread [he points to the chalice] and upon this cup, which we have set upon this Thine holy table; [he signs the cross over both three times, saying] bless them, sanctify them, hallow and change them, that this bread may become indeed Thine own holy Body, and the mingled wine and

---

[1] The bells are always tongueless, and are beaten on the outside by a short rod of iron.

water which is in this cup may become indeed Thine own honourable Blood; that they may be unto us all, help, and healing, and health for our souls, and our bodies, and our spirits."

After the Prayer of Thanksgiving, the people sing a short hymn in Greek. The priest now covers the bread and wine, separately, and then together; after kneeling he kisses the altar, and then goes round it, giving thanks for his call to that office, the deacon doing likewise.

At this point the priests and deacons come out of the sanctuary, where it must be understood the congregation only catch a glimpse of what is going on through the narrow doorway in the screen. I myself have only been able to follow the ritual by several times being placed in a very advantageous position right in front of the doorway.

At their appearing, the congregation, which is very promiscuously disposed about the church, all sit upon the floor with bowed heads, turned towards the east, while the Absolution is said, inaudibly, by one of the assistant priests, who then specially absolves those who are assisting him in the celebration. This Absolution is called that of the Son.

One curious point insisted on by the rubric is that in leaving the sanctuary the right foot must always be the last to be removed, as, in returning, it must be the first to enter. The right hand and foot throughout the East, more even by the Moslems than by the Christians, are considered honourable, and the left dishonourable. The single guardian angel of the Copts is always on the right hand: the Moslems have two guardian angels, one on each hand; on the right to record the good, and on the left, the evil deeds. The left hand is never used in eating, or in handing anything to another person; to offer it in greeting would be an insult. Nothing so immediately betrays the Western man, who would pass as an Oriental, as the use of the hands.

When the people have risen, the priest kisses the threshold of the sanctuary, enters, and censes the altar, the choir singing, "This is the censer of pure gold, holding sweet spices, in the hands of Aaron the Priest, offering up incense upon the altar. The censer of gold is the Virgin; her sweet cloud is our Saviour; she hath borne Him; He hath saved us; may He forgive us our sins."

After various censings, the priest again leaves the sanctuary, censing the pictures and the priests. A lesson from St. Paul is read in Coptic by a deacon or a layman, the priest meanwhile censing the choir. He then goes throughout the church censing the congregation, repeating again and again, "Jesus Christ, the same yesterday, to-day, and for ever, in one Person—Him let us worship, Him let us glorify."

He then returns to the altar, to offer inaudible prayer, while the lesson is being repeated in Arabic.

A lesson is now read from the Catholic Epistles, first in Coptic, then in Arabic. After responses by the choir, a lesson from the Acts of the Apostles is read, in the two languages. The congregation now divides itself into quartets, and they sing the Three Holies, each group singing a verse in turn. The text is preserved in the original Greek form.

In the sanctuary there are again traversings of the altar, which is kissed at each corner; and again the pictures are censed, and the choir and the congregation, while the reading is going on. A Psalm is sung, and the Gospel is censed, the bishop handing it to the priests to be kissed, and then kissing it himself. The celebrant must read the Gospel for the Eucharist in Coptic, the deacon then reading it in Arabic.

At this point the sermon is preached. Until a few years since only the old homilies were droned, but there is an increasing desire for fresh sermons, and some of the more educated of the Coptic priests are doing a great work for the uplifting of their Church by the use of their powers in the pulpit; even in the country I have heard men with considerable preaching gifts, to whom the people flocked to hear their message. The language of the sermon fortunately is Arabic, and when I recall the signs of the deep impression created by some of the sermons I have heard in Egypt (in mosque as well as in church), I feel again that, if a great modern prophet were to arise in that land of prophets, we might see a spiritual reformation sweep through the whole of the Church, indeed through the whole country; for the Moslem equally with the Copt is susceptible to the appeal of the spoken word, and is ready to show veneration to any man whom he considers saintly. The sheikh, as well as the priest, who has eloquence and is revered for a holy life, will never lack a congregation.

There are certain mosques in Cairo which are crowded for the Friday sermon long before the time of worship, because of the fame of the sheikh, just as there are churches filled to the doors when it is known that a certain priest is to preach.

After the sermon there are many prayers and responses, and much censing, with a repetition of the Athanasian Creed; at the end of which the priest again washes his hands three times at the south corner of the altar; he then turns westwards, and wrings his dripping hands before the people, as if to warn any unworthy member who dares commune without being pure, then dries them.

After more prayers, we reach the Prayer of the Kiss

of St. Basil (sometimes called the Prayer of the Reconciliation to the Father), at the end of which the deacon says, "Greet one another with an holy kiss," when the priest and the congregation all give the kiss of peace, by touching each other's hands, and then kissing their own; crying "Kyrie Eleison!" and chanting the hymn called *Aspasmos*, or greeting. This is a very moving scene.

At this solemn moment the priest pushes back the cover from his head, and removes the great veil from the bread and wine, saying "Offer, offer, offer in order—stand ye—with trembling—look eastward—let us attend; it is a mercy of peace, a sacrifice of praise." With the palms of his hands raised upwards and covered with a cloth, he begins the Liturgy proper of St. Basil of Cæsarea, to God the Father.

The congregation must now all stand up and not kneel. There is much prayer and response, and singing, when the priest takes the veil off the chalice, signs himself, the other priests, the deacons, and the people with it.

After dedication the deacon holds the censer, which the priest replenishes, and then holds his hands for some moments in the smoke, when he extends his hands over the bread and wine.

He then takes the bread in his left hand and covers it with his right, saying, "He took bread into His holy, spotless, and pure, and blessed, and life-giving hands," then holding the bread in his left hand, he signs the cross over it with his right, three times; he slightly breaks the bread at one side, using the same words as the Western Church uses. He must not, however, break the central piece of the bread, which is called the *Ispadikon*.

He now places the Sacred Host on the paten, and makes a profound bow in adoration. From this point he holds his thumb and forefingers joined, except when he has to touch the Sacred Host, until after the ablutions.

He now uncovers the chalice, and touches the lip of it with the joined thumb and forefinger of the right hand; then he signs the cross over the wine three times, with the same formula as that of the Western Church, until the people, prostrating themselves, cry, "Amen, amen, amen. Again we believe, and we confess, and we glorify Him!"

The priest again touches the lip of the chalice in the same way, and then tilts it slightly crosswise. Covering the chalice, he bows again in adoration of the precious blood, the people saying, "Amen. Thus we believe it indeed to be. Amen."

After prayer and response, the deacon says to the people, "Worship God in fear and trembling," and they all again prostrate themselves. An inaudible invocation by the priest at this point prays "that Thine Holy Spirit may come upon us, and upon these gifts here present, and may purify them to us." I believe the translation should rather be "Thine Holy Angel," although I could not take the responsibility for this reading. To the one or two Western observers who have been interested in the Coptic ritual the matter has been in doubt, and some of the Copts have themselves suggested that it should be understood in the sense of the Roman Mass, "that these prayers may be borne up by the hands of Thy Holy Angel unto Thine altar on high, before the face of Thy Divine Majesty . . . that we may be filled with all heavenly blessing and grace." A distinct invocation to the Angel, which comes later in the service, seems to confirm this.

Then follow many petitions and responses, and *Kyrie Eleisons*, with prayers (the priest having both his hands covered with the veil) for the Church, for our Pontiff the

Pope Abba Cyril, Pope and Patriarch Lord Archbishop of the great city of Alexandria, for bishops, priests, deacons, and all the seven orders in the Church of God, for all temporal blessings of water and crops, for the poor, the widow, the orphan, the stranger, and the wanderer.

The saints are held in remembrance, that through their prayers God will have mercy. The names of past Patriarchs are now read, and, with much censing, several prayers for the dead are recited, in a very mournful chant and with upraised hands by the priest, that they may be fed "in a green pasture, beside the still waters, in the garden of delight, the place whence sore-heartedness and sorrow and sighing have fled away, in the light of Thy saints."

The priest takes the veil in his right hand, and with the left hand on the altar, half turns to the people, and after certain invocations, silently makes the sign of the cross towards the people. After more invocations, responses, and *Kyrie Eleisons*, the priest kneels and adores the blessed Sacrament; rising, he takes the Sacred Host, breaks off a third part, and from that the small particle (*Ispadikon*), replacing the whole on the paten. There is a very elaborate ritual for the correct breaking of the bread, which I give in an appendix.

All the people now say "Our Father," and there are inaudible prayers at the altar, with invocation, to which the people respond until the Prayer of Absolution to the Father is reached.

At this moment all the people are prostrate on the floor, while the priest, with head uncovered, holding the *Ispadikon* between his thumb and forefinger, raises it as high as possible, saying in a loud voice, "Holiness unto the Holy!"

After this he again takes the little veil in his right hand, and stands, again half turned to the people, with the veil held extended towards them. He commemorates living men (at his own discretion), and then inaudibly prays for all men, for rest for those who have fallen on sleep, and for those who are alive, that they may be kept by an angel of peace; he prays for himself, "Let not my sins, and the abominations of my heart, deprive Thy people of the grace of Thine Holy Spirit."

He uncovers the chalice, the people crying "Kyrie Eleison!"; with the particle of the Sacred Host he makes the sign of the cross over the chalice; then he dips his finger in the chalice and makes the sign of the cross over the particle, and afterwards touches the rest of the Sacred Host with the particle, saying, and repeating, the words over the chalice, "The Holy Body and the Precious very Blood of Jesus Christ, the Son of our God. Amen."

Then the priest drops the particle into the chalice, covers it, and elevating the Host says, "This is in truth the Body and the Blood of Emmanuel our God," the people saying "Amen. I believe," to which the priest adds and repeats again, "Amen. Amen. Amen. I believe, I believe, I believe, and confess till the last breath, that this is the life-giving Flesh which Thine only begotten Son, our Lord and God and Saviour Jesus Christ took from our Mistress and Universal Queen, the Holy Mother of God, the Blessed Mary, and made it one with His Godhead without confusion or mixture or corruption, and witnessed a good confession before Pontius Pilate," and so on.

Then the paten is moved crosswise and replaced, and the priest kisses the altar three times. The choir now sings a *Te Deum Laudamus* in which in word and deed they "praise Him with loud-sounding cymbals—with cymbals of joy."

After inaudible prayers, the priest communicates himself with a third part of the Sacred Host, resting then awhile, with his thoughts fixed upon the holy Sacrament. Then he uncovers the chalice, raises it, moves it crosswise before him, and then with the spoon drinks a part, with the particle, two deacons standing on either side of him with lighted candles. He again rests awhile in contemplation, before taking the paten and turning full towards the people. All the congregation uncover their heads and kneel down, crying, "Blessed is He that cometh in the name of the Lord!"

It is at this point, it always seems to me, that the spiritual poorness of the Coptic Church is most sadly revealed. The priest stands there, inviting the great congregation to communicate, and he stands almost in vain, for while men will crowd to see the performance of the holy mysteries, they will not prepare themselves by fasting and confession to partake of them. Even the pious Copts communicate only about once a year, and that, strangely enough, in Lent; although confession is ordered at least twice a year. In the great cathedral at Cairo here, thronged to the doors as it is, the deacon has to make up for the absence of genuine communicants by pressing those members of the choir, who are children, and some of the infants even who have been playing in the sanctuary, to partake.

Possibly it is confession that is the obstacle, for I do not think that any Egyptian would regard the necessary fast from the vesper hour of Saturday as objectionable.

I fancy that to the Oriental, who intensely dislikes "overlooking," either physical or mental, confession must always have been a sore trial. It is certain that, as spirituality declined, confession was one of the first duties to be neglected.

During minority, baptismal innocence is presumed, and confession is not required, and so it comes about that it is the children who are brought to the altar. Often I have seen a mother bring her babe in her arms, the priest administering to the infant a single drop of the wine from the spoon.

The children who are to partake are marshalled by the deacon, and each is given a napkin, which he holds closely under his chin, until he has partaken, when he puts it close over his mouth, lest any of the holy elements should fall.

They walk past the officiating priest, and receive from him, standing, particles of the bread, placed in the mouth, the mixed chalice being given in the spoon, which is placed well into the mouth; and they go round the altar again and again, receiving each time they pass the priest, until the elements are exhausted.

The priest then moves the paten crosswise towards the people, turns and replaces it on the altar. He consumes what remains of the Host at each point of the cleansings, saying, "This is in very truth the Body of Emmanuel our God," and then, after cleansing the paten and the spoon into the chalice, he consumes what remains. Holding out the chalice, the deacon pours into it some wine, which the priest drinks. Then wine and water are poured over his fingers into the chalice, and he drinks it, wiping the chalice. Pouring some water into his hands he throws it upwards, saying, "O angel of this oblation, who flieth upwards with this hymn, remember us in the presence of our Lord to forgive us our sins."

It is a very old Coptic custom to hand the spoon to any person present who asks for it at the end of the Holy Eucharist; he lightly touches his eyes with it, kisses it, and hands it back to the priest, with a sense of healing and comfort.

After an inaudible prayer the priest goes to the door of the sanctuary, and a scene of extraordinary excitement suddenly takes place in the chancel. Men and boys rush so wildly towards the door of the sanctuary that it is no uncommon thing for them to slightly injure each other; being caught in the mêlée I have wondered myself how I escaped unhurt. At the door the priest finally washes his hands, and will throw the water poured over his hands by the deacon from a clay *gulah*, over the people. The excitement is caused by an intense desire to receive some of this water. It is a strange sight to see a great crowd of Eastern men with their heads uncovered, for they snatch off their red tarbushes lest a drop of the magic water should be intercepted from reaching their bodies.

The priest now stands to make the sign of the cross on the foreheads of those who approach him, while he recites the benediction. He then distributes small morsels of *corban*, bread cut for this purpose.

After all have inaudibly said the Lord's Prayer, the priest makes the general sign of the cross over them all, and returns, taking the chalice and the paten, to the sacristy.

There is no further service on the Sabbath day. It is puzzling to English people, however, to hear the Copts speak of their evening prayer, until it is realised that Sunday begins at sunset on Saturday, and the service then held is the evensong of the Sabbath.

It will have been seen how the Lord's Prayer is used

again and again in every service of the Coptic Church, and by the people whenever they pray; in each hour of Passion Week the following prayer, constantly said by the devout, reveals the importance attached to the Lord's Prayer: "Thine is the power and the glory and the blessing and the majesty, for ever. Amen. Emmanuel, our Lord and our King. Thine is the power and the glory and the blessing and the majesty, for ever. Amen. My Lord Jesus Christ, make us worthy to say, 'Our Father which art in heaven,'" etc.

CHAPTER III

Of the Bread and the Wine, of Holy Water, and the Extraordinary Fasts

IN the ordinary sense the Coptic Church does not use Holy Water, although there is not a page of its history which does not show that it has, in common with all primitive religions, a great reverence for water. The Epiphany tank is still a feature of every church in Egypt, and how many holy wells with magic power the churches contain, I do not know.

In the very early days the monks took water and blessed it for healing purposes. As a vehicle for magic it had special regard.

At a certain monastery the brethren washed in water in church, and the application of that water cured a sick monk. Wherever the great Anthony prayed, there water was said to spring up. If the Moslem goes to the holy well at Mecca for water to charm away evil, and to make blessed his shroud, the Copt goes to the Jordan for exactly the same purpose. The pilgrimage to Jerusalem, and the bathing in the sacred river, are so highly regarded that Coptic fellow-pilgrims who bathe together in the Jordan become brothers in such reality that their children may not marry.

In Christian districts the Nile itself is blessed, and

great benefits are expected at the season of Epiphany from immersion in the river.

It is interesting to recall that it was only in the year 1890 that Rome itself was induced to abolish the pagan expressions in the service of the Blessing of the Waters on the eve of Epiphany; the incantations, then set aside, to bring magic powers into the water belonged almost entirely to pre-Christian times in ancient Rome, with its augurs and birds and entrails, and spirits everywhere.

In Egypt we can still trace the cult of Isis in the Epiphany service, which is used to set forth the meaning and glory of our Lord's baptism, though it is not as pagan in its conjuring as the discarded service of Rome was. I give a few of the Coptic incantations still said over the water of the tank:

> Thou didst sanctify the floods of the Jordan, having drawn down upon them from heaven Thy Holy Spirit, and Thou didst break in pieces the heads of the dragons that were hidden therein. O our Lord, Thou man-loving God, Jesus Christ, come now again by the descent of Thy Holy Spirit,
> Sanctify this water, and give unto it the grace of the Jordan.
> Let it be a fountain of blessing,
> A gift of purification,
> A remission of sins,
> A driver away of sickness.
> Let it be a terrifier of demons,
> And let not all the powers of the foe draw nigh unto it.
> Let it be full of all angelic powers,
> That unto all those who draw therefrom, or who partake of it, it may be a purification of soul, and body, and spirit,
> For a healing of pains,
> For a sanctification of houses.
> May it produce benefits of every kind.

So terribly excited did the Copts present at the service of the Epiphany become, and so desperate not to forgo any of the promised blessing, that they threw off all their clothes in church and dashed, a seething mob, into the tank. There is little doubt, I think, that the ignorant thought by this means to wash away their guilt. It is only a very few years since that the scandal of the scenes created led to their suppression, at least in the cities of Egypt. The people must now be content with a sprinkling of the holy water by the bishop or priest.

Palm Sunday is still, however, the occasion of one of those many curious services in which magic water has a part. After the Holy Eucharist several basins of water are placed before the haikal screen, and a priest takes his place in front of them while the Gospel is read. The priest then consecrates the water by praying over it. The instant this consecration is completed, the congregation rush wildly towards the basins with the object of dipping their palm wreaths into them. What a curious turn for a church service to take, when, to restore order, the priest is sometimes obliged to beat the people with a stick he carries in case of need. Pieces of the dipped wreaths are worn by these Copts under their tarbushes during the whole year, being especially valued as charms against "the evil eye" and the sting of venomous beasts.

The Epiphany tank is in the narthex of the churches, near the west entrance, and there is generally a smaller tank in the nave, which is used in the same way on Maundy Thursday, followed by the sprinkling.

Nothing is wanting to invest these ceremonies with importance, and to suggest a magic rite. The clergy must be fully vested, and the bishop or Patriarch before the actual benediction must be vested in full canonical attire.

The water is censed, and stirred crosswise with the bishop's pastoral staff, and crossed with a special iron cross.

Travellers in Abyssinia speak still of wild nocturnal scenes in the Coptic churches there at this ceremony. Christians everywhere in the East believe that special graces are showered down at the Epiphany; dough will then rise without being leavened.

And when I am inclined to think that the East is too benighted, I recall the superstition of highly educated women at a vicarage near London itself, who stoutly averred to me again and again that the eggs laid by their fowls on Good Friday were proof against decay until the same day the following year.

"Concerning the collection"—a threefold offering is taken at the Sunday service, according to a rule which is very ancient. Three men, following each other, each carrying an alms dish, go round the church, during the service, and every worshipper is expected to put a contribution in each dish. One dish is for the clergy, one for church expenses, and one for the poor.

As it is nearly noon before the Holy Eucharist is finished, it may be imagined that the people in the church are famished. It is a strange sight to see them take from their pockets, the moment the benediction is pronounced, little cakes of bread exactly like the one used on the altar, and begin to eat them. Some of the small boys indeed have not waited for the end of the service to begin nibbling their cakes.

When the service was about two-thirds through, a verger appeared in the congregation with a large bag full of these eucharistic cakes, distributing them right and left, to any one who desired them, and receiving here and there a piastre or two in return. The reforming

and the Extraordinary Fasts 213

Copts object to this custom as distracting at a solemn moment in the service.

As a European stranger is always offered one of these cakes in any Coptic church, I have received a number in different parts of the country; and although I know now that they are never consecrated, I have not cared to eat them.

Every church has its own oven for baking the eucharistic cakes, which must be made of the finest wheaten flour, specially purchased out of the church funds.

The sacristan who distributes the cakes is specially appointed to make them, and he must chant, while doing so, fixed portions of the Psalms in a solemn manner. The dough must be leavened, and baked on the morning of the Holy Eucharist. The cakes must be round, and stamped only on the upper surface, with a device of crosses with a sacred legend round them. Women are specially forbidden to prepare the eucharistic bread.

My friend, Marcus Simaika Pasha, has taken great pains to preserve the proper design for the stamping, for he found that there had for a long time been an utter carelessness in the matter, especially in the country places. As the moulds had become worn and broken ignorant men had been left to repair them, and the priests had not troubled themselves in the matter. In many churches the design had degenerated into a mere meaningless travesty of the original.

Some of the loaves which I possess show great deviations, but at last the Patriarch has seen the wisdom of allowing Marcus Simaika Pasha to supervise the sending out from Cairo of new moulds for all the churches, the old ones being destroyed by the official decree of His Holiness.

The wine used is also made in church, some churches having their own winepress, others getting their supply from a church in Cairo in the Harat-az-Zuailah, where it is regularly made and distributed through the country in large wicker-covered jars, holding three to four gallons each.

Since the Moslem conquest there has always been a difficulty about the wine, as the idea of its use was genuinely repugnant (let us allow this much in all fairness) to all religious followers of the Prophet.

The use of wine was always a first point of attack when Moslem suppression of the Christians was afoot. About the tenth century all the vineyards of Egypt were destroyed, and the making or importing of wine absolutely forbidden, with the intention of stopping the use of wine by the Copts.

In their sore necessity Coptic dignitaries imported raisins and made wine secretly in the churches, and although raisin wine is prohibited in the early canons, the use has never been changed. It must be unfermented, and so distinctly sweet as to have no trace of acid flavour.

The use of the consecrated oil, or chrism, is regarded as of great importance. It is strange, however, to find, where such tenacity has been shown in preserving the ancient ritual, that the office of the Consecration of the Chrism was left in abeyance for two hundred years. It was the Patriarch John, who succeeded to the throne in the year 1676, who reintroduced it.

It was a very elaborate preparation, the most essential ingredient being the balsam grown in the garden by the Virgin's Well at Matarieh, near Cairo, where, according to legend, the Holy Family rested on their flight into Egypt.

There are several boilings of the rare spices, flowers, and aromatics, all precisely ordered, the oil being the pure olive oil of Palestine. The hallowing of the chrism is a ceremony of great pomp, the Patriarch and as many bishops and clergy as possible taking part in the presence of a large congregation. At one time it was an annual ceremony, but the intervals have grown longer and longer, until now it takes place only once in thirty or forty years, a large quantity being then hallowed. From the prayers used it is clear that the chrism is regarded as possessing a magic virtue against idolatry and witchcraft, a power of defence against the devil and his servants, and a power of healing both for soul and body.

The present Patriarch asserts that the chrism is only used at confirmation, at the dedication of a new church, altar, picture, or vessel. I think there is no doubt that the sanctity with which the chrism was regarded of old has been somewhat diminished.

The ordinary oil of healing (not to be confused with the chrism) is taken from one of the sacred lamps.

The pictures, or icons as they are called, which adorn the haikal screen in all Coptic churches, are of great interest, a few of them being masterpieces of early sacred art. All the pictures of any worth are painted on panels; canvas was first used two hundred years ago, and not a single painter of merit has appeared since then.

There are no pictures older than the thirteenth century. To that period belongs a very beautiful tabernacle or altar casket, at Abu Sifain, dated A.D. 1280. Dr. Butler's comment is that this solitary work of art is enough by its sole evidence to establish the existence in Egypt of a school of painters far superior to contemporary artists in Italy.

It is interesting to note that from earliest times all gifts to the Church have remained anonymous. There is a distinct feeling in the East, equally shared by the Moslems, that it is not fitting for man to obtrude his name under any pretence in the house of prayer. In the Coptic Church the name was suppressed even in the case of the burial of a patriarch or bishop, and although the custom has led to doubt and confusion vexing to the historian, we may still commend the principle of it.

There are no statues in the Coptic churches,—they are forbidden,—for as early as the fourth century Theophilus was so successful in his great campaign in every town in Egypt against the worship of idols, that there was no one left to adore the works of sculpture in the churches.

But it was not possible to root out the longing for the miraculous which lay behind the veneration of the statues of ancient Egypt, and very quickly comforting fables arose as to the magic power of the pictures of the saints.

Guimet describes the sacred picture found at Deir el Bahri, which shows how the old ideas would obtrude themselves. In the hands of the saint "are portrayed a chalice of wine and heads of wheat, under which Jesus appears, and on His sacerdotal robe, which is quite white, at the place of the heart is painted a brown square with four indentations which make of it a swastika, designed to draw the presence of the gods. Beneath the portrait are represented the boat of Isis, and the two black jackals, which for more than six thousand years have guarded Egyptian tombs."

Vasheh, the son of the Moslem Caliph, was in the tenth century converted by the miracle of St. Mercurius, making his solemn vow before the picture of the saint in the church of Abu Sifain, to which he had been providentially drawn by that saint. It is not surprising that a great and undue reverence is shown to the pictures of the church by the mass of the people to this day.

I have been taken to see many pictures, some of them in Cairo, to which wonderful powers are attributed, not always by the untaught and ignorant.

In the church of Harat-az-Zuailah in Cairo I have often seen the highly venerated picture of the Virgin Mary, in the midst of its little shrine, surrounded by people praying for help in sickness. One cannot repress a smile to hear such folk, when questioned, declare that "the Roman Church is the servant of idols."

On certain days a solemn service for the sick is held here, when candles are lighted at this shrine. The congregation, with its physical defects and failings, reminds one of the waiting-place of a great hospital; till the chanting of the priests begins, to the wild music of cymbals, bells, and triangles, and the people eagerly press forward for the laying on of hands.

Of all sections of the Christian Church, the Copts are the only one which, in its pictures, never represents terrors or tortures of any sort. They have no belief in purgatory, or the expiation of sin by suffering, and they never deal in the terrors of eternity.

Said the old Abba Sisoes, when certain men came to him to ask how they could escape the river of fire, and the gnashing of teeth, and the outer darkness, " I never think on these things; I believe that God is merciful."
" Did not a thief through one word inherit the Kingdom?" answered another of the early fathers.

This is the general sentiment of the Oriental, and the settled belief of the Coptic Church especially. And so it comes about that there is not a single picture to compare with those still found in ancient English churches, with skulls and skeletons, fires and grinning devils, and ingenious torments. The Last Judgment was frequently depicted over the chancel arch in England, and examples are still in existence which preserve the revolting details of such scenes.

All travellers know the painted carts of Sicily: the most common of the pictures represent a crowded hell, with Satan burning in a cauldron; and another favoured subject is that of a martyr being flayed alive at the stake.

In the Coptic churches these things have no counterpart: the devil is largely ignored, with all his works; the martyrs are pictured untroubled and serene. When St. George attacks the dragon, it is in fair fight, and the *coup de grâce* is sharp and merciful. In this the Copts alone have remained true to what Dr. Butler speaks of as the more refined and tender feeling of the Early Church, which, while it delighted to paint our Lord in glory surrounded by triumphant saints, yet left the doom of the wicked to the silence of imagination.

It is one of the benefits of its complete detachment from the Western Church at the time of the Council of Nicæa, in the fourth century, that the Coptic Church escaped the vulgar craving for artistic realism which afterwards found expression through depraved taste and a diseased imagination, working in an age of superstition.

Modern Coptic reformers, however, are opposed to the use of pictures, thinking they still give some excuse for idolatry. The reforming Patriarch Cyrillus in 1851 gave an order that church paintings were to be brought from all quarters to Cairo, where, adding every picture from the old cathedral, he made a great bonfire of them, many good pictures perishing in this way. In his address at the burning he used the ominous term "wooden pictures," saying, "These you used to honour and even worship. They can neither avail nor harm you."

The remedy was drastic but not effective, for under the present Patriarch modern canvases have been placed in the new cathedral—appalling daubs which cry aloud of the folly of the iconoclasts.

I have been told, in Assiout, of the zeal of one of the early converts to the teaching of the American Presbyterian Mission there, who, unable to bear the thought of the veneration paid to the pictures in the church, forced an entrance at night, took away the pictures, and destroyed them; and the same thing was done in other places, where reforming ardour was fanned by the American missionaries.

In some of the Coptic houses there are pictures of saints, before which tapers are lighted and prayers are said. Though to pray to saints is forbidden, it is known that many women pray and worship in their own homes before the pictures of the Virgin Mary, St. Michael, St. George, and St. Mercurius.

The practice of private prayer is strictly observed by the pious Copt. Like the Jews, he prays seven times a day—another instance of the way the Copts adopted the literal words of Scripture; it is enough that the Psalmist said, "Seven times a day do I praise Thee" (Ps. cxix. 164). Unlike the five daily acts of Moslem worship which require stated acts of obeisance, the Coptic prayers are often repeated while walking, riding, or transacting business. The more devout and formal Copts wash their hands, face, and feet before prayer, and some repeat the whole Book of Psalms during the "seven times"; others use the rosary to keep count of the frequent repetitions of the Lord's Prayer and the Kyrie Eleison which they rely upon exclusively.

The Coptic Hours of Prayer are:

>Midnight, or Matins.
>Dawn, or Lauds—at 6 a.m.
>Third Hour, or Tierce—at 9 a.m.
>Sixth Hour, or Sext—at noon.
>Ninth Hour, or Nones—at 3 p.m.
>Eleventh Hour, or Vespers—at 6 p.m.
>Sunset, or Compline—at 7.30 p.m.

Services are held in the church every Friday and Saturday evening. There is a morning service on Wednesdays, generally lasting about four hours. During Lent there is a service every day; as there is on all saints' days and feast-days.

On three occasions in the year there are special midnight services, which are very long—beginning at sunset and ending about one o'clock in the morning. During Advent there are services which occupy the whole night, consisting largely of hymns to Mary and her Son.

The relics of the Coptic Church, mostly consisting of bones of saints, are kept in the churches in long cylindrical boxes covered with rich silk or other stuff, looking like bolsters. Generally the bolsters may be found in a locker in the wall of the church under the chief pictures, where it is open to any one to take them out.

It is a touching sight to see the women, closely veiled, sitting reverently nursing these relic cases in earnest faith that the prayers they utter, mostly about personal ailments, will be answered. Every now and then they will stop to gossip, as they hand the cases to each other, the saints' bones inside rattling gruesomely.

It is generally believed that every church has a relic of its patron saint, and although the worship of them is forbidden, there is universal belief in their sovereign virtues.

As with their pictures, it is the early faith common to the Christian Church in the efficacy of relics which the Copts retain: the idolatrous honour and lavish setting of the shrines which grew up in the Roman Church they have in no way followed.

In the very early days of Christianity a belief obtained that every saint possessed protective and healing power, and a great veneration was felt for the tombs of saints and martyrs, Coptic history being especially rich in stories of miracles and wonders taking place there. Most of the monasteries rose on the sites hallowed by the devotion of saints. To the veneration of relics, of parts of the body or even the garments, or anything that had been touched by the saint, was a short step. One of the first stories related by Palladius, about the year A.D. 386, was of his companion monk, who possessed a blessed relic of St. John the Baptist, by means of which he cast out devils.

The Coptic Church is distinguished for the number and the length of its fasts. In this, as in so many other things, it carried on the practice of the ancient Egyptians. In the East the spiritual and material benefit of fasting has always been highly regarded. The yearly Fast of Ramadan has often been written about in the West, generally to be condemned as a pretence of any real self-denial, by observers whose knowledge of Islam has been too superficial to suggest to them even a suspicion of the extent to which fasts, even supplementary to that of Ramadan, are observed by pious Moslems everywhere. I know many men of this faith, some of them of great age, who fast regularly one day a week, and whose month of Ramadan is very rigorously observed from nothing but truly religious motives.

With the Copts, fasting should be one of the most important of all religious duties. It is a ground of pardon, and a way to salvation. A bishop fasts for a week after his consecration, while the ordination of a priest is followed by a month's fast; these being amongst a number of the special seasons of abstinence.

Of general fasts, Lent is the longest, and of course the most important. It lasts fifty-five days, during which time the people are forbidden to eat butter, meat or eggs, or fish, or to drink milk or coffee or wine; no food being taken between the hours of sunrise and sunset.

To truly observe the Fast of Holy Week the Copt should perpetually fast for the first three days with continual prayer; and then should fast from the Thursday afternoon till Friday evening, breaking the fast by drinking an infusion of myrrh in vinegar.

It is the custom in some districts to bake all the necessary bread at the beginning of the fast; the flat cakes become so hard that very long soaking is necessary before they can possibly be masticated.

The great length of the Lenten fast is accounted for by the joining on to it of the fast which is founded on the legend of Heraclius. The Emperor on his way through Palestine promised protection to the Jews; but at Jerusalem gave way to the entreaties of the Christians for revenge on the Jews for their cruelties, and for the pillage of the Holy City. They promised the Emperor that if he would break his bond they would institute a fast of one week each year. The massacre was ordered, and the Fast of Heraclius has continued until now.

The Fast of Advent lasts for forty days preceding the feast of the Nativity, and is less severe than Lent, fish being allowed.

The third great fast of the Coptic Church, called the Fast of the Apostles, begins with Pentecost, and lasts for about forty days; the length varying a little.

About a fortnight before Lent the Fast of Nineveh occurs, lasting for three days.

At the beginning of August the Assumption of the Virgin is honoured by a fifteen days' fast. On Christmas Eve, and the eve of Epiphany, a fast is appointed until sunset.

The obligation of these fasts is still generally recognised, though there is a growing laxity in the matter, under the more strenuous Western ideas of fixed hours of work, which increasingly obtain. Many of my friends discriminate as to the fasts they consider the most binding and those they must of necessity forgo. Many of those of the orthodox faith, however, keep the fast of Friday up to the hour of noon; and all fast on Sunday until the service of the Eucharist ends, whether they partake or not.

I do not agree at all with the suggestion I have sometimes heard in Coptic circles that the degeneracy of the clergy can be explained or excused on the ground of the severity of these fasts. The spiritual giants of the Early Church were the men who were most hard upon themselves in the matter of food, and there is rarely a suggestion that their powers were thus diminished. Over and over again one comes across the record of the hermit and the monk who had, in deliberate scorn of the body, subsisted from youth on incredibly small and poor rations, with terribly restricted sleep, preserving his physical and mental powers to an almost incredible age. Occasional lassitude of course asserted itself; but not more, I fancy, than can be attributed in ordinary communities to overeating.

The present Patriarch, and also the Bishop of Fayoum, may be mentioned as showing that in the present day this theory can be borne out. Indeed, my own belief is that it is through self-restriction that the Oriental always finds the way to a realisation of his best powers. Two of the most charming old men I have met in the East had both reached the age of a hundred and ten years. Their joyous alertness was delightful as they insisted to me that they owed all to the mercy of God, and to the keeping of fasts made more numerous and severe as their years increased.

There are seven feasts of the first importance. Christmas, falling invariably on the 7th of January; Epiphany; Easter; Ascension; Pentecost, when all women go to the church in the afternoon and distribute food to the poor, the priest dispensing incense in remembrance of the departed; Palm Sunday; and the feast commemorating the entrance of Our Lord into Egypt.

No church bells call the Egyptian Christians to worship; the ringing of bells, which from the time of Mohammed has always been distasteful to Moslems, was prohibited in Egypt in the ninth century, many of the old bells being carried off to the monasteries, where they still remain. In the records of the early monastic life which are left to us, there is constant mention of the calling of the brethren to pray by "beating the board."

The dislike of bells on the part of Moslems is so far connected with religious prejudice as to be based on a tradition that the Prophet disliked them. I know that to this day when visiting Europe Moslems find the ringing of the church bells a great physical trial, apart altogether from distaste for Christian customs. No old-fashioned Moslem will have a bell in his house; he summons his servants by the clapping of hands. To offer his children in ignorance a modern toy with bells attached would be a *faux pas*; knowingly to offer such a thing would be an insult.

The churches are neglected, and, especially in the country, little attempt is made even to keep them clean. If the ill-educated and ill-paid priests are ignorant of their history, and careless of their possessions, what can one say of the church attendants? As for the monks at the monasteries, their minds seem blank when they are questioned about the many points which interest the visitor; and that this ignorance is not an Oriental guise, is proved by the way in which they have given away, or sold for a pittance, the priceless treasures which the centuries had gathered in their far-off retreats. They have in some cases allowed even their uniquely exquisite screens of cedar and ivory inlay to be taken away. A pair of beautiful doors were bought by a Frenchman to decorate his home, from the Church of Al Mu'allakah, within the Roman fortress of Babylon, outside Cairo; but fortunately they have been secured by the British Museum. It would be a gracious as well as a judicious thing to return them to the church now that the authorities are alive to their value. The priest who sold these doors was never averse to a tourist hacking away a piece of the sanctuary screen with a penknife if he first offered a little *backsheesh*. Well might the intelligent Coptic laymen, while regretting the loss to their church of almost all its treasures, declare to me a few years since that while they had so little hope of any intelligent care of them as existed at that time, they felt that our National Museum was the safest harbour they could find. Even now, however, one occasionally stumbles across such things as beautiful screens, and even altar fittings, an ancient ark or an historic reliquary, in the lumber-rooms of the church houses.

Marcus Simaika Pasha has accomplished a great deal in showing to his compatriots the value the Western world puts upon such forgotten treasures, by recently forming a most interesting Coptic Museum in Cairo, as well as in many other ways.

A greater care is now taken of many of the historic Cairo churches by well-advised repair and restoration, and they are no longer the byword for dirt and want of sanitation that they were only a few years since, when I first knew them.

It is much to be hoped that the influence of this work will spread to the country towns and villages. In most of the country churches there seems to be no idea of even caring for the altar itself, for the state in which it is generally found is most painful.

Seeing that in the teaching of the Church the altar is regarded as the tomb of Christ, and the throne of God, it is amazing that the priests and deacons can see its cover torn, and begrimed with grease from the tapers and the ashes from the censer and the immemorial dust of Egypt, where dust asserts itself everywhere; while in tumbled disarray are torn books, dirty vestments, carelessly thrown on to it; the tabernacle turned over on its side: the whole giving the impression of a church dead and deserted—an impression only partly removed when the candles are lighted and the incense is burning, and the vested priests and deacons appear in the solemn service of the Holy Eucharist.

Reform, however, is impossible in any of these things until the priesthood itself is reformed, in its methods of selection as well as of training.

CHAPTER IV

The Beliefs of the Copts

HOW THEY SEPARATED THEM FROM WESTERN CHRISTENDOM, AND HOW THEY HAVE AFFECTED THEIR CHARACTER

THE Copts belong to the unchanged primitive Church which was defined by the Council of Nicæa in the year A.D. 325. She has rejected all later creeds, and she claims that not only has she refused to acknowledge any Pope but her own, but that she has remained fixed in her doctrine and organisation.

Through the stupendous movements of history, represented by two hundred years of Byzantine rule, through the invasion of the Arab Moslems in the seventh century, and all the sufferings and disqualifications of that domination, lasting for over twelve hundred years, the essential character of the Coptic Church has not changed.

To understand the position of this Oriental Church, therefore, it is necessary to do little more than briefly trace her history from the coming of St. Mark, about the year 45, to the rise of Athanasius the Great, who attended Alexander to the Nicene Council.

Universal tradition, both East and West, has connected St. Mark the Evangelist with the foundation of the Church of Alexandria. The Egyptian traditions say that St. Mark was a native of Pentapolis; he was one of the Seventy; it is firmly believed by the Copts that he was a servant at the feast when Christ turned the water into wine; he was the man whom the apostles met, before the Last Supper, carrying a pitcher of water; in his house the Passover was celebrated by Jesus; and it was there again, after the resurrection, that the apostles met secretly in fear of the Jews, when the Saviour appeared unto them.

It is curious that until quite recently the existence of Babylon in Egypt had been entirely forgotten in the West, so that we were always confused by thinking that it was to the Asiatic Babylon that the early Christian writers referred.

It is possible that St. Mark was accompanied on his journey to Egypt as far as Babylon (now wrongly called Old Cairo) by St. Peter, whose First Epistle is dated from that city. "The church that is at Babylon," of which he speaks (1 Pet. v. 13), was clearly intended to refer to the Egyptian disciples of his friend and amanuensis, St. Mark. It is not unlikely that a good deal of the Gospel of St. Mark was written during the stay at Babylon with St. Peter; the apostle's intention being to use it in the evangelisation of Egypt.

Mark's first convert in Alexandria was one Annianus, a shoemaker by trade; this man he afterwards consecrated as first bishop of the new Church, with three priests and seven deacons as assistants.

All the earlier writers speak of Mark as living in Egypt from this time until his death. It was probably in the year 62 that he gave his life as a martyr, being killed by the pagans whom he had enraged by protesting against their feast to Serapis. He was buried in the first Christian church, which he had built at Bancalia, near the seashore by Alexandria. For centuries after, the election of the Alexandrian Patriarchs took place at his tomb. If it is objected that tradition is stated as though it were history, I must say that all experience goes to show the probability of such traditional lore of the East having its origin in historic fact.

Within a century, a great Christian school had taken its place amongst the educational institutions which had made Alexandria the first city of the world—a school which has an imperishable honour from its connection with that early translation of the Bible into Greek which did so much to make it familiar to European nations. Alexandria gave to the primitive Church its most eloquent preacher, Apollos.

Through such men as Pantænus, and his more famous pupil, Clement of Alexandria, the Church of Egypt came into a wide prominence. It was Pantænus who carried the Gospel to India, in response to a request sent to the Patriarch.

In the philosophical and fairly tolerant atmosphere of the Eastern metropolis, the Church developed in comparative peace until the beginning of the third century, when it met the first of the great trials which were to test it, the persecution of Severus. A noble spirit of martyrdom was aroused; among those who gave their lives for the faith being Leonides, the father of that truly great man Origen.

At this time the Church of Egypt was the leader of Christendom, and the Novatian heresy—that to recant is an unpardonable sin—was referred to the Patriarch for settlement.

The divergence of the great forces of Christian life may be said to have begun in the Eastern direction given by the teaching of Origen, speculating on the nature of God; while, later on, the Western stream was defined by Augustine, who fixed the thought of the Church upon the doctrine of sin and atonement; after Rome had wrestled for the supremacy at the famous council between East and West at Sardica.

The fourth century ushered in what was, for Egypt especially, a period of martyrdom. The story of the persecution of the Coptic Church by the pagan emperors finds its horrible climax in the cruel and vindictive suppressions under Diocletian. All churches were to be demolished, all sacred books burned, every Christian in an official post was to be turned out of office, while all were reduced to slavery. The sufferings to which, through a series of years, the martyrs were subjected, almost eclipse any tortures of which there is a record.

So deep was the impression made upon the mind of the Church that the Copts have ever since reckoned time from what they call the Era of Martyrdom, using the first year of the hated Diocletian (A.D. 284) as the actual starting-point; thus the year 1914 is the year 1630 in their calendar.

It was the accession of Constantine to the throne, in 324, that brought relief to the harassed Egyptian Church. From this time onwards Christianity was the dominant religion of the Nile valley. For another century it continued to be a Church which united in one body all Christians, until the Council of Chalcedon.

But even in Constantine's time the cloud of internal strife and dissension—at first no bigger than a man's hand—began to gather. Constantine made the mistake of thinking the dispute was of little importance, which was eventually to involve the whole Empire, and in Professor Flinders Petrie's words "led to the overthrow of that great Gothic dominion which might have steered the world clear of the barbarism of the Middle Ages."

In a word, what developed into the greatest disputes in the realm of dogma, was based on the question whether "before time" means "from eternity." The Emperor might well advise that such a warfare, seeming at first to be little more than a battle of words, ought to be dropped without further distraction to the Church.

Above all Orientals, the Copt to this day carries on that love of disputing in which the ancient Egyptians had delighted, and which in early Christian times showed itself in the speculative writings of the early fathers. St. Anthony himself protested against this sore failing. The devils which possess man, he says, come with tumult and wrangling. It is recorded of a certain brother of that day that he asked a pious old abba, "If it should happen that a man fell into temptation, by the permission of God, for the benefit of his soul, what is it right for those to do who are made to stumble by the same temptation?"

It was a question characteristic of the East; no one who knows the Copt would be surprised to hear in Cairo to-day, after fifteen centuries, exactly the same query. When the great Moravian missionary, Danke, went to Egypt in 1786 he could make no opening for his message for a long time, while the Copts were interesting themselves by putting theological posers to him, which to us seem less than trivial. In 1840, Mr. Leider, who went to Cairo for the Church Missionary Society, had to plough the same stubborn furrow. The Copts who came to his meetings struck despair to the heart of that good man by insisting upon disputing, for seven precious days, the proposition "whether angels have wings in reality or not."

It was what is called the great Arian controversy in the fourth century that began to disturb the whole of

The Beliefs of the Copts 233

Christendom, but especially that Church of Egypt, in which it began. With apparent innocence, a young presbyter of Alexandria, whose name was Arius, a man of whose character it is recorded that he was austere and upright, in his eagerness to defend his beliefs against that heathen charge that the Christian doctrine of the Trinity taught a plurality of Gods, got himself entangled in definitions of the Trinity which were taken to imply a denial of the deity of Christ.

The Patriarch, recognising that this teaching would lead to what has since come to be called Unitarianism, did his utmost to reclaim the young man, and when he found this hopeless, excommunicated him. This act only fanned the great controversy, in which the name of Athanasius, who became Patriarch of Alexandria, stands out most prominently in defence of the deity of Christ.

The story of the many exiles suffered by this great and sainted father of the Church during the forty-six years he occupied the Alexandrian throne (ending in the year A.D. 373) would alone serve to illustrate the distractions by which the Church at this period was torn.

The dispute became the centre of political intrigue through the unfortunate fact of the Court party at Constantinople favouring Arius. When the Emperor called the Council of Nicæa (the first of the famous Ecumenical Councils),[1] and its decision went against his wishes, he used his sovereign force to get what had

---

[1] It is interesting to remember that the Creed of Nicæa was expanded into the form which the Church of England (in common with the whole Catholic Church) uses in its Communion service at the Council of Constantinople in A.D. 381. The Coptic Church differs only in omitting the phrase "God of God," and in affirming the procession of the Holy Ghost to be only from the Father.

been lost by argument. He would have Arius restored to the priesthood; and when Athanasius resisted, he appointed an Arian Patriarch.

The great body of the Church in Egypt would not recognise the imperial appointment, fiercely supporting Athanasius; almost as much for reasons of national patriotism, as for doctrinal significance.

At this point the rival Church (which survives to this day) was established in Egypt, called the Greek Orthodox Church.

The political conflicts with the Emperor insidiously undermined the spiritual power of the Coptic Church, and the degeneration was accelerated by the bitter rivalry between the Church of Egypt and the Church at Constantinople. It seems as if almost the only passion left at the time to the Egyptian Church was to maintain her ecclesiastical supremacy.

If the Council of Nicæa made the divergence in doctrine which separated the two branches of Christendom, it also struck the blow which deprived Alexandria of the position, until then universally acknowledged, of being the paramount See. Till then, Alexandria had always decided for the whole of Christendom the date of Easter; at Nicæa, the Western date was adopted. Apart from the authority of the Church, the astronomical science of Egypt had always been acknowledged in this matter. Egypt retains to this day the ancient mode of reckoning for Easter, and the city of Alexandria still maintains its prestige in the claim of its Bishop to fix that date for the Coptic Church. Easter, strangely enough, is a festival which is hailed with joy both by Copt and Moslem alike. It decides for all men in Egypt when winter is over, and the day on which to hail the spring, when all the folk of Egypt shall

The Beliefs of the Copts

make festival together by going into the country "to smell the zephyr."

Out of the first theological disputes others grew, until the last of the Eastern controversies in which the Western Church had any part arose; when Rome, from the paramount position she had gained by the middle of the fifth century, cut off once and for all, by excommunication and disestablishment, the Egyptian Church.

This was called the heresy of "one nature" (Monophysite), a dispute, so far as words go, having a more trivial basis than any before—for practically it turns on the use of the words "in" or "of."

Nestorius had previously asserted that the two natures of Christ, the human and the divine, were so separate and distinct as to prevent one nature from qualifying the acts of the other nature. This was condemned in Council, and the unity of the two natures asserted.

The old Abbot Eutyches, in the enthusiasm of his advocacy of what he conceived to be the orthodox position, asserted that while Christ was God and Man (on which all were agreed), yet the Egyptian Church must say that both natures were united in Him, instead of being co-existent in Him; that therefore it is irreverent to speak of two natures, as that implies imperfect union, whereas in Him there was no imperfection, the two natures being absolutely one God-man.

The Greeks and the Romans insisted on excommunicating Eutyches; but the Coptic Patriarch, Dioscoros, refused to submit to this decision of the famous Council of Chalcedon. When one thinks of the unrestrained rowdyism which characterised the proceedings of this Council, it is not difficult to believe that the whole business was used by Rome more as a weapon to finally crush the claims of Alexandria than to purge Christian doctrine of error. The decision was made the excuse by Marcian (consort of the Empress), not only to dethrone the Patriarch, but to confiscate the property of his Church.

It was only a small minority, however, that entered into possession of the stolen churches; for the loyalty of the Copts remained true to their Patriarch, and ignored the authority of the Melkite, or imperial Patriarch, who was consecrated by the Emperor's orders by four Egyptian bishops who had deserted to him.

A still more passionate patriotism was roused in the hearts of the members of the Egyptian National (or Jacobite) Church, as it came to be called, by this action of the alien Emperor.

It was this that led to the deadly feuds which disgrace the time, when men stained the very altar itself with the blood of the officiating priest, who was made the victim of strife which had little to do with religious considerations.

I am convinced that it is to the double patriotism, thus engendered, that we must look to find part of the secret of that deep and abiding loyalty to this Church, which, however long it may have smouldered, has always kept the vital spark, ready to set ablaze any movement that has ever had the power to stir the indefinable instincts which this passion left in the minds of the Coptic people.

When Heraclius attempted, in the seventh century, to reconcile the two factions, the Coptic Church would have none of it; the old fire was stirred in their determination to preserve their Church as the embodiment of their national instincts, for which they had fought since the Council of Chalcedon.

The doctrine which had been made the excuse for their persecution had now become to them the shibboleth of their most cherished aspirations. Their Patriarch had become more to them than a religious head—he was to them as the king of the land of their birth. They had been forced to fight and suffer for religious freedom in such a way as to involve the defence of their national existence. This had become an ideal, the defence of which settled the course of all their history.

So horrible were the persecutions to which they were again and again subjected by the Byzantine rulers, that the untrammelled Arabs, when they burst in upon them, found them disheartened, and even callous as to any sort of political development. The invaders, under the inspiration of the impassioned call of their Prophet from idolatry to the worship of the One God, seemed, in those early days of their faith, to have become possessed of the secrets of a primeval vigour which enabled them to sweep all before them.

As for the depopulation from the great number of the Copts spoken of in the early Christian days, I fear that here again Western prejudice is too apt to adopt the view, which the Copt allows to stand uncontradicted, that bloody persecution, and the worldly attractions offered by Islam, altogether account for the decline.

European Christian writers have found it a congenial task, the results of which were sure of a welcome by their Moslem-hating public at home, to dwell on the devastation wrought to the Egyptian Church by the tyranny and injustice and persecution of the Arabian invaders. So deeply is all this ingrained in Western prejudice, that it is almost useless to point to the evidence of centuries of Moslem toleration, and to the steady stream of Coptic defections that were based on nothing more than the worldly advantages arising from the profession of faith in the one God and in Mohammed the last of the prophets.

Sufficient count has never been taken of the extent to which the Coptic nation, in the fourth century, started, by way of monasticism, on the road which, for a very long time, seemed as if it must lead to nothing short of a national extermination. In Sohag alone there were at one time ten thousand monks and twenty thousand nuns. In one place it was said the whole population was under monastic vows. About Thebes, the "sons of the monastery" of the blessed Pachomius numbered over eight thousand. The holy man Abba Thor, in his desert monastery, ruled over a thousand monks; but he was quite eclipsed by one of the great cities in Thebais, for there the communities of religious men and women, all pledged to celibacy, grew to such an extent that it was computed there were no less than ten thousand monks and twenty thousand virgins; and this while the movement was far from having reached its zenith.

We read without surprise that "Egypt was filled with monks"; and in that sentence was the death-knell of everything that might have carried the Coptic people to the position of one of the noblest nations in the subsequent history of the world.

It was into a country thus weakened that the Arabs forced their way; and they saw at once the necessity of turning that great stream of emigration from Arabia into Egypt, which was kept up for many years, to save the rich and fertile land, watered by the Nile, from depletion.

No doubt, in the early days of the conquest, there

The Beliefs of the Copts

were a great many conversions to Islam, and it is this mixture with the Arabs that has, when one considers the matter on broad lines, made of all the people of Egypt one nation, as near together in ethnic appearance as in manners and customs.

It was a Copt, Dr. Fanous, a man of culture and possibly the greatest living orator in Egypt, who declared to a great gathering of his fellow-Christians at Assiout, that the Copts and the Moslems "have indeed been divided, yet really they are one and united, and the only difference is one of faith. From this point of view they cannot justly be looked upon as distinct elements. Whatever they may be called, the Moslems and the Copts are the veritable descendants of the People of Egypt of seven thousand years ago."

When Lane was writing, eighty years since, he calculated that there were but one hundred and fifty thousand Copts in the whole of Egypt; at the present time these have increased to between eight and nine hundred thousand.

The only material advantage now left to draw the native Christians to the side of the Moslem majority[1] is the firm belief that the Moslems enjoy the favour and preference of the English rulers; and this may be thought to have but little weight with the descendants of those who through so many years stood fast against all temptations to desert their faith in Christ.

The Coptic communities in the cities and towns go on growing in proportion to the marvellous increase of the whole population; it is in the villages that the thoughtful Copts to-day see a danger of a total extinction of their race by a gradual and almost unconscious absorption into the Moslem faith.

[1] The total population of Egypt is now about ten millions.

The very causes which encourage the Coptic increase in the towns are leading to their disappearance in the country. Many hundreds of villages have no church, and no priest ever visits them. In the days when opposition roused a man's pride in the profession of the Cross he made efforts to preserve the faith in which he gloried.

In these days the only religious function left in which the remote country Copt exerts himself, is to carry his children to a distant church for baptism, neglecting all the other sacraments. In every way he lives the same life as his Moslem neighbour, and between them there is no sign remaining of religious contention. Is it surprising, when the Church does nothing for him, that his knowledge of Christianity becomes more and more weak, until it takes very little persuasion, on the part of a sheikh whom he respects, to draw him into the ranks of those on whom he is dependent for society and neighbourly offices—the men whom he sees daily at their prayers, and going regularly with deep satisfaction to worship God in the mosque.

This is a strange result of the Christian occupation of Moslem Egypt. Some Coptic friends of mine have turned with entreaty to unofficial England, hoping that some help might come from a country taking such deep interest in missionary work. It is difficult, however, to see how any help is possible, unless the opportunity arises to assist in the revival of the whole Coptic Church, so that it may itself go forth to seek out and care for the scattered members of its flock.

I like to recall that charming picture of Miss Whately years ago, in the intervals of her school work in Cairo, going to the villages to carry the light of the Scriptures to the poor and ignorant. Sitting one day in an entirely

Photo: Dittrich.
THE EGYPTIAN VILLAGE OF KENEH, LARGELY COPTIC, WHERE THE DRINKING VESSELS ARE MADE.

Photo: Dittrich, Cairo.
THE BEAUTIFUL BANKS OF THE NILE.

The Beliefs of the Copts 241

Moslem village, two nomads of the adjoining desert, to whom she had previously read the Bible, brought to her a friend to "hear your book." The man was a Copt, living alone with his family amongst Moslems in a distant village, through which the nomads passed. They had told him of Miss Whately's reading, and wished him as a Christian to enjoy it, as they in their turn delighted in hearing their Koran. The poor man was enchanted to hear the Scriptures in a language he could understand, and confessed himself ashamed of his total ignorance of the Bible.

The native teachers trained by the American Mission have reached a good number of villages, and many chapels have been built, where small gatherings of Christians are held. From Coptic centres like Assiout a number of zealous itinerant teachers go out from the chapels to the little hamlets to preach.

I have never been more impressed than when I accompanied one of the daughters of a leading Coptic family in Upper Egypt on such a mission one Sunday afternoon. We crossed the Nile, gleaming under the golden blue sky of an early spring day, in a little row-boat, making for a village hid in the distant palm groves.

Was this the Egypt of the veiled and secluded woman, of the horrid infidel and fanatic, of the shrinking Christian afraid to disclose himself? were questions I asked myself. When our little band arrived at the village we were received with pleasant salaams by Moslem and Copt alike as we walked along the dusty ways towards the insignificant meeting-place. The news of our coming of course preceded us. A few people joined us on the road, and as the girl preacher passed the mud huts I saw here and there the face of a woman peering out to catch a glimpse of and to attract her winning smile, for she was veiled only for protection from the sun, and in no way hidden.

One old Moslem woman caught the girl's robe as she passed, and kissed it, murmuring, "The lady of Jesus," which I found was the beautiful name that had been given her.

As soon as we had arrived at the dusty barn in which the service was to be held, the poor people began to gather.

Of course part of the barn had been screened off for the women, but from where I sat I could see the little group behind the screen, one or two of them mere girls, with babies at their breasts, sitting on the dusty mud floor, and wistfully drinking in the sweet words of that wonder of wonders to them, a girl speaker of their own country. Because I was an Englishman, no objection was shown to my sitting there; no native man would have been allowed to catch a glimpse of such a hareem.

On the other side of the partition were about thirty men and boys, whose every expression spoke of their delight in the story told, in prayer and speech, with such fervour and charm by the Egyptian girl—a delight sufficient to make them forget the religious differences between the followers of Mohammed and Christ.

How strange it was to hear the girl's sweet voice singing well-known English hymns in the Arabic tongue. If there had ever existed any sort of fanaticism, which I think doubtful, it had been driven out by the spell of a simple girlish eloquence. For a full hour she spoke, and, even then, a sigh of disappointment marked the end of her speech.

I do not know if any Moslem converts are to be made by such work; the future only can tell if Egypt is to be turned to the Christian faith by a newly awakened fervour in its native adherents.

But of this there is no doubt, such calls as this to a better life can never be altogether lost with a people who, like the Egyptians, are naturally pietistic, and with whom there is such a deep appreciation of that piety which leads to a scorn of the pleasures of the world, that they will everywhere venerate the ascetic, and listen to his teaching, no matter what the nature of his faith may be.

This disposition is shown clearly in the experiences of this girl missionary of Assiout. A certain learned and elderly sheikh frequently discusses with her, in perfect courtesy and frankness, the claims of Him of whom Copt and Moslem alike speak as "Our Lord Jesus, on whom be blessings and peace," and the two patiently compare together the Bible and the Koran stories of Christ.

The sheikh has never said one word which could be thought to indicate a desire to desert the Arabian Prophet; but he has admitted that the story of the Cross, told as this girl tells it, has a beauty and a significance he never suspected from the Moslem version of it.

One day this girl arrived in a distant village where there was not even a barn prepared for her. As she looked for the shade of a palm tree under which to draw her audience, she passed one of those large tents which denote a wedding or a funeral. As it was at present unoccupied, she entered and mounted the little platform on which the singers or the Koran readers sit, according as to whether the scene is one of rejoicing or woe, and a crowd of poor village folk soon surrounded her.

In the midst of her oration a Moslem sheikh appeared. "Did she know," he asked, "that this was a funeral tent, in which later on the Holy Koran was to be read to the mourners?"

"Yes," she had thought it might be such a tent. But, she asked, "Was it not a place where men were coming to hear of the comfort and help which God has for His suffering children?"

"Yes," answered the sheikh.

She too had a message, also from God, for she held His Book in her hand; and she wanted to tell them also of the comforting words of our Lord Jesus.

"Was this indeed the Book, written in Arabic?" asked the sheikh, who knew no language but Arabic. One of the greatest gifts to Egypt of the American Mission is a cheap Arabic version of the Bible.

The sheikh, like the Prophet, "on whom be blessings and peace," had reverence for the Book of the Christians. He only wished he could read it himself.

The girl on her part spoke respectfully of the Koran, which she had carefully studied, and of Mohammed, whom she regards as a great teacher.

"Then," said the sheikh, "you shall read and explain your Book to my own people, after you have finished preaching to these poor folk" — the village people, who had by this time gathered in the tent.

And such was his influence with the Moslems who gathered later on, that my young Christian friend was allowed to read and explain the Story, which she first prefaced with the English hymn, turned into Arabic, and set to an Oriental monotone—"the old, old story of Jesus and His love."

CHAPTER V

A Sketch of the Aged Coptic Patriarch, Cyril V.

BEFORE I ever visited Egypt I had heard of the wonderful old man, Cyril v., successor of a hundred Popes, bearer of a title which was held by the head of the Christian Church while Rome was still a city of secondary account in its Councils. It can only excite a smile nowadays to refer to the time when the Pope of Alexandria excommunicated the Pope of Rome. Lord Cromer had spoken to me in England of the Patriarch as the greatest reactionary force in Egypt; remarking that "he was ruling there when I first went to Egypt; when I left he was in full power, and he still rules." Lord Cromer was called to his wonderful work in Egypt in the year 1877, and the present Patriarch had then been on his throne for two years, and as no man is eligible for the dignity who is under fifty years of age, it was not at all unlikely that Cyril, as my Coptic friends averred, was close upon his century of years.[1]

It was with deep interest that I availed myself of the audience which had been arranged with this extraordi-

[1] All Egyptians over middle life are vague as to their exact age; it is not known how old the Patriarch is—with a grim humour he diminishes the number of his years as he advances. When I visited him he told my friend who was with me he was eighty; obviously a joke, for he had spoken of being ninety years to the same person a year or two before this.

nary man, "providing that his health allows of his receiving visitors when the hour appointed arrives." It was on a Sunday morning that I was taken to the house adjoining the cathedral in Cairo : noon was the time chosen, as the celebration of Holy Eucharist would then be over, and certain priests free to attend the reception, especially one of the few priests who speak any English, the Patriarch's nephew. The Patriarch's own room is called "the Cell," to recall to him his monastic life, the duties and the high aims of which are set before him in the prayer of ordination. He must maintain his monastic rules, and is compelled to add to them certain regulations calculated to preserve bodily purity.

The house, which is really the administrative headquarters of the Coptic Church, rather than a residence, is spacious and cleanly, with a wide hall and staircase, the chief rooms being on the first floor. The small reception-room was sunny and bright, having very little furniture, but with several coloured portraits on the walls. Two of these were of our English Sovereigns, King Edward and King George, both of them pointed out to me with satisfaction by my Coptic friends. The other was a lithographed portrait of the Patriarch himself —recording a handsome, ascetic face ; he had been drawn in full canonicals and wearing the enormous crown presented to him by Menelek, King of Abyssinia.

There was no provision in the room for the assumption of any sort of state ; indeed, I was asked to give up a small chair of ordinary pattern, in the window, which I had taken, as it was said the Patriarch generally sat there with his back to the light, owing to the weakness of his eyes.

Presently the old man, who bears the great title of "the most Holy Pope, Patriarch of Alexandria and all the land of Egypt, Nubia, Abyssinia, Pentapolis, and all the preaching of St. Mark," came in, attended by three or four priests. He was clothed in the plain black Coptic robe and turban, faded and threadbare. A man of tall, slim figure, more emaciated than in the portrait, with a lingering of good looks scarcely touched by senility, he moved without any of the physical drag which extreme old age so often imposes; it was by the dimness of the eye alone that one would suspect the weight of years which otherwise he seemed to bear so lightly.

As the introduction was made I kissed the fleshless hand, noticing that it was free of any sort of episcopal ring. Before speaking more than the usual Eastern greeting the old man raised his hands outspread to the level of his breast and recited, as the Eastern Christian custom is, the Lord's Prayer; as the protecting *selesma*, or consecration, I thought.

He then turned to me and asked after health, and home, and friends, showing solicitude, and paying gentle compliments, with that grace and charm of which only the Oriental has the secret. Of England and all that our country had done to bring security and religious liberty to Egypt he spoke with enthusiasm; and he referred to Lord Cromer in terms of profound respect, the profounder perhaps because, when these two strong men had often wrestled strenuously for what each had considered right, the Patriarch had generally gained the victory—by way of a subtle Oriental strategy, and a knowledge of the working of the minds of Eastern men, deep enough even to thwart the mighty power of which the British Agent was the representative.

In answer to my inquiries, he complained of not feeling very well: though he would not be persuaded to sit down, so that every one remained standing throughout the whole interview.

As we were about to withdraw, he signed to a priest to bring him two of the little brass charms which he always presents to visitors, according to the Eastern custom that it is to those who honour one with a visit that gifts are made. These he blessed, and handed to us, with the expression of good wishes for our spiritual welfare. Of little intrinsic worth, they are treasured as a souvenir of an interview with an historic personage.

I learnt much about the life and opinions of Cyril v. from dignitaries of the Church and leading laymen, from the young reforming party, as well as from those who respect the ancient traditions for which the Patriarch contends, and support his conservative action.

Of this every man is agreed, that the private life of their Patriarch is one of purity and great simplicity and self-denial. The man who has absolute control over the revenue of the Patriarchate, reaching perhaps to as large a sum as £35,000 a year, the greater part of which he might if he chose spend on the exalting of his office, and with large power over the monastic revenues of over £80,000, chooses to live a frugal existence within the limits of a personal expenditure of not more than £60 a year. He builds schools, and repairs churches and monasteries; in Old Cairo he has just built a nunnery—which I have visited—for a sisterhood which has until now been very badly housed; he supports with the money all the causes, especially those of the poor, which appeal to him. But for luxury, or that display which so generally appeals to the Oriental when he has the opportunity of asserting his dignity, he shows a supreme indifference.

But there can be no doubt that what is called reform makes little or no appeal to His Holiness Cyril v. The party which, under the influence of the English rule, would like to hurry the Church into drastic changes, has always found in him a rock of offence; the skill of his subterfuge, the genius for tactics which invariably leads to success against every sort of opponent, often by ways that are dark, has sometimes provoked a dislike that in times of crisis has become frantic at its impotence against such uncanny power.

Those who support the Patriarch will say that he is perfectly sincere in believing that his duty and responsibility have always been to guard the Church from schismatic change, leaving the Church to his successor as he found it. He is truly suspicious of the so-called reforms so often urged upon him, and he doubts the pro-English party of the Copts who would lead a Catholic Church into Protestant heresies; as he has always had doubts of the proffered sympathy of English clerics, longing to reform his Church, suspecting that what they are really seeking is to pervert his flock from the true faith. He knows that these foreign reformers have, when speaking to English people at home of the need of such work as theirs, often referred to "the soul-destroying heresy of the Coptic Church"; to which criticism he has never lacked effective retort, for it must be admitted that he is in a safer position than Church of England reformers, when suggestions of heresy are in question. The Coptic Church has from the day of its early separation from the Western Church denied the title of "Orthodox," not only to all the churches of the West, but of the East, except to monophysite bodies. This contention may excite the scornful smile, but we should remember that the assumption was originally due not to arrogance, but to the protest of the national Church of Egypt against the innovations of Constantinople—not to presumption, but to the early fidelity of the Copts to the belief and customs of their forefathers.

As for the young Coptic reformer of to-day, he has travelled a long way from the position of his fathers, on a road made alluring by the increasing firmness and security of the English occupation, and he is apt to forget that such men as the Patriarch were reared in an intense hatred of the English Reformation, and an intolerance of the iconoclasm of the early Western missionaries who attacked the Coptic Church in the last century.

Lady Duff Gordon, writing fifty years ago, said that the Copts would rather have a Moslem than a heretic ruler, above all the hated Greek; and they did not want other Christians to get power. "The Englishman the Copt looks on as a variety of Moslem—a man who washes, has no pictures in his church, who has married bishops, and above all who does not fast from all that has life for half the year." Indeed, the Englishman's heresy is so extreme that it is regarded as a thing not even to be mentioned, unless he draws attention to it by attempts to convert the Copts. The immediate predecessor of the present Patriarch would not eat with Lady Duff Gordon, and was otherwise rude to her; he hated the Protestants "who ate meat all the year round like dogs." The Moslems, he declared, were at least of an old religion! At the period when such views were held, the present Patriarch, Cyril v., was already a man approaching middle life.

The opponents of Cyril think him obstinate through ignorance, and unscrupulous in gaining his own way;

they deplore the Church's rule which sends to the distant monastery to choose a Patriarch from amongst men unlettered, untravelled, mostly of ignoble birth. But when they have got at grips with the problem they would like to solve, they have found that orthodoxy is the last thing that can be dislodged, and that the power of this Oriental potentate has deep roots in a universal passion of attachment in the hearts of the people, who, when put to the final test, support the ancient office, and all it stands for, before every other consideration.

A young Coptic friend of mine, burning with zeal for the reform of his Church, and in one aspect regarding the old man with feelings little short of hatred, yet speaks to me, with glowing eyes, of the thrill he has (using an English colloquialism he says, "His hair stands on end") when he hears the Patriarch recite the prayers of the Holy Eucharist. It is very interesting to find in the history of the Oriental Church how often the almost hypnotic effects of the Patriarch's prayer has, on great occasions, turned even the current of history.

The Patriarch is selected by a Council of the chief of the clergy and the laity, from monks designated by the Superior of the Convent of St. Anthony, near the Gulf of Suez. The bishops, too, are always chosen from the monasteries, so that there is no translation possible. To be eligible the man chosen must be free born, of free parents, and the child of a mother's first marriage, or "a crowned mother," the crown not being permitted to widows. He must never have slaughtered an animal with his own hand, nor otherwise have shed blood. (I think for the reason that David was not allowed by Jehovah to build the Temple, because he had shed blood.) His moral character must be such as was described by St. Paul to Timothy and Titus; and his orthodoxy must be unquestionable. Provided he can recite the sacred offices in Coptic, and is familiar with the vernacular language of the people, very little of learning has ever been required of either Patriarch or Bishop. There have been Patriarchs who could not read.

If there is no unanimously accepted candidate for the Patriarchate, the names of all those who are eligible are reduced to three by a process of voting, when a solemn ceremonial of casting lots is resorted to, the intention being to trust the matter finally to God Himself within the sanctuary—as He elected St. Matthias. Pieces of parchment are prepared, each bearing a name of one of the three candidates, with an extra scroll bearing the name of Jesus Christ. These are deposited in an urn which is placed under the altar. The Holy Eucharist is then celebrated, and for at least a day and night, sometimes longer, prayers are continuously offered. A young child is brought, and draws one of the scrolls from the urn. If it bears the name of one of the candidates, election falls on him at once; if the name of Jesus is brought out, it is taken as a sign that none of the three are approved of God, and the whole process is gone through again.

It has to be admitted that the rule of sending to the monasteries for all the men who are to govern the Church is the greatest possible hindrance to advance, seeing that these desert institutions have long since sunk to a low level of spiritual life, and to an intellectual poverty which is contemptible. The inspiration and fervour which called them into being, and for a considerable period made them the home of a truly saintly monasticism and the centres of learning, languished long since, and no attempt seems to have been made to check the flood of formalism, ignorance, and indifference which has overwhelmed them.

One pitiful sign of this is the way in which the rich literary treasures of the monasteries have been scattered by their rulers, who were incapable of realising their value. The British Museum now possesses more ancient Coptic books and documents than all the monasteries of Egypt; and the travellers who bought or purloined them found that sometimes a bottle of liquor was regarded as generous barter, or that the promise of straw-stuffed hassocks, to take the place of unique tomes on which generations of monks had stood in church to keep their feet out of the draught, was thought to be a good bargain for the monastery.

There is scarcely anything so disheartening to the intelligent Copt of to-day, who desires to see the spiritual life of his Church revived, as the contemplation of the life of the monasteries, which still retain important functions and great revenues. In his bitterness he declares that these are nothing but the resort of ignorant men of low origin, who seek only a lazy and untroubled existence. It is admitted that there is scarcely a single dignitary in the Coptic Church who can claim to be of good family.

Remembering the remoteness and the unbroken monotony and rigour of the life of these desert monasteries, with the long fasts; and observing, as I have myself done, the Patriarch and most of the bishops living lives of monastic severity long after all but compulsion of conscience has been removed, I think this is too stern a judgment. There must still be some sort of spiritual call drawing men to these quiet refuges from the world.

The weakness of the system is, that proved character and ability in the priesthood count for nothing, and men of talent and long experience in the work of the Church are often obliged to submit to the rule of the ignorant—

or even illiterate—novice; with the result that paralysis overtakes all the best endeavour of cleric and layman alike, and there is an ever-recurring set-back, as one desert recluse succeeds another, as Patriarch and Bishop, with no advantage from what his successors may have learned in the practical school of responsible life.

Those who are interested in the future of the Church hope that at the proper moment a strong and wise combination of those Copts who are agreed on the need of reform may be able to bring about a peaceful reformation, beginning first with the translation to the Patriarchate of the Bishop who has proved himself the best fitted for the high office.

The next great need, doubtless, is to prepare the way for an educated priesthood, to be decently supported out of the available funds. As to the Patriarchate, there is no lack of precedent for overriding the rules which stand in the way of the Church's advance. The monastic rule has certainly been set aside once or twice in the past; a married man even has been chosen who was a merchant and not a monk, with the best results—to recall this to Oriental conservatism should be helpful in preparing the way for reform.

There is something quite romantic about the troubled story of Cyril v. after he was called to the Patriarchate. Well may men have dreaded this office to such a degree that to this day the Patriarch is always brought in chains from the peaceful monastery to his restless abode in Cairo—relics of the day when he had to be literally dragged to his new post.

Centuries ago a dear old mother, when she saw the son of her heart dragged from the retreat which she had hoped was to shelter him from the storms of life until he entered the desired haven, to assume this fearful dignity, exclaimed, in the bitterness of misgiving, "I would rather have seen you in your grave!"

Monks before now have cut off their ears so that they might be ineligible for the office of Patriarch. As early as the days when Athanasius was Patriarch, there was vulgar plotting against a man who had been raised so high. The leader of a schism persuaded Arsenius, Bishop of Hypsele, to go into hiding, so that Athanasius might be charged before Constantine with his murder, a mummied hand being produced as evidence of the crime. Intrigue may in these days be a little less crude, but its practice is still dear to the Oriental mind.

Cyril v., the hundred and twelfth successor of St. Mark, was in his youth a monk of the monastery of Baramous, in the Natron valley, where he was distinguished for the holiness of his life. His predecessor had been an ignorant and bigoted man, whose resentments of the proselytising of the American Mission read like a story of Oriental despotism and revenge of the Middle Ages.

When he died in 1873 a large number of Coptic laymen consulted together and drew up a scheme of reform, based on a canon of their Church, too long ignored, which declares that in all important matters the Patriarch must consult pious and learned men, both priests and laymen. They determined to gain the assent of any new Patriarch before he was finally elected to office.

Delaying the election, and acting with the sanction of the Metropolitan of Alexandria, who stands next in authority to the head of the Church, and who during a vacancy acts as Vicar-General, they formed two Councils—one of the clergy to deal with ecclesiastical affairs, and the other of laymen, for civil matters; and in each diocese similar Councils were formed.

The bishops accepted the scheme, and the Khedive gave the necessary sanction. Time was given to test the working of the plan, and when it was found to be satisfactory the prelates took the necessary steps for the choosing of the Patriarch.

In the early days of Cyril, a Theological College was started in Cairo under able direction. It was in dealing with this College that the new Patriarch first showed that Oriental determination to have undisputed sway, which almost always asserts itself in the East in men who discover that they are in the possession of great power, and are naturally gifted with that subtle faculty to master the forces that would contest their assumption.

Supreme power in the East, indeed, seems invariably to find its way into the hands of men skilled in intrigue; it is this that has always offered such possibilities to men of subtle intelligence, no matter what their birth, of raising themselves above every natural obstacle to advance. It is this that gives the zest of a great game to life to certain men who know how to play it. It is this too that keeps the public life of Egypt from ever showing any attraction to men of steady principle.

If those who win the shifting rewards of this game could only realise it, they are all the time defeating their own ends, for I think it may be said that so long as Britain rules, the repugnance which mere intrigue will always arouse, will lead to a constant curtailing of the field in which the shameless game can be played. And the steady, and less artful, part of the nation may one day be willing to emerge from the obscurity which the fear of the tricks of the superlative conjurer in high places has forced upon him.

The Patriarch's first move, then, was ruthlessly to abolish the College, which he could not absolutely control. To the protests of the Council of laymen he turned a deaf ear; their importunities did not wear him out, but themselves.

Cyril made for himself, as the Patriarchs had often done before, friends of the mammon of unrighteousness; he remembered a reforming predecessor, who not so very long ago had sought to bring about a union between the Greek and Anglican Churches,[1] and had in so doing aroused the suspicions of the Moslem authorities, so that the traditional cup of coffee is said to have ended a noble life.

Cyril v. quietly commended himself to the ruling power, so that behind him there would be "the sword of the infidel" if days of stress should come. Then he settled down to his steady course of masterly inactivity; doubtless his policy was well considered, and in his own way his desire was to serve his Church.

The Oriental never forgets; and memory, especially of wounded pride, can bridge the centuries. The Patriarchs have never lost the suspicion of Western Christians since the establishment in Egypt, in the eighteenth century, of the Uniat Church, which consisted of those who were permitted to follow the doctrines and ceremonies of their own native Church on the condition that they ackowledged the supremacy of the Pope of Rome and rejected the jurisdiction of their own Patriarch.

To such a state of paralysis had the reformers, who had hoped so much from the assenting Cyril, been reduced by his methods, that it was not until 1890 that the leaven of rebellion asserted itself in the new generation that had risen up. The Tewfic (meaning "pioneer") Society was then formed with the objects

[1] Cyril IV., 1854-61.

of gaining Church reform and of advancing various causes for the good of the people. This movement gained sufficiently in the interest of the people to rouse the Patriarch, who promptly went to the Khedive—Tewfik was reigning at that time—to persuade him that the aims of the Society were treasonable. The Khedive was not to be so moved, however; he happened to be the wisest, as he was the most highly principled, of his line, and when he had made careful inquiries he advised the Patriarch to yield.

Excommunication has always been the dreaded weapon in the Catholic Church; the Coptic Patriarch has always known that to Oriental Christians it is the climax of terror and despair. Athanasius, Bishop of Sarabon, who had given his support to the new Society, was made to taste the bitterness of excommunication. The cruelty of this edict roused the whole reforming party to fierce rebellion, and they, following the example of the Patriarch, committed once again the grave fault of appealing to the Moslem rulers—asking them to break the papal will.

The reforming party arranged a great popular demonstration in Cairo, delegates coming from the chief Coptic communities of Egypt. A deputation was appointed to wait upon the Patriarch to urge the reassembly of the Council, and the need of reform.

They were met by the statement that Cyril did not see any need for a Council. When the deputation showed determination, the old man wept—one suspects diplomatic tears—but withdrew, leaving them to themselves.

A public meeting in the courtyard of the Patriarchate was suggested; upon which Cyril sent to the Moslem Governor of Cairo to beg for police protection.

He then called a Synod of his own, which was attended by all the bishops, the abbots of the monasteries, and the chief priests. A paper was presented to them for signature directed against the reformers; most of the prelates signed the document without reading it, but to the honour of the Church some of the most able and enlightened of the priests—and the hope of the Church lies in the fact that such men are to be found—declined to assent. An edict was issued ordering that this document was to be read in all the churches.

The Patriarch had evidently determined now to fight again solely for unquestioning supremacy. The effect of all this was to so vex the reforming party that they, too, lost sight of every interest but that of gaining the upper hand; until the contest degenerated on both sides into nothing but vulgar plots and counterplots.

The crisis happened to take place at the moment when the youthful Abbas succeeded Tewfik as Khedive. The authorities were obliged to take notice of the quarrel, and the Prime Minister of the day, Mustapha Pasha Fehmi, doubtless under Lord Cromer's advice, favoured the views of the reformers, who now obtained Khedivial decrees against their Christian Pope. Cyril, however, defied them, and the strange spectacle was seen of Moslem authorities demanding admission to the cathedral to enforce the will of the Government—only to find the doors barred against them.

An amazing *coup* was, however, effected, by which the Patriarch was exiled to a desert monastery in Nitria; the Bishop of Alexandria being sent a prisoner to another of the desert retreats.

What forced Lord Cromer to give a deciding word of such import, when his settled principle was to stand aside from all religious disputes, was no doubt the spirit of rebellion shown by the Patriarch against the Khedivial decree ratifying the election of the Council.

His Holiness sent a telegram, in unmeasured and discourteous terms, to the Khedive, declaring that he would never recognise the Council; he wrote to the Sultan of Turkey, as the Khedive's overlord, complaining of the action of His Highness; he appealed to France as the power most likely to be willing at that time to make trouble for England; and he cunningly sought to persuade the Russian Agent that here was an opportunity to drive in the diplomatic wedge for which he might then be supposed to be searching.

The native political situation changed again. It is always changing in Egypt, for the subtle combatants here are generally well matched, and Oriental intrigue, however clever, can never build on anything stronger than shifting sand.

A conservative Moslem, Riaz Pasha, became Prime Minister, representing a party never favourable to a Coptic revival, and genuinely shocked at rebellion against legitimate hierarchical authority. Riaz saw that the vast majority of the Coptic people, whatever the reformers might think, were desolated by the removal of the man who was still their head. And then, too, Cyril's parting thunders of excommunication had brought the whole Church almost to a standstill, drying up the comforting wells of absolution and benediction, and depriving the people of all the seven sacraments, including those of baptism and matrimony, unless they were prepared to run the dreadful risk of unsanctioned and illegitimate celebration.

An irresistible hunger made itself felt for the restoration of the hierarchy; and the only man who could have prevented the recall of the Patriarch, the British Agent, now felt that he had gone far enough in a quarrel, as he put it, "between the temporal and the spiritual authorities of a creed which was not his own."

I think it is clear that the Patriarch, who had been removed by the British Agent's word, had finally proved himself master of the situation, and the worldly wisdom of the political ruler of Egypt was forced to bow before this subtle priestly influence.

Never within memory has Cairo been the scene of such a thrilling popular ovation as greeted the Patriarch when he returned. The crowds held up the city, and the great sea of enthusiasm swept aside every idea but that of passionate rejoicing at the restoration, the Moslem populace celebrating the great event equally with the Copts! The people wept for joy, and sang the praises of the exile, as though a god had been brought back to them, the traditional enemies of centuries falling upon each others' necks in congratulatory emotion.

If evidence were needed that this passion of attachment to the Patriarch is universal, the triumphal journey of Cyril through the Nile valley, as far as the Sudan, in 1909, is convincing. He called at many towns, and everywhere scenes like those of Cairo were re-enacted. Nothing was lacking that a people could do to show veneration and devotion; there was indeed something almost barbaric in the abandon of the simple folk, both Moslem and Copt, of the remoter towns. At Assiout there was a significant incident. A petition was presented to His Holiness begging for reform. At the moment of its presentation the Bishop of Deir-el-Meharak cried, "Tear it up, tear it up!" And the Patriarch assented, and flung the pieces back to the deputation.

The victory of the Patriarch was complete and

permanent. Never again would British Agent venture to force his ideas upon him; never again would Council, or deputations, have the same assurance in confronting him with objectionable demands. He came back to power as a giant refreshed, and he used his power as a giant.

He would neither recognise the Council nor suffer it to continue its work. He encouraged those clerics who were orthodox in their support, and only with great reluctance did he eventually tolerate the bishop and priests who had refused to bind themselves to him.

He turned again, with cordial appreciation, to the Moslem authorities; who reciprocated by recommending him to the Turkish Sultan for a decoration; which he accepted! If he seemed to compromise, by choosing four prominent laymen to form an Advisory Committee, experience has shown that he never meant to do anything but dictate to them—any promise of reform he gave, under pressure, was left in abeyance; and if he consented to the reopening of the Theological College, he insisted on men of the old unlettered school being in charge, and even then it was with extreme reluctance that he ordained any of its poor pupils.

As for the Tewfic Society, it goes on still, doing an excellent work, especially for education, holding silently and patiently to its propaganda of reform while the long years total up for the marvellous old man who has curbed its early enthusiasms.

Some of the bitterness has died out of the controversy. On the one side, the life of the Patriarch, when he is left to a peaceful and undisputed sway, soothes antagonism; for doubtless, in his own strange and Oriental way, he follows the Master whom he is sworn to serve.

On the other hand, the excellent men who are most concerned to see their Church advance have risen superior to the first longing to score mere diplomatic victories. They show a desire for peace; and exercise, with chastened and saddened minds perhaps, a patience that proves their Christian sincerity.

Occasionally the Patriarch can, by the gentle and tactful persuasion of such a man as Marcus Simaika Pasha, be wooed a little into the way of reform. In spite of his great age, however, there is no opening for those who might think to score at the expense of a failing memory or a declining force of will. Such men quickly discover that there is no memory in Egypt so tenacious, of even trifling detail, as that of their Patriarch; and that his yea still means yea, and his nay, nay. His will was still strong enough to receive, with seeming acquiescence, even Lord Kitchener's suggestions for the formation of a new Council, with modified powers, and then to do little or nothing to carry out the suggestions.

The Patriarch alone has power of ordination of both priests and deacons. Ordination is performed not by imposition of hands, but by the act of breathing. He has sole power over all the churches, and over all the revenues; if he thinks fit he can appoint his own treasurer to any parish, who must collect all revenue and send it to the Patriarch, who pays a pitifully small sum to the priest in charge, applying the surplus to general church purposes at his discretion.

This great power must remain the subject of constant discussion; and since the Khedive, as the head of the Moslem Church in Egypt, has been deprived of the control of the *Wakfs*—or pious revenues—(in 1914), serious proposals have again been made equally to deprive the Patriarch, by appointing a Commission, or creating a Government Department. It is too great a responsibility to be left in the hands of one man. It would be quite possible to form a Coptic Council, competent in every way to deal with it; for there are enlightened men available, of considerable financial ability, and of known integrity.

What such Coptic leaders chiefly ask is, in a sentence, that the rich endowments shall be used for the education and betterment of the condition of the clergy, the institution of schools in monasteries, the good and wise administration of the endowments in order to secure larger revenues to be spent according to the wishes of the pious donors, and the rendering of properly audited accounts. They want to see the monasteries reformed, the clergy uplifted, the poor benefited; all this to lead, as they trust, to social and moral reform, and a spiritual awakening for the whole Church.

CHAPTER VI

A Visit to the Venerated Bishop of the Fayoum, Amba Abraam

THERE is a man in Egypt whose name is unknown to the ruling class, and who is yet the most talked of and the most deeply venerated man in all the valley of the Nile. Although he is a Christian bishop he is just as much a saint of heaven to the Moslem as to the Christian ; and the Christians who join in the daily throng that seek his spiritual help and blessing number Copts and Greeks and Romans—the latter being by no means confined even to natives of Egypt.

Before I even thought of seeking an audience of this wonderful old man I had heard Catholic people as far away as France speaking of the Bishop of the Fayoum and Gizeh in Egypt as an ascetic in whose powers were confirmed all the signs which our Lord had said should follow them that believe—" In My name they shall cast out devils . . . they shall lay hands on the sick and they shall recover."

This old saint, whose power is known over all the Eastern world, is in the direct and unbroken succession of those early Christians who—again in the words of our Lord—spoke with new tongues ; they took up serpents ; and if they drank any deadly thing, it should not hurt them. These words have been understood alone in the East. When the Western Christians comment on the manifestations of Oriental Christianity, it should be kept in mind that these " signs " are all included in the first promise of the risen Christ to them that believe (Mark xvi. 17, 18).

No matter where I had gone in Egypt, I had heard again and again of the Bishop of the Fayoum ; and incredible stories were told to me of his self-denials, his fastings, his mystical wisdom, his power of divination, his faculty to exorcise evil spirits and to cure all manner of sickness ; and of the comfort his words gave to the afflicted both in soul and in body ; of his unstinted kindness to the poor, whom he helped out of a coffer which was like unto the widow's cruse; and how, with flashes of insight, he reproved the evil-doers who thought to deceive him, the spiritual force that was in him seeming to overtake such even when they had left his presence. And of course the power was attributed to him, as it is to all Eastern saints, of being able to confound all thieves by a sort of spiritual detective gift.

Many stories are told of his detachment from every sort of mundane claim, and of his contempt of the needs of the body which was like that of the saints of old. As he has now reached nearly a century of years, the veneration always felt for him has gained in depth as he has survived one generation after another of those who have felt his influence.

It was one thing, however, to resolve to seek an audience of the saint, and another to wear one's way patiently through all the hindrances conjured up by the suspicions of the Oriental Christians, who alone could help me; who, while they were charmingly courteous, and to all seeming more than willing to do what I asked,

the Fayoum, Amba Abraam 267

were all the time questioning themselves in their own minds if it was to the advantage of the Copts that an Englishman should go behind the Oriental veil which hides a life that they fear may not be really understood or approved of in the light of a standard differing from their own.

It is, as we know, a matter of self-conscious pride to the Copt that he is a fellow-Christian with the Englishman; but he is not content with that: he wants the Western visitor to see only those phases of his Christianity which approximate to that of England. And so with the refined skill of the East he will, in most cases, lead the inquirer aside from everything that the Oriental in him has made indubitable, but which is, if he could only realise it, the chief interest of the Western inquirer, as well as being the last thing ever to be suppressed or eliminated.

Nothing could have been kinder than the terms of an invitation I received to visit the beautiful capital town of the Fayoum province, and to stay with one of the leading Coptic families there. I was, however, versed enough in Eastern life to know that I might, so far as the Bishop was concerned, travel hopefully, but never arrive. And even when I was met by all the chief men of the town of Fayoum, who overwhelmed me with promises that nothing that I wished should be left undone, and that they had no desire but my satisfaction, I still knew that a contest of patience and wit was only just at its beginning.

As to what really happened in the days when I was waiting for a summons from the Bishop, I can now, looking back, piece together from various sources a story that was by no means clear at the time.

There were many private conferences on the part of

my friends, and many subtle suggestions as to what line they should take with me. They were all proud of their Bishop's fame, but those who had travelled in Europe felt, for one thing, that an Englishman would be disappointed to find a Prince of the Church living apart from any semblance of state. One of these men, at least, had visited the Bishop of London in his beautiful palace at Lambeth, and several of them had seen the spacious refinement which surrounds even a provincial bishop of the Anglican Church.

Their first secret move was to call upon a rich Coptic layman, whose house was the most palatial in the town, to persuade him to allow the Bishop to take up his quarters there, so as to provide a suitable background for my audience.

Consent being given, the next visit was to the Bishop himself. But here the dream of a palatial setting for the solemn play-acting was instantly vanquished; the old man had not left his private chamber for some time, and, feeling the physical limitations of his hundred years, had no intention whatever of ever leaving it again, except to be occasionally assisted into the church to which his dwelling was literally attached. When he was pressed, he flared up, declaring that under no circumstances would he leave his chamber for any sort of other house, much less for one of the palaces of the rich. The deputation came away with a feeling of that hopelessness which leads the Oriental very easily to a condition of lassitude in which he abandons his projects.

They then visited me, to assure me that they found, with deep regret, that the Bishop's health precluded any possibility of his receiving me. This suggestion, however, I resisted, as politely as possible, as I knew the old man was being resorted to daily by scores of the native people. I had come a long way on purpose to see him, I said; would not some one tell him this; I was sure he would not send me away unsatisfied.

A mere hint of the truth was now, in despair, revealed to me: the apartments of the Bishop were mean; he cared nothing for comfort; the people who served him, knowing that he made no demands upon them, neglected to keep the house clean. There were even odours to be encountered on the staircase leading to his apartments.

I was not ignorant of the fact that the Coptic churches, concealed in the days of the persecutions from the outer world by the huddling together, barnacle-like, against their walls, of all sorts of unsuitable buildings, had in many cases become noisome from the want of sanitation. The description by Mr. Somers Clarke of the entrance of a country Coptic church came to my mind: "A little commonplace doorway down a narrow lane, a small door, thick, and studded with heavy nails, an evil stench, and we find ourselves in the reception hall." Very earnestly I declared that I cared for none of these things; I only wanted to see and have speech with the Bishop.

Another deputation returned to the church house. A distinguished Englishman (I had no control over this unblushing deception), they told the Bishop, was anxious for an audience; would the Bishop appoint a time when he might be kept clear of the native throng?

The old man apparently had no liking for the idea of being sought out by travellers as a celebrity; this was not his Master's work. If the Englishman was poor, or sad, or ill, or had need in any way of spiritual ministration, or counsel, *then* he would see him, but not otherwise.

Again I was told what was not the old man's answer, but that a serious relapse in the Bishop's health that day had made it impossible for him to fulfil his earnest desire to see me.

Still the troublesome Briton would not be satisfied, or say *ma'aleesh* (do not trouble), as the polite and easily turned aside Oriental would. Fortunately ill-manners are excused to the English by the Egyptian, on the ground that it is our national habits that are peculiar, and we are not altogether to be held accountable for them. Oriental courtesy will often cover the rudeness of a European guest, with this as a sufficient excuse; the host will still go on striving to create a feeling of satisfaction and content in his visitor, so long as there is a chance left of meeting his wishes. I *ought* to have said *ma'aleesh*, but if I could not show this politeness—well, I had left my friends in trouble which they must still struggle as my hosts to overcome.

These men looked very gravely concerned when I maintained my protests, with an assumed mulishness that I knew well enough would intrigue them to try again to remove that direst of trouble to them, the displeasure of a guest.

A Coptic friend, whom I have known in Cairo for some time, now had a brilliant inspiration. Had I not a weak throat; had I not, two years before, made a long stay in Egypt purely for health reasons? That was enough. The Bishop was quickly informed that an Englishman out of health sought his blessing.

"Bring the poor man to me," he said at once, and appointed the next afternoon at five o'clock for the visit.

When the deputation returned with this news (they forgot now to be even plausible about the Bishop's ill-health) we beamed upon each other with restored good

the Fayoum, Amba Abraam 271

feeling, like a party of children who, after prolonged sulks, are overjoyed to "make it up."

I recalled what I had read of that early Coptic saint, Anthony, who when persons of rank often sought, in vain, to tempt him from his hermitage, had but one reply, "As a fish dies out of water, so a monk dies out of his cell." The only chance of gaining an interview with St. Anthony of old was to claim his intervention for some one in distress.

The last thing that hindered the happiness of a great Coptic gathering of friends that evening were the misgivings, which now cropped up again, of what I might think of the state in which I should find the Bishop living. By every kind of delicate suggestion and apology they tried to prepare my mind for the visit, so that I might put the most favourable interpretation possible on things.

The next day we set off in the carriages of my host, to be driven through the picturesque town (at that dashing pace which is the Egyptian's delight) to the out-of-the-way slum in which the church of Fayoum is hidden.

Our hostess is one of the modern Coptic ladies who have travelled much in Europe, speak English very prettily, and have discarded not only the veil, but every semblance of the black mantle designed to make the Eastern woman inconspicuous out of doors.

As my wife was also to visit the Bishop, our hostess accompanies us, although she has from the first never ceased to murmur her gentle protests against the proceeding; she is thinking of the horror of domestic dirt which she herself has thoroughly learned in England; for no Egyptian lady who has once experienced what our passion for cleanliness means ever fails to adopt it,

She carries back to her native country a divine discontent, through which a little steady reform is at work in a way which of all things will make most for the true advance of Egypt—the fostering of a happy efficient home-life.

The appearance of our cavalcade makes a stir in the mean streets, so that a little crowd has gathered at the entrance of the church, where two or three priests are awaiting us, to give us formal welcome. There is evidence that an attempt has been made to sweep the little courtyard and the stairway, but centuries of dirt easily defy such casual onslaught. As for the odour on the staircase leading to the Bishop's apartments, I fancy nothing short of demolition to the foundations of the building could dispossess a thing so "old established."

My companions now became silent with depression at the thought that their intrigues to keep a disagreeable secret should have been overcome—a thing, however, I could not help feeling, they were more disposed to hide than to remedy. One of them, a graduate fresh from Oxford University, having surreptitiously fortified himself, offered me a lozenge of formamint.

We reached an outer apartment, dark and bare as a garret in a ruined tenement, the floor black with grime, the walls naked as the builder left them ages since, except for the dust-laden festoons of spiders. The windows were opaque with dirt, and much of the glass was broken. In this apartment we waited, while the chief priest passed once or twice in and out of an adjoining room, whispering comments in Arabic to our party which I could not hear.

Now the word is given, and we are ushered into a chamber, proving to be rather larger than the anteroom; in much the same condition, and equally bare, but for a

THE DOMES WHICH ARE CHARACTERISTIC OF ALL COPTIC CHURCHES.
At the Desert Monastery of Anba Bishai.

ON THE ROOF OF A COPTIC MONASTERY.
With the illimitable desert stretching away in all directions. There have been times when the monks have subsisted almost entirely on the dates grown as shown within their own stronghold.

square bed, and two chairs obviously imported for the occasion.

On the bed, sitting in the Eastern posture, and wrapped in a threadbare robe of black, with a black plaited turban on his head, sat the frail, emaciated form of the Bishop.

Introductions were made, the old man being particular to know correctly the names of those who were strange to him. He took the hand of each visitor in turn, but kept his own hands all the time partly concealed in the wide sleeve of his robe. The instinct of every Oriental is to kiss the hand of any man for whom he has deep veneration, but Bishop Abraam, I found, will never allow his hand to be kissed, if by covering it in this way he can avoid it.

It was with deep emotion that I looked into the face of this modern saint. To doubt his right to the title was impossible, for the power of a pure and beautiful soul made itself felt at once, with a force that was almost overwhelming.

The eyes looked out of a calm, grave face, fringed with a small white beard, which in no way obscured the sensitive mouth. The turban was worn farther back than is usual, leaving the broad unwrinkled forehead to suggest that the ascetic, in this case, had been governed by a fine intelligence.

That the Bishop was a centenarian seemed difficult of belief; he might be as weak as the frailness of his body suggested, but nothing about him even hinted that the mind was touched with age; and when one caught the steady glance of his eye, and heard him speak, the physical limitations were forgotten, which perforce made of his bed the throne from which he ruled his diocese and ministered to the larger world of suffering humanity.

The two chairs were placed close to the bed, so that my wife and I might sit near to the Bishop. He then questioned me earnestly about the Church in England, and the Bishop of London, who was visiting Egypt at that time, for he had heard of him, and that I was acquainted with him, and that we had met in Khartoum. Then he turned to more personal matters, and was concerned for our general well-being.

To my request that the Bishop would give us his blessing, he asked, in a very quiet voice, one of the priests who were present to bring to him his hand-cross. I had often heard of this particular cross, which had been held in blessing over tens of thousands of Egyptians, and was believed by most of them to have in itself mystical powers. It is the cross the Bishop has used all his clerical life, and I know that he himself is so attached to it that he considers his powers would be disturbed by its injury or loss.

It is usual, I believe, in every Christian Church to kneel in receiving a bishop's blessing; but on no account would Amba Abraam consent to any person kneeling before him—to God, he said, alone was such obeisance due. He was distressed that I felt obliged to kneel, but when I explained that my first reverence was to God, and then to His good servant, he gently gave way.

Taking the cross in his right hand, and holding it closely over our heads, the Bishop poured out, mostly in the Coptic language, in tones of rapt devotion, the wonderful prayers and blessings of his Church.

Of the mere words, I of course recognised little, except the oft-repeated "Kyrie Eleison!" (Lord have mercy!). But I was thrilled nevertheless by the childlike earnestness of the man who uttered them; never had I heard prayer which seemed to establish a link with the

the Fayoum, Amba Abraam 275

Throne of Grace with such instant security; it seemed as if earth fell away, to leave this man speaking in the clear presence of God Himself.

The form of the blessing was so very Oriental that I afterwards asked the one priest present who knew both Coptic and English well, to transcribe it for me; and I give it here, omitting only the passages that were personal to my wife and myself. If I should relate the long-drawn-out endeavours by which I got this translation I should have to tell a story of many months' ingenious persistency on the part of faithful Coptic friends and myself, which any one who knows the *bookra* (to-morrow) of the East would read with sympathy. The Coptic form of the Lord's Prayer is of interest. I give the whole form as the priest wrote it.

In the name of the Father, and of the Son, and the Holy Ghost. Amen.

Our Father, who art in heaven: hallowed be Thy Name: Thy Kingdom come: Thy will be done on earth as it is in heaven: Give us this day the morrow's bread: and forgive us our debts as we forgive our debtors: and lead us not into temptation: but deliver us from evil: through Christ our Lord. Amen.

Thanksgiving.

Let us thank the Maker of all good, the merciful, the Father of our Lord God and Saviour Jesus Christ, because He has protected, kept, accepted, and pitied us, and has brought us to this hour. Let us ask Him to keep us for this day, and all the days of our life, in peace. O God, our Lord and Master, the upholder of all, the Father of our Lord God and Saviour Jesus Christ, we thank Thee in every case, for everything, and at every time. Thou hast protected, assisted, kept, accepted, pitied, supported, and brought us to this moment. For this we beseech and ask from Thy holiness, O Lover of souls, that Thou wouldst confer upon us to fulfil this holy day, and all the days of our life, in peace and fear. From every envy, trial, evil deed, the counsel of the wicked, the rising up of the hidden enemies as well as of those that are seen, preserve us and all Thy people, and Thy holy place. What things are good and helpful grant us, as it is Thou that has given us the power to crush serpents, scorpions, and all the power of the Enemy.

Lead us not into temptation, but deliver us from evil, through the mercy and kindness of Thine only Son, our Lord and Saviour Jesus Christ, whom we love, and to whom, as well as to the animating Holy Spirit, we offer glory and honour now, for ever and the ages of ages.

SHORT PRAYERS FROM THE SERVICE OF THE MASS.

We ask, God the upholder of all, the Father of our Lord God the Saviour Jesus Christ, we beseech and ask from Thy holiness, O Lover of souls, remember, O Lord, the safety of Thy Church, the one holy, universal, apostolic Church, extending from one end of the earth to the other.

Remember, O Lord, our revered Patriarch, the head of the priests, Amba Kyrollos, preserve him and us for many years and days of safety.

Remember, O Lord, our meetings, and bless them, and grant that we may not be hindered from complying with Thy holy will.

Grant us, O Lord, and those coming after us, houses of prayer, houses of purity, houses of blessing. Rise up, O Lord, let Thine enemies be scattered, and let all the enemies of Thy Holy Name flee before Thy face. May Thy people increase through Thy blessing to thousands of thousands, and myriads of myriads, and accomplish Thy Holy Will, through the grace and goodness of Thy Holy Son, our Lord God and Saviour Jesus Christ, to whom, and to the Holy Spirit, we offer glory and honour, now and for ever. Amen.

THE LAW OF FAITH (recited by the Bishop in Arabic).

We believe indeed in one God, the Father, the upholder of all, the creator of heaven and earth, and what is seen and what is not seen. We believe in one Lord, Jesus Christ, the only Son of God, who is born from the Father before all ages, light out of light, a true God from a true God, born and not created, equal to the Father in essence, by whom everything existed, who, for our sake, we, the people, and for our salvation, descended from the heaven, took a body from the Holy Spirit, and from the Mary the Virgin, was born a man, and was crucified on our behalf in the time of Pilate. He took pain, was entombed, and rose up from among the dead in the third day, as it is recorded in the books. He rose up to the heavens and sat on the right of His Father, and will come in His glory to redeem the dead and the survivors; whose kingdom never ends.

We believe in the Holy Spirit, the animating Lord, springing from the Father, and to whom, as well as to the Father and the Son, we prostrate ourselves. We believe in the Holy Spirit, the speaker through the Prophets.

We believe in one holy, universal, and apostolic Church. We confess one baptism for the forgiving of sins.

We expect the resurrection of the dead, and the revival of the next age. Amen.

Kyrie Eleison! Kyrie Eleison!! Kyrie Eleison!!! (Repeated in threes, twelve times.)

THE LORD'S PRAYER.

A PRAYER CALLED THE JUSTIFICATION [1] (recited in Coptic).

O Master, the Lord Jesus Christ, the only Son of God, the Word of God the Father, who hath cut all the bonds of our sins by His redeeming and life-giving pains, who hath breathed in the face of His righteous Apostles and pious disciples, saying to them, " Accept the Holy Spirit. Those whose sins you forgive, are to be accordingly forgiven." Now also, our Master, Thou hast before Thy righteous Apostles conferred upon those who work in the priesthood in Thy Holy Church the power to forgive sins on earth, and to tie and to untie all the bonds of oppression. Now, also, we beseech and ask from Thee, O Lover of souls, on behalf of these Thy servants who bow their heads before Thy glory, to endow them and us with Thy mercy, and to cut, on our behalf, all bonds of oppression or injustice. If they have sinned towards Thee in anything, either knowingly or unknowingly, by doing or saying, Thou, O Lover of men, knowest their weakness. O God, grant us the forgiving of our sins! Let us fear Thee! Lead us according to Thy righteous and holy will, because it is Thou who art our God, to whom, as well as to the life-giving Holy Ghost, we prostrate, and offer glory and honour, now and for ever, and to the ages of ages. Amen.

---

[1] The priest's note says: " In Arabic the word would be *Tahlil*, which would call the prayer 'the asking of pardon,' but according to the meaning of the Coptic word it means 'justification.'"

THE BLESSING (recited in Coptic).

May God bless and pity us. He manifests His face and exercises His mercy towards us. O Lord, save Thy people, Bless Thine inheritance, Preserve and lift them up for ever. Dignify the era of the Christians. By the power of Thy animating Crucifix, by the entreaties made on our behalf by our Mistress and Queen, the Mother of God, the holy and righteous Mary, and the righteous leaders Mikhail, Ghabriel, Raphail, and Surial; and the four animals having no bodies; and the twenty-four priests. The Cherubim and the Serifium, St. John the Baptist, and the one-hundred-and-forty-four thousands, and my masters the Fathers and the Apostles. Our Father, Peter, and our Teacher, Paul, and the rest of the Apostles, and the three pious youths, Sidrak, Misac, and Aptanach. The blessed Archdeacon Stephenus the first martyr. My Master the King St. Gurgic, and St. Tadros el Mishriky Viloptaire, Voriaus, St. Aba Mina, Aba Boxtor ibn Romanous, and all the martyrs. The great St. Amba Antonius, and the righteous Amba Paula. The three pious Makars, Amba Jhon, Amba Beshaway. Our two spiritual fathers, Maximus and Dumadinyous; Amba Moses, and the forty-nine martyrs. All those who put on the cross, the righteous, and all the wise virgins, and the angel of this day. Their Holy Blessing, grace, power, love, and help will be with us for ever. Amen.

O Christ, our God! O King of Peace! Give us Thy peace. Forgive our sins, for Thou hast the power, the glory, and the honour, for ever. Amen.

In the name of the Father, the Son, and the Holy Ghost, one God.
Blessed be God, the Lord, the upholder of all. Amen.
Blessed be His only Son Jesus Christ, our Lord. Amen.
Blessed be the consoling Holy Spirit. Amen.
Glory and honour to |the Three, the Father, the Son, and the Holy Spirit, now and for ever, and to the ages of ages. Amen.

THE LORD'S PRAYER.

The blessing over, the gentle old man again inquired, in tones of tender solicitude, as to the welfare of all, myself and family. In Oriental terms he spoke of the pleasure such a visit had given him.

Turning to a priest, the Bishop asked him to bring to him certain little gifts, consisting of as many coloured *manâdîl*[1] as there were members of our party. Taking these separately in his left hand, he held his little cross over them and blessed them, in the name of each of us in turn, handing them to us as a souvenir of the visit.

It is usual in the East, as I have already noted, always to make presents to visitors; this trifling gift was at the same time a sign of politeness and a symbol of the poverty in which the Bishop lived; it is the form the Bishop's presents always take, and because of the personal blessing going with it, the little red handkerchief, distributed all over Egypt, is treasured in thousands of homes, doubtless as a sort of holy talisman.

We now saluted the Bishop and withdrew. The chief priest, Abd-el-Sayed, accompanied us to the outer gate, where quite a crowd of natives of that quarter of the town were awaiting our appearance—and before the final leave-taking he formally addressed us, as we stood in the open court, in these words:

"Your visit has brought us great honour this day. The Bishop Amba Abraam, the speaker, and all the people of El Fayoum, take a great delight in your visit. Accept our deep thanks. May God preserve you for ever. Amen."

So long as any Coptic record has been kept it has been usual to address visitors to the churches and monasteries in this way—generally at vastly greater length.

I may here make one or two remarks on points arising out of the Bishop's blessing—largely the outcome of personal inquiries of the bishops and priests and other living authorities.

The "Kyrie Eleison!" is the one oft-repeated cry

---

[1] The Arabic word for handkerchief. These were red, stamped in black of a coarse quality, possibly of the value of a penny.

which, out of its dead language, can be recognised in every service of the Eastern Church. From earliest times this cry has gone up to heaven, almost without ceasing. As for the repetition, Western observers who, like the late Bishop of Salisbury, think it mere wearisome nonsense, will never understand the East until they realise the deep need there is in the Oriental mind, quite regardless of whether it is Christian or Moslem, Buddhist or Hindoo, for a passionate expression of the soul only to be gained by prolonged concentration on certain words or short phrases. If the dervish travels towards the eventual ecstasy by crying a thousand times " Allah ! Allah ! ! " the Oriental Christian who seeks communion with God takes the same path, which to the Western mind has always seemed meaningless and tiresome. One of the early Coptic saints, the blessed woman Thäis the Harlot, dwelt in a solitary cell for three years, incessantly crying " Kyrie Eleison ! " ; "and hers was a great reward." [1]

If the Copt uses a rosary, it is to keep count of his " Kyrie Eleisons," so that he may say them in his daily prayers the correct number of times, always divided into threes. If he is alarmed, this is the first cry to come to his lips ; if he is in dire need, it is the same. In old days all the nation prayed to God to replenish the Nile when the flood had failed, crying as one man, " Kyrie Eleison ! " the Moslems giving up their " Allah Akbar " in the intensity of their desire to compel the great God by much asking—and more than once, history says, the miracle of a second flood was the result. And if the Moslem crowd at other times mocked the Christians by mimicking the sacred formula, it should also be recorded

---

[1] Anatole France has drawn a delicately beautiful picture of the life and trials of Thäis in his novel of that title.

the Fayoum, Amba Abraam 281

that many Copts have thought the Western Christian to be outside the pale when they found that they never prayed " Kyrie Eleison ! " two hundred and one times.

From earliest times the Coptic Church has made supplication in the name of the angels mentioned in the prayer used by the Bishop. The archangel Mikhail (whom we call Michael) is of great honour in Egypt. In the folk-lore of the fourth century onward, Amelineau found frequent use of the interjection "by the intercession of the angel Mikhail." He is known to have taken the place of one of the most popular of the pagan gods. It was in the fourth century that Pope Alexander publicly destroyed the brazen image of this idol in Alexandria, turning the temple into a church ; the people only consenting on the promise that the patronage of the archangel would be found better than that of the idol, and that the yearly feast should be continued unaltered. To this day the heathen feast is continued in honour of Mikhail.

The translation of the last prayer used by the Bishop, being made for me by a Coptic priest, is of interest, as it differs slightly from previous translations into English. Angel names were mingled with the names of heathen gods. The most prominent are those used in the Bishop's prayer—Michael, the conqueror of the dragon (Rev. xii. 7), who also exercised healing functions; Gabriel, Raphael, and Uriel; Enoch, as the heavenly clerk, took the place occupied in former times by Thoth.

Having seen the Bishop, whose fame will doubtless keep his name alive for centuries in a land where saintliness is still the chief claim to lasting memory, I became deeply interested in the many stories about him which the mention of his name in any part of the country, however remote, at once elicits.

One of the strangest things to the Western observer is to find that in the crowds which daily resort to this Christian dignitary, many of them having made very long pilgrimages, to gain his personal blessing, there are as many Moslems as Christians. There is no difference in the eager faith they all show in his power to help them in all their sorrows and difficulties—a fact which may well give pause to those who have been taught to regard fanaticism as the first characteristic of the followers of Mohammed.

Questioned as to their reasons for thinking they can get good from a Christian bishop, all these simple folk can say is that he is a good man, and to Allah all good men are acceptable; the Bishop prays to God, as they do, and he is a disciple of our Lord Jesus, "on whom be blessings and peace."

As for the power which God has given the Bishop to do good to poor men and women, have they not heard of it for many years? they have seen with their own eyes the sick who have been healed, and those who have had devils cast out of them. Did they not know that the Bishop's insight could strip bare the craftiness of the thief, and that it was impossible to escape if one deceived him? A man once went to him—they told me—"to beg money to bury his daughter." The Bishop suspected that the man was a rogue, but he gave him the money he asked, saying, "The punishment you deserve God will give you." When the man got home he found that at the moment the Bishop was speaking with him his daughter had suddenly died.

It is related of many of the old monks of the Egyptian desert that they read men's thoughts, understanding the things that were passing in their minds. Abba Paule had the gift, which had been given unto him by God, of looking into the soul of every man, and of knowing what his soul was like.

It was Diodorus who, in speaking in those days of divination, said, "The soul foresees future events in the phantoms she herself creates." When the blessed Ammon was living in the country of Nitria, they brought to him a lad who was suffering from hydrophobia. Looking upon the boy's relatives he rebuked them, saying, "Get ye gone; it is in your hands to cure the lad. Restore the value of the widow's bull which ye slew secretly, and your son shall be restored to you healed." This they did, and, after Ammon had prayed, the disease left the boy.

It was another Ammon who, when travelling down the Nile in a boat, knew in his own mind that the brethren at a monastery he was passing had need of him. At that very moment, indeed, they, being in trouble, had set out to seek him. He met them on the bank of the river and quieted their fears.

I have spoken of the poor robe in which the old Bishop was wrapped. It was literally like to the robe of an early Coptic recluse, one Abba Isaac, who maintained that "the manner of the apparel which a monk ought to wear should be such that if it were cast outside the cell for three days no one would carry it away."

Bishop Abraam's rule of poverty is just as absolute and as free from any double meaning as that of the fathers of his Church; and was in no way a poverty which was waiting to manifest itself after £10,000 a year has perforce been spent in automatically maintaining what we vaguely term "suitable position."

A rich layman just before my visit did not like to see his Bishop in this threadbare cloak, and so went out and bought a garment, soft and sable. Returning to that upper room, he begged the Bishop to discard the old robe; here was a new one. With a wan smile the old man took the robe, and tucked it under his pillow. Later on in the day, in the crowd which thronged him, he saw a poor ill-clad fellah, shivering with cold. "Ah!" he said, "the Lord hath been mindful of thee this day, for here is a cloak waiting for the first man who has need of it."

And when the poor man got out into the daylight, he saw that such a cloak was unsuitable to a country fellah; he would sell it, and buy a coarse *gallabieh*, then he would possess both a cloak and spare money to buy food. The man he offered the cloak to was, by chance, the donor, who recognised his gift! Knowing the Bishop, he felt that remonstrance of any sort was useless, so he re-bought the garment, hoping that when the Bishop found that he had done this, he would be persuaded to wear it.

Again, however, the cloak was tucked under the pillow; and again a poor man received it as of the Lord. And now doubtless the threadbare cloak will persist till the day when the Bishop exchanges it for a glorious robe which time cannot corrupt.

There was once a Coptic brother called Paphnutius who had two tunics in eighty years; and even this "spiritual excellence" was excelled by a holy gardener at one of the monasteries in the time of Pachomius, for he had only one garment of linen, which he used to put on when he was about to partake of the holy mysteries of Christ, and then he would take it off and lay it aside, so that he might keep it clean, "and it lasted him for eighty-five years."

His was the day when a monk sold even the few dearly loved books which filled the hollow in the wall of his cell, and from which he gained mental profit, and also the brethren who borrowed them; but the claims of the widow and the orphan must prevail if he would " have life."

Here, in the twentieth century, the succession of those earlier followers of Christ truly survives in the life of the Bishop of Fayoum, to carry out in all their literal simplicity the teachings of the Man of Galilee, who Himself having nothing, sought as disciples only those who would sell all to follow Him.

The Bishop was at one time possessed of private means; and this is how, long years since, he arranged to use them. Calculation showed that his income was a little over two pounds a day; so a simple arrangement was made by which a trusted servant appeared every morning at the bank, from which to bring to the Bishop, in a bag, the value of two pounds, in half-piastre pieces.[1] This bag, too, was put under his pillow, when the Bishop could no longer leave his bed, and during the day he distributed the whole of the contents to those of his visitors who were in monetary need, and in the end he gave away all his capital.

The Bishop's personal expenses are almost nothing, for he never has been known to eat anything but a few boiled beans and bread; the men who attend to his simple wants being the "servants of the Church."

But it must not be supposed that all the people who seek the Bishop are poor; the sorrows of the rich are as sure of spiritual consolation from him as are those which poverty fosters. And the rich visitors never despair in their grateful attempts to enrich the old man. Innumerable are the gifts of gold; but he never looks at them, and never once has he even counted the contents of the purses pressed upon him. "This is from the Lord" is

[1] A piastre is worth about $2\frac{1}{2}$d.

all he says; and following his own instinct and faith, he always waits until the Lord sends to him the poor man or woman ordained for that particular offering.

One of his clergy, the Rev. Abd-el-Sayed, in speaking of the Bishop, said: "His love for his people is above all other love. How often is his hand raised to ask God to bless his people and to assist them. All his days he spends for the glory of God. No one ever saw him caring about anything else in this world. I believe as a boy he ran away from home to enter the monastery. When he became head of that monastery the only complaint made against him was that he spent everything on the poor, and even got into debt for this reason. He was always extravagant in this cause; indeed, before he came to Fayoum the Patriarch had brought him from his monastery to keep him by his side, not only because of his goodness, but because he made some trouble by giving away too largely of the monastery's revenue. The people of Fayoum are for ever proud that they went at that time to Cairo to beg the Patriarch to send them this noble man as their Bishop. He has given a very great name to this province, and has brought honour to all the Christian people of Egypt by his pure name."

The Bishop's power in exorcism of evil spirits has perhaps brought him more visitors from distant parts than any of the other gifts by which he is famous.

Knowing a highly intelligent young Copt in Cairo, the son of a blind singer at the Cathedral there, who had witnessed a cure of a near relative, effected by the Bishop, I thought it would be interesting to get the story in his own words.

This young man belongs to the class, unfortunately becoming rare, of the exceptionally well-educated Copt, well-read in French and English, as well as in his native Arabic, and holding a responsible post in the Government Service, who nevertheless preserves a passionate attachment to the Christian religion, and to the services and teaching of the Orthodox Church. The modern young Egyptian of Cairo, whether Copt or Moslem, is too much prone to an easy-going materialism.

This is the young man's story of the exorcism, which I will leave exactly as he wrote it :

"The Bishop Abraam has a never-failing power against evil spirits, relieving large numbers both of Christians and Moslems every year, who are possessed by them. My young aunt had an evil spirit, and she became a source of great trouble to all our family. Many doctors tried to cure her, but failed. When she was under the influence of the fit, she used to yawn much, and to stretch her arms forwards and backwards, crying incessantly. Unconsciously, of course, she talked much nonsense, cursing everybody; then she would ask to have her feet washed with soap and cold water. This was always done; but in a short time she would tear off all her clothes and roll on the ground, the scene being terribly painful to her family.

"Bishop Abraam was not then confined to his house, and because my father was a servant of the Church, we begged the Bishop to visit us if he ever came to Cairo.

"At last he sent a message that he was to pay a visit to the Patriarch, and on a certain day he would come to our house. Wishing to honour a distinguished guest in our Eastern custom, we prepared a banquet; but when the Bishop entered the room, and saw this, he sternly rebuked us, and would not eat at all, declaring his first business was to see the sick woman.

"My father being blind, I had to take the Bishop to my aunt's room, he carrying his hand-cross.

"Whether from excitement I do not know, but the moment we appeared, my aunt fell in a fit; crying in an awful voice, 'Take away this fire. Oh! I am going to burn!'

"The Bishop was praying earnestly, and moved slowly to where my aunt lay. He then laid the cross on her head and said in firm tones, 'In the name of Jesus Christ I command you to go out and leave her!'

"I shall never forget the agony of this moment, for my aunt distorted her mouth, and uttered a fierce cry.

"The Bishop did not move the cross from her head, and simply repeated his command. Then the spirit, apparently wrestling against the superior power, said, through my aunt, first, 'I will go out through the eye'; then 'through the ear'; then 'through the mouth'; but the Bishop each time sternly rebuked it, saying, 'Go out through the foot.'[1]

"Then my aunt began to rub her eyes, stretch her arms, and move her hair away from her forehead as if she were awaking from sleep. She then half raised herself, and gazed at the Bishop, who was now smiling. He asked her to get up and show him her foot. Others of the family now came into the room, and we all looked at the foot; there was a red cross of blood on the big toe, which I distinctly observed.

"My aunt was frightened at seeing the blood, but when she was told what had happened, she got up and took the hand of the Bishop and kissed it. The Bishop blessed us all, and then said we might prepare for him a small dish of beans, which he ate with a piece of bread. Thanks to the righteousness of Bishop Abraam, my

---

[1] In many cases of exorcism I have heard it declared that the spirit sought to leave its victim by these organs, which it is believed would thus suffer injury—the formula of driving it out by the toe is always followed.

aunt has ever since had the best of health; she is now married and has three fine children."

Many stories are told of the uprightness of the Bishop, and of his absolute fearlessness of dignitaries. He was once summoned by the Patriarch to attend as a member of a Council for the excommunication of a priest. This priest was charged with having allowed a bishop, who was under the ban of the Church, to enter his church, and with giving him food to eat, and a place to sleep in; all this being prohibited by the Church Law. The weapon of excommunication has never been laid aside for long by the Coptic Church, and its operation has always been drastic and final.

The Council assembled, under the presidency of the Patriarch, and the charge was read. The Patriarch then immediately announced that the priest must be excommunicated, writing the judgment, and handing it to Kallini Pasha, one of the Council, to add his signature and then pass the document to the others.

Bishop Abraam was sitting next to the Pasha. He took the paper and read it, and then said, "I cannot see why this priest should be turned out of the Church. Did not Jesus Christ command us to be kind to the poor, and to be considerate to strangers?"

Handing the paper back, he said he would not sign it, and when the startled Pasha remonstrated, saying, "The Patriarch has decided, and the verdict is according to Church Law," he replied somewhat brusquely, "Why was I called to this Council, if I am not to express what I think?"

Any one who knows the Oriental dread of the consequences of blunt speaking, especially when it runs counter to those in authority, will realise the alarm that seized the other members of the Council. One of them whispered, " Do you know that the man you are speaking to is Kallini Pasha?" "Who is Kallini Pasha?" asked the old man. "Did not Moses speak to God Himself? Leave me in peace." He then left the Council room and went downstairs. A member went after him to say that the Patriarch wanted him, but the Bishop replied, " Blessed is the name of God! I will not go up the stairs of this house[1] again in my life, unless that judgment is brought to me, and torn up, while I stand here."

The Patriarch yielded to this man, who is the Church's " true master "; the priest was acquitted, and is still in full charge of his country church and parish.

The Bishop follows the early ascetics, not only in the matter of food, but in denying to himself much of the sleep which nature demands. Of the great Anthony it was said that most of his days dawned on him without his having had any sleep. In cultivating that complete scorn of the body to which they attained, many of the early recluses arranged their caves so that they could neither sit nor lie down, so that sleep should be impossible. During the night season, one of them declared, a man might see many things that appertain to the spiritual life; to refrain from sleep, as from food, conquered temptation; and, moreover, a man might thus emulate the angels in heaven. It was Abba Sisoes, of the Cairo of his day (Babylon), who, to vanquish sleep, stood all night on a dangerous crag in the hills, being rescued by an angel, who then forbade such an expedient.

The Bishop of Fayoum often spends whole nights

---

[1] In the Patriarch's house in Cairo, like all other houses in the East, all the rooms of any importance are on the first floor. The ground floor is used for storage, for lumber, for stables, anything but human habitation, for which it is considered positively injurious.

in prayer, sitting in the one position. It was the desire of the ascetic to reach a condition of impassibility, and amongst Coptic saints there have been those who have so neglected the body that in their emaciation they were unable to stand up. One poor old body—the monastery gardener I have spoken of—who would never allow himself a comfortable position, became so bent and stiff, that when he died it was impossible to strip off the skin garment wherewith he was clothed, and, as his simple brethren recorded, "We were obliged to roll him up in cloth like a bundle, and bury him in that state." This is that "haven of impassibility" of which they spoke; and to this haven the Bishop of Fayoum has attained.

Around such a figure, especially in the mystic land of Egypt, and with the descendants of a people who sought wisdom and guidance from oracle or seer, it is not surprising to find the mists of fable already gathering, arising out of a profound belief in certain powers, many of which I feel sure the Bishop would not claim for himself. It is possible that any man leading such a life would develop powers which to ordinary men would seem to be abnormal. Such a man might be expected to see visions, and in this land of divination the gift of premonition would naturally follow. "Any pure heart can foretell things to come," said the blessed Mar Anthony, the first hermit of the Egyptian desert, expressing an ancient belief which never grows old.

It is not difficult to see in the crowd of eager suppliants who throng the courtyard and the outer rooms of Bishop Abraam a picture of the crowds who sought divine guidance in the ancient temples of Egypt, where God was supposed to speak by signs and oracles through the priests. Whether we believe, with Garnault, that these people were the victims of the charlatan, or, with Maspero, that the priest did indeed speak by divine inspiration in the name of God, the inscriptions remain to show us in what a noble tone men spoke of their experiences in the temple. "I came to seek divine wisdom; I stated my petition before my ancestor, asking his advice. And when the audience was over I turned away from these mysteries with my face aglow from the joy that filled my heart, because I had heard my God speak to me as a father to his son." Such is the account which the hieroglyphics give again and again.

Or we may see the descendants of the crowds of sufferers, like those who sought the sanctuary at Ptah Sotmu in Memphis, where for long ages the gods had been sending dreams to reveal remedies to the patients who came to sleep in the courts of their temples; the same people came to the temple to ask for the detection of thieves who had injured them. And when the Christian religion came they resorted to the monk for like help. Shenouda, the Christian recluse of Akhmin, was constantly appealed to by those who had been robbed, and, by some power he exercised, was successful in naming the thief and compelling restitution.

And to-day the people, differing very little in feature or dress from these early crowds, and whose mental outlook is much the same, insist on treating such a man as this saintly Bishop as their oracle as well as their physician.

Like St. Anthony, the Bishop, always declaring that "It is God alone who can grant relief," does everything possible to turn men from that personal adulation which the Oriental is too prone to lay at the feet of any man with spiritual power.

The teaching of the Coptic Church in the matter of priestly healing, as in most other things, is founded very literally on the precepts and example of our Lord and His Apostles. And to its credit, it should not be forgotten that, along with the use of holy oil in anointing, in the laying on of hands, and the casting out of evil spirits, the bishops and priests, and even the Patriarch himself, have often seriously studied medicine and attained great skill in it; so that many of the cures effected have been the result of science as well as of faith—surely a perfect combination in the ministrations of the true physician, whether cleric or layman.

In the ancient church of Abu Sifain, near Mari Mina, there is a picture of one Saint Kultah, who is shown holding in his right hand a wand pointing to a casket in his left hand; the lid of the casket is raised, and shows six little compartments for drugs. In mid-air is shown a cross, on one side of the picture; on the other, a crosier.

It was in the eighth century that the Patriarch Politian was summoned to Bagdad, by the famous Caliph Haroun-al-Raschid, to cure a favourite slave-girl, being promised certain Church privileges in Alexandria as a reward.

Even the early monks would not let the people depend for their cures, as they were only too ready to do, entirely on prayer and the magic of the holy oil. The monk of Ancyra was only one of many who laboured for the sick that their ordinary bodily needs might be supplied, and "he brought them the binding up which helped their healing"; and of the anchorite, Apollonius, it is told that he carried about pomegranates and dried cakes, and raisins, and eggs, as the things which are necessary to the sick.

I have no doubt, however, that these ancient fathers, when they gathered the herbs which they knew to be medicinal, used the incantations which, if properly used, are still generally believed to add to their efficacy.

The greatest effort ever made by the Coptic Church to stem the tide of the lax and superstitious ideas which grew so alarmingly in Egyptian soil was made by Mark ben el-Konbar, in the twelfth century. His teaching was for a time successful, but the deep-rooted customs of the country have always clogged the advance of those who wish for such reform.

There is a solemn service in the Coptic Church for the laying of hands on the sick, after the celebration of the Holy Eucharist on Sunday morning. Candles are lighted before the picture of the Virgin, and the priests stand at the doorway of the sanctuary chanting the Scriptures to the weird clanging of the handbells and the cymbals.

The unction, or anointing, of the sick, based on the teaching of St. James, is one of the seven sacraments of the Eastern Church, and it is in no way used as a last rite for the dying as in the Roman Church. The Coptic Church understands sickness in a very wide sense; there is a sickness of the body, a sickness of the soul which is of sin, and a sickness of the spirit, or affections. Anointing is practised in every case, not only on the bodily sick, but on penitents, and even on the dead.

When performed strictly according to the old rites, the first act of the anointing is to fill the lamp with seven branches with the purest olive oil of Palestine, placing it on a stand before the picture of the Virgin. Incense is burnt while the Scripture is read and prayers recited. Then while the priests continue the service the chief priest lights, one by one, at stated intervals, the wicks, making the sign of the cross over the oil.

The sick person is now brought to the door of the sanctuary, and the chief priest holds the Gospel in its silver case, and the hand-cross, over the sick man's head; he then lays his hands upon the sick man's temples, reciting the orisons, while the other priests severally give their benedictions. One of them takes the Gospel and reads whatever passage on which he chances to open. The cross is again uplifted, and a procession is formed and passes round the church, bearing the lamp and lighted tapers, while prayers are chanted for healing through the intercession of saints and martyrs. Coming back to the sanctuary, the sick man is anointed with oil, in the form of a cross on his forehead, and on either wrist.

If the person for whom the service is held is too weak to attend, a substitute is put in his place, for this service is never performed outside the church. Seven priests are required for the full ritual.

By one of those curious practical turns of the Oriental mind, which surprise the superficial observer, it is a positive though unwritten law that in every case of recovery from sickness the first public act shall be a visit to the public bath.

In speaking with the people who resort to the Bishop of the Fayoum, one finds at once how largely they are ruled by superstitions little differing from those of their early Christian forefathers, when the very symbols of the Christian religion were used to replace those of the fallen gods of the Pharaohs. Belief in the magic of the cross is universal; it has a double power, for the mystic force behind the *ankh*, or "sign of life," of the Pharaohs was transferred to the Christian symbol. Dr. Budge says that "Those who are familiar with the magic of the dynastic Egyptians find few miraculous occurrences in the histories of the monks, of which parallels do not exist in the pagan literature of Egypt."

In Egypt, Spiritualism had its birth. Even in the vulgar development of the *séance*, with its table-rappings, Egypt was accomplished in the fourth century—the table (history relates) rapped out the name of a successor to Theodosius the Roman Governor.

The first magicians lived in Egypt, and possibly it will be in Egypt that the last of the race will survive. Every village knows of the gipsies, with their wonderful book of sorcery and magic. This is the land of the *afreet* and the *ginn*—the Coptic fellah believes in the race as fervently as his Moslem neighbour, and is especially scared of calling up a *ginn* of an alien faith to his own, even as the early Christians were dreadfully afraid of the god Serapis at Alexandria.

You may read of a monastery ghost in the fourth-century records. Is there not a suggestion of hypnotism in the story of the same date, of the rich young monk who, vexed by the passion of lust, wandered in the desert praying that he might be delivered from this temptation, and so be able to return to the nunnery which he had built, and which needed his oversight? Angels came to him, and they laid hold of him by his hands and feet, and one of them took a weapon and mutilated him, "not indeed in very truth, but only apparently and in a phantom-like manner," or, as we should say, by suggestion. The cure was complete and permanent, and Abba Elijah lived to conduct the great nunnery at Thebes with every credit.

No edicts of the Christian Church have been able to suppress the belief in magic, but, if we are inclined to condemn these poor folk, who will have it that there is magic power in the holy oil, the wine, in the blood of the martyrs, and in the relics of the saints, and in the various forms of holy waters of which the Coptic Church has an especially varied and lavish supply; and who will believe all sorts of fables, and embellish all the sacred stories with a miraculous folk-lore, the very suggestion of which the West has almost forgotten; we may still remember that Coptic edicts have been issued against these things, and good men like Bishop Abraam of the Fayoum sincerely wish the people to adopt a more simple faith.

The poor woman who comes to the Bishop with an unbearable headache will, however, insist, in spite of anything he may say, that the pain will depart by the mere touch of the Gospel case, or the cross, which he holds over her in blessing. An English lady was visiting some poor women in Cairo, and seeing that she had a Bible in her hand, one of them said, "Let me lay the book on my poor aching forehead; that will cure me." In the same way this group of poor souls sitting on the floor before the altar of a side chapel, nursing the curious bolsters in which the relics of saints are wrapped, as they croon their prayers, firmly believe that magic powers will come from mere contact with the precious bones; and I have found the Moslem woman sitting in the Christian chapel nursing the relics and looking as intensely expectant of blessing as the Copt.

Men will go on desiring to kiss the hands of the Bishop, in spite of his objections, believing that by kissing the hands of a priest they will purify themselves; in the same way that in church they will rush to the door of the sanctuary at the end of the Holy Eucharist, hoping to catch if but one drop of the water sprinkled by the officiating priest, in which he has just laved his hands, because they think that the touch of the man who has handled the sacred elements must have magic power to bless them, especially in sickness or physical disability.

As for the general teaching of the Coptic Church on this particular subject, I think we must admit that it is only a little removed from the practice of the early Western Church. Confronted with the mass of pagan superstition which, by adapting itself to the Christian religion, had taken a firm hold on the masses of the people, our own Church, from time to time, made those protests which, through the decision of the Synods and the great leaders of theology, have come down to us. These very protests, however, took for granted the marvels of magic, but denounced them as ungodly and devilish, while allowing that there was a higher form of magic that was divine.

It is to be expected that out of this teaching the *sacramentalia* was regarded as having magic attributes, and that, again in spite of papal prohibition, the belief still lingers in the Coptic Church, even amongst the priests. It is related of an old monk that he frequently ate the ashes of the incense as a blessed food; many are the remedial and magic uses of the holy oil, the holy water, the incense, the consecrated salt, and even the wax from the altar candles.

These poor people clamouring at the Bishop's door have inherited, too, without any change or misgivings, all the fables which gathered round the Gospel story in the first days, beginning with that wealth of anecdote about the Child Jesus, and the miracles, even of the Holy Infant's touch; and they will relate these to you with a childlike faith, which is shocked at any sign that you, a Christian, can have any doubt of their authenticity.

These poor fellaheen have never had an ancestor who could read or write, but in the East it is always enough that they have heard with their ears, and their fathers have told them these things.

They have, for instance, all drunk at some time at the spring at Matarieh, just outside Cairo, that sacred spot at which the Holy Family rested when they fled from Herod; did I not believe, they asked me earnestly, that that unfailing spring of fresh water was the miraculous gift of Jesus? There is no doubt it has been so regarded from earliest times; and when the journey to Egypt was more difficult, many pious Europeans made the pilgrimage specially to drink of this water.

There is another holy well in Cairo, the existence of which is never suspected by the visitor, for it is deliberately preserved as a secret. Once a year the Church of St. Mary's, in the Harat-az-Zuailah, is the scene of a remarkable gathering of people representing every nationality and religion in Egypt, who crowd there to possess themselves of some of the sacred water of its well. I owe it to a friendly native Christian that I saw this well, and that I can give an account in the words of an orthodox Copt, showing how the people themselves regard the story of the sanctity of this water.

A few years after the Mohammedan conquest of Egypt, a Moslem person killed another Moslem, and threw him just at the door of the Harat-az-Zuailah church. The matter was reported to the Mohammedan Governor of Cairo, who, having learned that the body was found in front of the door of the church, gave an order that unless the Copts in Harat-az-Zuailah gave a satisfactory explanation as to how the man was killed, they would all be prosecuted.

The news was alarming. The man was dead,

nobody knew anything about him, the Copts were quite innocent of the crime, but still they must explain. They had to give their explanation in one week's time.

Three days passed, and they were entirely unsuccessful in finding the facts. The priest of the church resolved to die of hunger under the old picture of the Virgin Mary, which you (my friend is referring to the author) saw in the Harat-az-Zuailah church, and which has a door of wire-netting with small pieces of cloth tied to it. He tied up his neck with a fine rope, which he attached to the wire door of the picture. He fell fast asleep, and lo! the Virgin Mary appeared to him in a dream, and told him, "Get up from your sleep, take some water from this well, and pour it over the dead man. He shall return to life and tell his story."

The priest awoke from his sleep, startled and amazed, and did as he was told. The dead man moved, returned to life once more, and related all his story to the Governor. The Mohammedan criminal was arrested and confronted with his victim. The priest explained how the dead man returned to life, after which explanation the murdered man fell back lifeless as he had been before.

The news of the well then spread over all the country, and the Christians had afterwards to suffer very much, "as the Mohammedans thought that they were able to bring life back to the dead, and they always asked them to do so for their dead, but it was impossible to do such things again."

After I had written the above sketch, I heard of the death of the sainted Bishop of Fayoum. From friends in Fayoum and in Cairo I have received particulars of his passing. A representative was at once sent from *the Fayoum, Amba Abraam* 301

the Patriarch to report on the personal property of the Bishop, and the only things he found were the hand-cross and a walking-stick. He had given to the poor all the money he had, so that the chief Copts of the town had to contribute the money to pay the funeral expenses. Over twenty thousand people attended the funeral, all mourning as for a personal friend. The poor people of that countryside are desolate and quite inconsolable. He has been buried in the cemetery of one of the desert monasteries.

I am able to give a purely Coptic version of the Bishop's life, translated from a little book published in Arabic, since his death, by a Coptic priest who knew him—the Rev. M. A. El-Baramousi El-Saghir:

Amba Abraam was born in a village called Galada, in the Assiout province. His parents were true Christians, and they brought him up on sound Christian principles, which he always followed.

He was sent to a *kuttab* (or village school). When he left this *kuttab* he was deeply interested in reading the Bible, Church songs, etc. At the age of nineteen he entered the Monastery of the Virgin Mary, known as Deir El-Moharrac, which is near to Assiout, and of which some speak as the place where Jesus stopped when He fled from Herod the King. He was very popular in the monastery. The monks got very fond of him, especially the Head, the Rev. Abd-El-Malik. The duty of Amba Abraam was, at that time, to receive the visitors and to attend to the sick.

It was necessary to take the opinion of the monks present in the monastery about any one who was going to be nominated as a monk; so the Chief held a meeting of all the monks, and asked their opinion about the character of Amba Abraam, and whether he deserved to be their companion and brother. They all spoke favourably of him, and consequently he was nominated a monk, and was then called Bulos Gahabrial El-Moharrakawi. He has been always a good example in the monastery. He used even at that time to give all he possessed to the poor. He had a strong will, and was able always to rule himself.

There was a Bishop at Minieh at that time called Amba Yakovous. He was very fond of spending his time with the monks. He chose

Bulos Gahabrial El-Moharrakawi to be his companion, and wanted him to stay at Minieh. The Chief of the Monastery did not like the monk to live away, but he had to fulfil the duty of obeying the Bishop of Minieh, who was higher in Church rank; and so Bulos Gahabrial El-Moharrakawi went to Minieh, and was authorised to take charge of the Visitors' Department, and keep an eye on the Bishop's house in general.

The Bishop of Minieh used to admire him very much, and some time later, when he wanted to go back to his monastery, the Bishop before he left promoted him to the rank of Reverend, and asked him to pray for him. He encouraged him, and showed him great admiration.

So he lived quietly in his monastery for some time with his brethren, who had great reputation at that time for their piety and purity. Being all admirers of him, they now joined in asking the Patriarch to appoint him Head of the Monastery, and he was officially appointed to this influential position, which enabled him to exercise his generosity.

He continued five years as the Head of the Monastery, during which the institution was known as a shelter for thousands of the poor.

During his tenure of this office he cultivated a four-acre garden, increased the buildings, and raised the morality of the monks, from whom there are now Bishops. The present Bishop of Abyssinia, as well as Amba Locas, Bishop of Keneh, Amba Marcos, Bishop of Esneh, and others, were monks at the monastery under his presidency.

After five years as Chief of the Monastery he resigned, and went to another monastery called Deir-El-Baramous. He was followed by a great number of monks, who could not live without him.

Deir-El-Baramous is one of the oldest monasteries in Egypt. At this last monastery he did not take an active part in managing affairs, but he took apartments for himself and his followers, and engaged himself in prayers and religious study, always showing great sympathy with the poor; he used to share his clothing with the bedouins and fellaheen in the neighbourhood.

In the year 1597 (Coptic) he was chosen Bishop of Fayoum and Gizeh. When he got this important position, he showed great attention to the poor and the widows and orphans, and he lived exactly like one of God's men. He never cared about wealth. His food was always very simple. He used to spend his nights in a narrow room on a rough bed—he never used a bedstead until the end of his life, when he was strongly advised to do so, on account of his age.

When his name got widely known as the friend of the poor, his house was crowded with needy people, come from every part of the country. Consequently, he brought a nun, who was at one time Head of one of the nunnerys in Cairo, and asked her to take charge of the poor. This woman once thought to give to the Bishop food of a better quality than that given to the poor. This fact was unknown to the Bishop, but one day he decided to go and have his dinner with these poor people. It was a surprise to him to see that the food offered them was different from his own. He therefore approached the nun, and asked the reason why this was done. She did not utter a word in reply. He took the keys from her. She was greatly shocked, and has been lying ill ever since.

I should not be exaggerating if I called him our father Abraham, for his faith and love to strangers; he might be called Moses for his patience; or David for the purity of his heart; or Elijah for the eloquence of his tongue; or Paul for the strength of his proofs.

I once stayed a week with the Bishop of Fayoum. These are the things I saw during my stay. A woman of Balout, a village near Manfalout, in Assiout province, was ill for a very long period of time. She had spent all she possessed on doctors, with no good result. At last she heard the people talking about the Bishop of Fayoum. This woman was doubtful whether the Bishop's blessing was given only to Christians, as she was not a Christian herself. However, she was taken by four men of her relatives to Fayoum. In addition to all her other ailments, she was dumb.

When they arrived at the Bishop's house, they laid the woman before him, requesting him to pray for her. So he continued praying for her for three days. After these three days, the woman was able to walk in the streets, and went back to her village, telling the people about the result of the Bishop's prayers.

Another man who had changed his Christian religion, and left his wife, was brought to him. The Bishop tried in vain to influence him to go back and live with his wife, and follow his original religion. The man did not listen. The Bishop said, "God knows what to do with you." So the man went, but died shortly afterwards.

I saw great numbers of women coming from all parts, with different diseases, and all were cured through his prayers.

His annual visits to the people of his diocese were unique of their kind. The first thing he used to do when he entered a village, was to ask about its poor people. During his stay in villages he used to think a great deal about the peaceful relations between the community, and do his best to make them live on friendly terms.

He used to examine carefully any candidate for the ministry. He used to consider greatly the people's will, and unless the candidate was very popular, he would not appoint him. He used to follow the saying of Paul to Timothy, "Do not be hasty in putting your hand on one." Very often he preferred poor candidates to rich ones. In any case, the approval of all the people was very essential.

In the year 1618 (Coptic) the chief Bishop of Abyssinia visited Egypt. He was one of those nominated monks by the Bishop of Fayoum. After being received in Cairo by the Patriarch and the Khedive, he went through some of the capitals of the provinces. Then he intended to visit his old monastery. He asked his old Bishop to accompany him on this visit. He granted his request. They were joined by the Bishops of Alexandria and Esneh, and others, and they stopped at several places in response to invitations from Coptic notables.

In Abu Kerkasa they were the guests of Adib Bey Wahba, who was until that time without a son. All the Bishops joined in asking the Bishop of Fayoum to pray for him, that God might give him a son. So the Bishop prayed that God would, after a year's time, give him a son. The Bey believed strongly in the Bishop's prayer, and after ten months God granted the prayer of the Bishop, and Adib Bey Wahba was granted a son, who is now about twelve years old.

In remembrance of the Bishop's visit, Adib Bey Wahba used to visit the Bishop every year, and he used to kill a number of beasts for the poor, and give meat and other things to the poor and needful. During recent years, owing to his age, the Bishop was unable to make his tour in the villages.

He was a self-denying man. Once the Patriarch wanted to promote him to the rank of Metropolitan, but he courteously refused it.

What makes the generosity of this Bishop more appreciated, is the fact that he never made a distinction between different religions and creeds. He was always ready to give when asked, and he never delayed a prayer when needed and when requested to make it. Most of his time was spent in praying, especially for the poor.

THE SAINTED BISHOP OF THE FAYOUM WITH HIS WONDERFUL
HAND-CROSS.

This photograph, which was taken of the Bishop on one of his last public appearances, without his knowledge, is the only one in existence. The author owes its possession to Coptic friends in the Fayoum.

CHAPTER VII

Does the Ancient Race of the Pharaohs still survive in Egypt?

IT would form a curious study to show how successfully the Copts for many centuries managed to hide themselves from the observation and even the very knowledge of travellers and sojourners in their own country, who profess to have made a complete study of the dwellers by the Nile. There can be little doubt that the Copts have all the Oriental secretiveness, added to a very natural suspiciousness, bred of the oppression of certain of their Moslem rulers; but for the possession of which qualities they might have been almost entirely crushed out of existence. If the Copts hid in fear from their infidel compatriots, they had scarcely less cause to conceal themselves from the Christians of other lands, who hated what they regarded as the Coptic heresy as much as they detested the infidelity of the Moslems.

When the First Crusade captured Jerusalem, in 1099, they forbade any members of the Coptic Church to enter the holy city, so little could they discriminate between the Egyptian Moslems, who defeated them at Askelon, and the Eastern Christians who were in sympathy with them.

When the Crusaders invaded Egypt, in 1204, they

massacred indiscriminately the Christian and Moslem inhabitants; possibly because, like that Bishop of Salisbury who had led a Crusade eleven years previously, they considered such Christians as heretics worse than infidels.

St. Francis of Assisi, when he joined the Sixth Crusade in Egypt, in the year 1218, was unaware of the very existence of the Egyptian Church. Centuries later that great English traveller, Bruce, who travelled through Egypt and Abyssinia, and received the greatest help from a State official who was a Copt, never even suspected that there was such an institution as a Christian Church. Lane's ignorance of the Copts, and the injustice of his characterisation, based on very slight evidence, may be put down to the secretive cunning of those Copts with whom he had dealings.

While the Moslems gave Lane some confidence (although I feel perfectly sure they were never in doubt that it was an Englishman in native disguise who was taking such an abnormal interest in them), he only succeeded in gaining anything like familiar speech with one Copt—a mean soul, whose abuse of his fellow-Christians carries the bitterness of its injustice to this day.

A great deal of the morbid prejudice against the Copts which marks the attitude of many Englishmen in Egypt of to-day takes its rise from Lane's work, to which all inquirers about the Egyptian people are referred. This attitude again induces the old Oriental evasiveness, and so the abysmal English ignorance of these people gets little chance of remedy.

I must say that even in these days of British rule and protection, reliable information is only got from the Copts with the utmost patience and difficulty, however sympathetic the inquirer may be.

If an English visitor gains the interest of the rich and travelled Copts, it is necessary that he should be on his guard against the impression they are fain to create that there is little or no difference in manners and customs, as in religion, between the English and French, whom they imitate, and their own race.

A recent writer, Mr. John Ward, judging the Copts by the life of one or two very rich families with whom he stayed, declared, "The Christian virtues are all practised. The man a husband of one wife. The lady of the house sits beside her husband at the family meals," and so on; and goes on to express the views, so carefully suggested to visitors in such households in Egypt, that the Copts are far removed in all their ways from their Moslem compatriots.

The facts are that these few rich houses, whose generous hospitality I have enjoyed, do not represent Coptic life at all; and the freedom of their ladies, of whose charm and modesty I can speak, is not, unfortunately, a thing of which the average Copt shows at present any sort of approval.

As for the upper-class Moslems, they are too proud to play any sort of part in representing themselves as anything but Oriental in habit and thought, and it will never be fully known how bitterly they resent the pro-English leadings of the wealthy Copts.

If one applies for information to the Coptic clergy, one is met either by economy of fact, which is more misleading than silence, or by genuine ignorance; if to an intelligent Government servant—of whom there are many in Egypt—one gets a picture drawn of Coptic life which has little relation to the truth, as one slowly finds, if pertinacity gives no rest until the true life of the people has been discovered.

No Copt with any education will speak to a stranger of the primitive folk-lore; of the crude superstitions from the early centuries which everywhere obtain, colouring all life and especially the religious beliefs of the people; of the Oriental customs, which are so common to the life of Egypt that there is very little, if any, difference between Moslem or Copt. All have the mistaken notion that something has been gained for the Coptic cause if a writer, especially an Englishman, has been sent away with a picture, no matter how far from the truth it may be, which an astute and secretive mind has imagined meets the preferences and prejudices of the visitor, and leads him to flatter its subject.

The Copts complain of the scorn with which the English official classes treat them, and the impatience of their Moslem fellow-countrymen, and seem utterly incapable of realising that they are largely responsible for the mistrust that has brought this result upon them.

The English writers whom the Copts regard as their best friends, because they have uncritically recorded what they have been told, have indeed been those who have done them the most serious disservice. When Professor Butler declared that "before the law and before the government there should be, in strict justice, neither Copts nor Moslems, but one community of Egyptians," he was saying a wise thing which the Copts would do well to take to heart.

It is writers who are always telling them that (after fourteen hundred years) the Arab is an intruder in Egypt, and the country really belongs to the Copts; that because "the genuine Egyptians are the Christian Copts" they ought to have special treatment at English hands; that their faults are largely the faults that come from oppression; who would indeed keep alive for ever a hatred of the Moslems by dwelling on the past, while flattering the Copts by attributing to them virtues they do not possess;—it is such writers who, with the most friendly intentions towards them, have not only failed to help the Coptic cause but have hindered it.

The cleavage between Copt and Moslem, thus fostered, dates only from the British occupation; the two have no innate antagonism, as history has again and again proved. From the English the Copt has gained nothing by the cleavage, but rather the claims he has made to special favour have resulted to some degree in a denial of bare justice. The English ruler disliked the self-assertion; when it was based on any reference to "fellow-Christians," it became positively distasteful; and in his endeavour to show he was free from bias, the English official has proudly drawn himself too far from the central point of impartiality.

Such ill-informed views as those of Dean Stanley, that the Coptic Christians of Egypt are "the most civilised of the natives," views which have been re-echoed again and again by those who know little or nothing of the Egyptian people, their wish as Christian writers alone being father to the thought, is resented by the Moslem section of the community, not merely as a libel upon themselves, but as a misstatement of facts which they suspect has been cunningly fostered.

Mrs. Butcher, who in her very able *Story of the Church of Egypt* never has any hesitation in blaming Moslem persecution for all apostasy, when she comes to the details on which her sustained attacks on the Moslems are based, can even speak of *backsheesh* as a purely Moslem vice!

As an Englishman and a Christian I wish (as others who have seen a good deal of the country have done) we could take such flattering unction to our souls, that the Copts of to-day, because of their faith, are generally ahead in morality, as well as in culture, of their compatriots. Years ago Miss Whately, the sister of the Primate of Ireland, worked patiently amongst the poor of Cairo, for their moral good. Her conclusion was: " I cannot say I ever saw much difference between them; there is no superiority on the part of the Copts, either in manners or conduct."

And what was Lord Cromer's verdict, when he had finished his long course as the greatest ruler Egypt has ever had? In his *Modern Egypt* he said that, for all purposes of broad generalisation, the only difference between the Copt and the Moslem is that the former is an Egyptian who worships in a Christian church, whilst the latter is an Egyptian who worships in a Mohammedan mosque.

This is distasteful reading, but if it is to be made obsolete let us admit that the ostrich artifice towards the true condition of these ours fellow-Christians can only delay those who desire to help towards a better and more consoling state of things.

How little there is in common between the orthodox Christianity of Egypt and the teaching, say, of the Church of England, is seen when they are brought to the test by the responsible authorities of both Churches.

An English Association, seeking in the name of the Anglican Church to further Christianity in Egypt, began its work by "refusing all tolerance to the soul-destroying heresy of the Copts," thus bringing down to our own times that hereditary Christian dislike between East and West, of which I have spoken.

Those Churchmen must have been strangely lacking in historical memory who were astonished that the present Patriarch, coming from a desert monastery, one of those places where men brood over insult and injury in the undisturbed silence of centuries, was so suspicious of the advances of Dr. Blyth, the Bishop of the Church of England in the East, that for a long time he declined to receive him.

I have no doubt the Patriarch thinks it presumption, coming from the Church of the Reformation, to speak of a reunion of Christendom, especially when he recalls the way his flock has been drawn from the fold of his ancient Church by the Christian missionaries of America. The Patriarch has never been one of those Copts who have sought favour with the English of any class; indeed, he has always preferred to commend himself to the Egyptian Moslem authorities rather than to those of the British Agency.

It is not surprising, in view of the ignorance about the Coptic people which prevails, that little attention has been given by historical scholars to their ethnology; or that what consideration the Egyptian Christians have received has often been trivial and misleading.

The very name of the Copts has been the subject of random guessing by men professing to be writing with authority. The name Copt ought to be written and pronounced Kypt or Gypt, as it is pronounced by the community themselves. It is undoubtedly derived from the ancient Greek name of Egypt, Aiguptos. Whether this Greek name was in turn derived from the ancient Egyptian name of Memphis, Hakaptah, or not, does not especially concern us, but the common error of tracing the word "Copt" to the name of the town of Coptos, now called Keft, in the Keneh province, is absurd.

In the first place, there was no reason for changing the designation of a whole nation when the Egyptians changed their religion, and certainly a more important town would have been chosen to supply a name. A common nickname for the Copts by the Moslems is "gins Pharoony," from genus Pharaonicus—used by men to their fellow-countrymen, who themselves boast of being Arabs and sons of Arabs.

But whether the name of Copt takes us back to Pharaonic Egypt or not, many of the secular customs, as I have shown elsewhere, link them to the ancient people. It is to the Coptic language, however, that I think the student of the future will have to look for what is the "most reliable evidence of the people's origin."

Dr. Sobhy, of Cairo, and Claudius Bey Labib, a distinguished Coptic scholar, have made a painstaking search in modern colloquial Arabic, of which they have given me the advantage, which has resulted in the finding of more than twelve hundred Coptic words used side by side with Arabic words. Sometimes they discovered whole sentences, and popular sayings, in pure Coptic, used by the Egyptians of to-day, with no knowledge of their origin. Some of these have come to be regarded as mere gibberish or jargon.

There is a common expression often used in the place of the words "something or other"; it is pronounced *kani mani*. When Dr. Sobhy first came across the expression he thought it merely an example of meaningless alliteration. He found, however, that a complimentary Arabic phrase was often added as a rhyme—*dukkan el zalabany*, meaning a pastrycook's shop; reminding him that *kani mani* were the Coptic words for honey and butter.

It is in the expressions used between mothers and their babes, and by the workers in the fields, that many such instances are found; and especially

Pharaohs still survive in Egypt? 313

in the speech of the boatmen on the Nile—where one would expect to find the least change in the colloquial expressions.

It is thought that the Copts numbered about six millions at the time of the Arab conquest, in the seventh century; Eutyches, the earliest historical writer on the Coptic Church, estimates them at eighteen millions, which must be an exaggeration, unless he included the actual population during the early Roman rule.

Of the few scholars who have dealt with the subject, some have detected traces of negroid origin in the Copts; while others, like Rosellini, considered there was evidence of Jewish and Roman blood.

Denon in his *Description de l'Egypte* makes the fullest comparison of Coptic physical characteristics, with the result that he was satisfied of a remarkable correspondence to the human figures represented in the paintings and sculptures of the ancient race.

There is truth, perhaps, in all these theories. In different parts of Egypt the Christian people are found to differ somewhat from the general type, according as these different influences have predominated. The Copts of Lower Egypt, particularly in the provinces of Dakalieh and Sharkieh, are much darker than usual, except in Mansura. In Upper Egypt, the Copts of Sohag, Girgeh, and Minieh are dark, while almost the whole of the inhabitants of Ahnoub, near Assiout, are fair-skinned and have blue eyes.

The colour of the skin, taking the whole country, ranges from pale yellow to dark brown; it is never muddy, but always clear and smooth.

The eyes are generally dark, but the shades vary from black to a light brown—spoken of in Arabic as honey-coloured. They are usually inclined to almond shape; but they are not exceptionally distant from the nose, as has often been stated.

The nose is generally straight, but occasionally hooked a little downwards and enlarged at the tip; it is rarely aquiline.

The mouth is of medium size, the lips full and well shaped, and the teeth white, strong, and regular. Sometimes the ears are large. The Copts are of medium height; they are scarcely ever very tall.

The hair is always black or dark brown, sometimes smooth and glossy, but more often wavy and frizzy; never crisp or curly.

Where, in the cities, there are variations from these general types, it is accounted for by foreign marriages. There is a certain admixture of Armenians; though in the present day there is an inherent prejudice between the Christians of Egypt and those of Syria, intermarriage goes on to a certain extent. Marriage with Greeks is almost unknown.

Professor Elliot Smith, in a valuable report, made some comparisons with the bodily measurements of the men of to-day, which suggest that there is very little difference in this respect between the ancient Egyptians and their descendants.

Skulls of Copts of the early centuries have been examined, and they have been found to be almost identical with those of the skulls of the Pharaonic mummies; and the same form of skull is found amongst the modern Egyptian Christians.

A certain deviation of skull, which came about the fifth century, was traced by Professor Elliot Smith to the mixture with the Syrian race which took place. It was at that time that the Council of Ephesus was held for the excommunication of Nestor for heresy, which led

Pharaohs still survive in Egypt? 315

to a close connection between the Coptic Church and the Syrian Church of Antioch. A great number of the priests of Syria then moved into Egypt; later, Syrian monks were so numerous that they had a monastery of their own in the Natron valley, which has existed from the tenth century until to-day.

No doubt these monks had a great following of secular folk to whom are attributed that type occasionally met with amongst the Copts, with wide noses and large oblong eyes, and the bushy beard which is never seen in Egypt on any other man.

Occasionally one does come across traces of negro blood; and amongst skulls examined, some have been found with negroid characteristics.

The Copts were always great slave-holders, and at one period concubinage was common, although the Church issued stringent injunctions against it, with threats of excommunication.

The Eastern laws governing the holding of slaves, which were observed in all their humane kindliness no less by the Copts, who had no compulsion in the matter from the Koranic dictates, explain at once how the negro type would persist after the Church got its way as to the female slaves. The father would never repudiate the children of such a union, and there was no law to brand them as illegitimate. Colour prejudice was—and still is—quite unknown, so that these children were all married in their turn into the community in which they were born. Moreover, any slave who bore a son to her master, from that instant became free, and was treated with the honour of a wife.

But with all this, I think sufficient attention has never been given to the Jewish element in the Coptic people. It is not a popular suggestion, I know, but the prejudice which has gathered through the long Christian era against the Jews, and which the Copts share to the full, ought not to make us stupidly blind to historic fact.

From the days of Jeremiah, when Johanan the son of Kareah led a band of Jews down into Egypt, there had been a steady stream of emigration of Jews from Palestine.

In this connection the very ancient tomb preserved in a synagogue at Old Cairo, which the Jews have always persisted in declaring contains the body of the prophet Jeremiah, is of great interest.[1]

By the first century, we have the authority of Philo for saying the Jews resident in Alexandria, and in the country from the desert of Libya back to the bounds of Ethiopia, did not fall short of a million.

The various philosophic influences to which this community had been subjected in Egypt had reduced the old conservative party, such as existed in Jerusalem, and such as became St. Paul's most relentless persecutors, to a small minority. The majority had the most lively progressive tendencies; the dominant school were led by such a man as Philo, seeking to reconcile Judaism with Greek philosophy.

[1] Until a few years since, a roll, which all agreed was written by the prophet Ezra, was preserved here, with a curse on any one who should remove it. It was only through the treachery of a Jew that its existence became known to outsiders. Two zealous antiquarians forced their way into the synagogue, discovered the roll, and tried to unloose it. Evidently it had never been opened for centuries, for the remains of a serpent were found in its hiding-place, where it must have taken refuge. The edges of the roll were so glued by the discharge of the serpent, that it was found impossible to separate them without great damage. The antiquaries, after seeing enough to satisfy them that it was of marvellous age, departed, hoping to make a further examination under favourable conditions. But the guardians took alarm, and a fresh hiding-place, unknown to Gentile prying, has been found for the roll.

There is a good deal of evidence that the first appeal of the Christian faith was almost entirely to the Hellenistic Jews, little attempt being made at first to reach the masses of the native Egyptians.

The "Gospel according to the Hebrews" was read chiefly by Jewish converts. The "Gospel according to the Egyptians" implies by its title that it was intended for use either by the native Egyptians, as distinct from the Alexandrians, or else by the Gentile converts, in distinction from the Jewish.

It will be recalled that the earliest Gospels in circulation in Egypt were not the Canonical ones; in Clement's day these two Gospels—to the Hebrews and to the Egyptians—were still in general use. It is generally believed that these two documents preceded the four Apostolic Gospels in Egypt, and were most likely the ones used by the earliest Christian community there.

"It is purely a matter of conjecture, although perhaps a correct conjecture," says Harnack, "that more Jews were converted to Christianity in the Nile valley than anywhere else."

Egypt is the home of asceticism, and it is most likely that Christianity was looked upon at first by the Jews as a call to a new and deeply spiritual Way, which could only be reached through Judaism. As time went on, it is reasonable to suppose that these Jews became absorbed into the Christian Church which was fast covering the country.

What strange development is it in Egypt that leads to the feeling of repugnance for the Jew to-day, which denies him, alone of all men, admittance to the Coptic church during service? The Moslem even is never refused admittance. I have stood through the whole celebration of the Holy Eucharist with a well-known sheikh at my side—but to the Jew the door is closed.

And amongst the common people in Egypt the last word of insult is to call a man a Jew! After an Egyptian has smiled indulgently at such epithets as dog, or ass, or buffalo, to call him a Jew will generally open the floodgates of Oriental wrath.

I think that in the case of the Copts it cannot be the old grievance of the usury of the Jews, which in all other parts of the world has been so largely responsible for this hatred. For the Copts themselves are the "bankers," to use their own term, or in plain words, the chief money-lenders, of Egypt. In this business they have been astute and hard, so that some of their princely fortunes have been built up on methods which have helped to embitter the victimised Moslems (taught in the Koran that the usurers' business is sinful and despicable) against the whole race.

I have met one or two wealthy Copts whose relentless and unscrupulous pursuit of gain by means of adroit usury had turned them into the type of brutal harpy, the only suggestion of whose existence, fortunately for most of us, comes from melodrama; as the only man who could be a match for them would be a Mr. Justice Raffles.

I have heard the suggestion that it was because he found men of this type, with ability, and the strength to exert it, that Mohammed Ali, the maker of modern Egypt, and the first of the Khedivial line (he reigned from 1811 to 1848), and later on Ismail (1863-79), put the financial affairs of Egypt into the hands of the Copts.

Those were the days of some very cruel acts of financial pressure, when money was extorted, and property often craftily seized, in ways that were barbarous.

An old friend of mine often speaks to me of a raid he remembers as a young man on his father's flocks, when the marauding emissaries of Ismail took away every head of cattle from the large farms, without any sort of excuse. But the youthful blood of my Moslem friend being up, he called to the family retainers, and with a fine daring they galloped on borrowed horses to the Khedive's farms a few miles distant, and recaptured the cattle. The sequel was truly Oriental. Ismail laughed at the original theft done in his name, but he admired the spirit which would not sit down under it, and sent for my friend to compliment him, so that ever after they were good country neighbours. The Copts in such employment would not, however, commend themselves to the affection of the people.

Seeing the epoch-making developments which had their birth in Egypt, through the early passion of the Christians for monasticism, a brief note may be permitted on an extraordinary development of Alexandrian Judaism, by which a community of Jews, settled near Lake Mareotis, formed themselves into an ascetic brotherhood. Philo[1] describes how each member of the brotherhood lived in a separate cell, called *monasterium*, in which he spent his time in mystic devotion and ascetic practices, and especially in the study of the Torah, and in reciting the Psalms; practising the while great self-denial. Women, he says, were admitted into the Order; they spent their time in caring for orphan children, and they listened "behind a separating wall" to the Law as read by the men at their devotions. Which incidentally may be thought to dispose of the oft-repeated charge that the dividing screen was the later invention of the terrible Moslem.

[1] In *De Vita Contemplativa*.

By the fourth century asceticism was the dominant force in Egypt. It is not impossible that it was out of this early tendency in Egyptian Judaism that the whole movement sprang.

It was persecution which first turned the thoughts of the most saintly of the early Christians in Egypt to the peace to be found in desert retreats—first in lonely caves and cells, and then in the monasteries which had been built in places equally remote from the ordinary life of the world.

By severest self-repression, by the vexing and humiliating of the body in every possible way, by crushing all natural instinct, men thought they were living the life of the angels, and were taking the only way to the salvation of their own souls, which indeed, especially in Egyptian monasticism, was the sole aim of its followers.

Very literally, the hermits and monks (and nuns, for it must be remembered that women always had a great part in this movement) considered that in this way they were making the desert "to blossom as the rose."

If the desert blossomed—and indeed many a fair and fragrant flower did bloom in its parched soil—everything that was most vital and helpful to the life of the Church and the nation wilted and died.

When the later persecutions of Byzantium came upon the Copts, most of the power for a noble resistance had been lost; they fought and bickered, intrigued and plotted, and retaliated with bloodthirsty passion, in the spirit of their oppressors.

There is little wonder that the Arabs found the conquest of Egypt a matter of little difficulty, and that the first impression they received of Christianity there was unattractive to those hardy sons of nature.

Photo: Dittrich, Cairo. A COPTIC WOMAN OF THE POORER CLASS.

Photo: Dittrich, Cairo. A COPTIC PRIEST.

At one time all Copts were required by the authorities to wear the black robe and turban, which are now retained as their out-door garb by the priests alone.

Much has been written about the many persecutions of the Copts by the Moslems, and the Western bias with which the story has been told has taken too little account of the toleration shown by the first conquerors, and by certain of the later rulers. The many acts of ill-mannered self-aggrandisement and pride on the part of the Copts when they were in the enjoyment of liberty, which often aggravated the Moslems to cruel reprisals, have scarcely been recorded. Those who know the Oriental temper appreciate the significance of such stories as that of the rich Copt (it was a double offence that his wealth was gained by usury) who in old days rode through Cairo with incredible arrogance and display, and caused those who did not render him obeisance to be chastised; and of the wrath of the Moslem authorities at such reports, and the savage use they made of their superior power, by ordering such public humiliations of the Copts as were diabolical in their ingenuity. The Copts should thereafter wear distinctive dress in the streets, so that all men might know they were mere Christians, and point at them the finger of scorn. They should not escape notice even in the baths, for naked they must wear bells round their necks. If a Copt presumed to ride either a horse or a mule, the first Moslem who met him might slay him and take his goods. The Copt might ride the lowly ass, but then only with his face to the tail.

Bitter and cruel indeed were those days, when enmity and persecution so pressed upon the Christians that all their skill and cunning were given to preserving their lives, and that only in hiding.

Their churches were built over by every sort of erection so that they might escape observation; their church bells had long since been silenced. The people huddled together in their own separate quarters, which they fortified as far as they dare, disguising their dwellings as they had done their churches.

It may be said that for hundreds of years the Copts practically buried themselves alive, their very existence passing unsuspected by even Christian visitors to their country.

The English officials who, in these days of our supremacy there, in the curious mistrust and dislike they show of the Copt, unknowingly are basing their dislike on the objectionable manners bred of such an existence—a shrinking lowliness of bearing, which is called servility; a sly glance seeking for the line of least resistance, which Lord Cromer calls "trimming"; an economy in the use of truth, until they see their way clear, which goes by a sterner name.

And if the Copt mentions religion, as a claim to favour, the Englishman cannot disguise his nausea, never reflecting that the Copt has for centuries, in the nature of things, looked upon this as the first claim on fellow-Christians both to receive and to give help.

The dislike thus engendered in the English leads to far-reaching judgments, some of them unjust; so that many of the Copts are declaring that they were in a better position, especially after Mohammed Ali had removed their disabilities, a century since, than they have ever been under the British rule.

If the Englishman would look below the surface, he would find that the fundamental elements in the Coptic character are of higher worth than could be imagined by those who judge him by the distorted manners he has acquired.

For one thing—and this of the first importance in a Briton's judgment—the Copt is not altogether a craven, as is so often said; though, more than any other Oriental,

Pharaohs still survive in Egypt? 323

I admit he does go in deadly fear of exciting ill-will. But a great deal of his history cries aloud against the charge of cowardice. The tenacity of his early patriotism, and the unswerving loyalty to his Church, from which no prospect of gain, either from Constantinople or Rome, could turn him aside for an instant, confirmed the splendid triumphs of the early martyrs and the endurance of the saintly fathers—of whose incredible attainments those of St. Simeon Stylites, at Alexandria, are but a single instance.

It is said, with easy self-assurance, that the Copt is not a fighting man, with no reference to the fact that from the year A.D. 642 he was never allowed to bear arms.

The Copts at intervals all through the centuries of oppression have shown signs of a latent heroism, apart altogether from those great powers of stolid resistance which alone have preserved their existence. If they only suspected themselves of fear, they, with an Oriental complexity of mind, again and again branded themselves and their loved ones with the cross, so that, perforce, they should not deny their Lord when the time of trial came.

What more beautiful story, in all Christian history, is there than that of the followers of Christ, who having apostatised to Islam under great pressure, later on, in response to the preaching of Matthew their Patriarch, decided to return to their allegiance to the Cross at whatever cost.

Cairo, that city of many weird religious phantasia, never saw a stranger or more moving sight than when in the year A.D. 1389 a procession entered its gates consisting of a great stream of men and women, strained with suppressed emotion and stern with resolve, who as they marched, cried aloud, "We are Christians!

We renounce Islam and its Prophet! with shame we confess that we deserted Christ for fear of persecution!" In this way they sought to expiate the desertion of their faith, knowing that it was by this road that they would put themselves beyond the terrible fear of again proving traitors.

The Moslem crowd surrounded the men and women with vilifying cries, while the sheikhs demanded their submission. With one voice, again and again, they replied, "We are Christians! We are Christians! We have come in this way to atone for our grievous sin; by death we may perhaps gain the pardon of the Saviour whom we denied!"

When it was found that not one of them would yield either to threat or promise, it was determined to make an example of the men first. One by one they were beheaded, before the eyes of the women. These, however, remained firm, crying the more that they preferred death to the betrayal of their Lord. The chief Kadi, becoming enraged by the constant rejection of his demand, ordered the guards to take all the band of women to the foot of the citadel and there behead them all. This was done; although even the Moslems in the crowd cried out against the Kadi for taking the lives of women by beheading.

To come to our own times. At the fall of Omdurman to the Mahdi many Copts were killed and others were forced into worship in the mosque. Of those who survived those days were two well-known Copts, one named Boules, who so successfully defended himself, in his own house, that the Dervishes promised him his life to save themselves the trouble of bringing up the heavy guns. The other, Ibrahim Bey, owed his life to a black servant.

It can never be known how many Copts refused at that time to give up their faith. The natives told of one, however, a Copt from Berber, who, when brought before the Khalifa Abdulla, said that his fathers before him were Christians, and that he would prefer death to the denial of his faith. Even while he bowed his head to the stroke, his friends interposed and begged the Khalifa to give them time to teach him the new faith, saying he was mad and ignorant. On his second appearance, he still persisted and declared that he would rather die than give up Christ. The Khalifa discharged him as a lunatic; but on the next Friday in his sermon in the mosque he took the bravery of this Christian as his subject, expressing the doubt that any one of his congregation would be willing to die, in cold blood, for Mahdism.

During those thirteen years of awful misrule at Omdurman, the Copts and other Christians managed to collect in a quarter by themselves, and though they had to appear regularly at prayers in the mosque, their children were baptized secretly by Sitte Katerina, the wife of a Greek merchant, who was possibly the bravest of them all.

If such stories as this—and they are by no means solitary instances—are attributed to religious emotion, it is fair to recall that at the time of the French invasion the Copts showed not only courage but resource. It was a man named Jacob, with his Coptic recruits from Upper Egypt, whom he had trained, who fortified his house during a three days' massacre, and afterwards with great skill and courage fortified and guarded the whole Christian quarter in Cairo. It is stated (and has never been denied) that Napoleon took a number of young Copts from Egypt to serve in his army in France, where several of them rose to the rank of captain, and one became a general. It was Tewfik Bey, a Copt, who later was the hero of the garrisons of the Red Sea Coast.

Those Frenchmen who have had intimate relations with the Copts—and the French people have always shown a capacity to understand the Egyptians beyond that of the English—have never shown the same sort of contempt for them. They have never spoken of them as cowards. Amelineau wrote with enthusiasm of the calm courage of some of the leading country Copts, who like his intimate friend, Abd el Schahid Botros, head of a rich family at a village between Girgeh and Abydos, weathered the storm raised by the rebellion of Arabi Pasha in 1881–82, showing remarkable qualities of diplomacy and self-restraint in turning aside the anarchy and fanaticism which, in the lower orders of the people of any country, always finds an outlet as soon as ordinary government is overthrown.

CHAPTER VIII

The Egyptian Christians and British Rule

The Author has thought it best to leave this chapter exactly as he wrote it, in the last days of peace, in 1914.

AS I have never had the slightest inclination—possibly owing to some sort of temperamental eccentricity—to approach any of the people of the Orient with that prejudice which seems to be natural to the majority of Englishmen, I think I shall be on safer ground if I quote the exact words of an English writer, whom I take to be an official, as expressing the views on which the British official attitude towards the Copts is based.

"When the English came into the country in 1882 they adopted, it must be admitted, an attitude of mistrust towards the Copts, not unlike that felt in Europe with regard to the Jews. This attitude becomes exaggerated when put into words—it is so undefined and unexpressed —but there can be no doubt that it did, and still does, exist amongst English residents as a whole. The somewhat servile manner of some of the Copts annoyed the British official. By reputation, if not always in actual fact, they were too fond of strong drink. Sometimes a Copt seeking employment in the office of an Englishman would make his petition in the name of the Saviour who died for both of them—a peculiarly distasteful means of approach, the substance of which on first thoughts the Briton was inclined to deny with some heat. Moreover, it was felt, not entirely in jest, that while the Moslem Egyptian never told the truth except when he intended to deceive, the Copt omitted to tell it on all occasions."[1]

I have shown elsewhere how far I think this sort of judgment is founded on what is superficial observation and the hasty conclusions of temper, rather than on patiently acquired knowledge and experience. If I am right, it will not be difficult to see how, based upon such data, the widespread injustice of personal treatment, as well as the course which politics would take, would lead to grievance and discontent.

And as time has gone on, I fear it must be admitted that very little has been done to seek a truer knowledge of these people, by looking beyond mere superficial manners to the deeper springs of life and character; or to find, perhaps, historical explanations of certain habits of mind which irritate Englishmen, reared in a land of vigorous freedom; or to admit excuses for conduct which might be admitted to be the outcome of centuries of severe constraint.

It was the English who delivered the Copts from an existence that was only made possible by lowly deportment, if not by "trimming" and intrigue. As for the mention of the Cross in the ordinary concerns of daily life, of course it is repugnant to Englishmen, with their reserve and shyness about any mention of sacred matters. But here again it might be considered how entirely the Oriental differs from us, and that in a close community like the Copts, the one bond must always have been that of the Christian religion. How could they know that with the English our deepest feelings are offended by

[1] *Blackwood's Magazine*, August 1911.

references which to the Oriental are the most natural? And Lord Cromer was right—for the Copt himself *would*, if he had the power, show favour to other Christians.

I hope I have made it clear that I have no sympathy with those who would encourage the Copts to expect any sort of preference above the Moslems, or to think that they have a single claim, historical or personal, to any such treatment. But we need not give them less than equality, in our desire to show that we are impartial, or deny them justice to prove our dislike of certain traits that are distasteful.

If the way in which their claims are presented does irritate us, we might still consider such claims on their merits, and agree to such facts as admit of plain proof.

None of these things were done by Sir Eldon Gorst; and although since the irritable outburst of the last of his reports was written the temper shown to the Copts has been more restrained, things still stand almost as he left them. A cessation of their mild agitation for consideration of their claims has been purchased by the vague promise of future readjustment, with threats, not at all vague, of the consequences of any sort of renewal of their plaint.

The points for which the Copts ask consideration are perfectly clear. They come under five main headings:

(i) Since British rule began they have been debarred from holding the position of Mudir, or Governor of a province, or of Mamur, the chief administrative magistrate of a district.

(ii) The Copts employed by the Government are compelled to work on Sunday, because Friday has been made, by the English, the day of rest, in deference to its being the Moslem day of prayer.

(iii) The Coptic community is not properly represented upon the Government councils and committees.

(iv) They are obliged to pay taxes for the support of many schools wherein the religious teaching is solely Islamic, and very inadequate provision is made in any of the schools for giving any sort of Christian teaching to their children.

(v) They wish to call attention to the enormous sums spent by the Government for Moslem religious celebrations, such as the sending of the Holy Carpet to Mecca every year, while no countenance or support is given to the Coptic religion.

The first injustice seems to me to be the greatest, as it is also the most galling. If I am right in judging that the keeping of the Copts out of the higher administrative posts of the country is the work of mere political expediency, it will be easy to imagine how the best part of the Coptic community is stultified and humiliated by hearing that the "diplomatic" reason, given far and wide, is that the Copts are lacking in the necessary ability to occupy such posts.

At the very moment that our Agent was declaring to the people of Great Britain, in his reports, that the Copts must be condemned to such a measure of extinction, in the affairs of the country, because of inadequate ability, the Prime Minister of Egypt, who had risen to power by sheer merit, was himself a Copt.

As for the qualifications for the exercise of administrative authority, who can be ignorant of the fact that Egypt has again and again been ruled, to all practical purposes, solely by Copts?

But still, the Coptic cause has been ill served by certain sympathetic English writers whose advocacy has led them to assert (and this has often been asserted) that the people of this race are not only equal to, but far ahead of, the Moslems in skill and in character. In what may be called the office work, in book-keeping, and the details of the routine of administration, they have shown superior skill. In the private concerns of the country there is scarcely a single estate, or a business concern, in Moslem hands, which is not ruled in those departments by a Copt, whose ability and integrity are freely acknowledged by their employers.

At the same time, the Moslems who rise to power are possessed of no mean gifts of organisation; those gifts that go to the astute selection and management of men, to initiative, and a certain clearness of foresight and judgment. But I believe that, speaking generally of their ability, the Copts and the Moslems are almost indistinguishable. I admit that the consciousness of belonging to the conquering race gives to the Moslem an air of dignity and self-assurance which seems to mark him out as a ruler. But is it not possible that, with proper encouragement, impartially administered under our rule, it would soon be found that the Copts would in large numbers recover the spirit so necessary to command?

If this grievance is not the outcome of what the English, rightly or wrongly, have thought was a political necessity, how is it that until the Occupation the posts in question were never regarded as altogether closed to the Copts?

I have many Moslem friends in Egypt, and when they are questioned it is evident that they have caught the suggestion entirely from the drift of the British policy, of all they have to say in favour of Coptic exclusion. Strange as it may seem, it is from the English that the idea even of religious disqualification has come, for when pressed the Moslems never attempt to support it by precept or precedent of their own.

The late Sheikh Ali Yussef once said, in the days before he had taken the cue from the policy of Sir Eldon Gorst which led the sheikh to that hatred of the Copts which he afterwards exhibited in the newspaper he edited: "There is no difference between the ability of the Copts and the Moslems."

As for the religious question, we have the evidence of an Englishman. Professor Sayce said recently: "When I first knew Egypt, in the pre-Occupation days, the religious antagonism between the Copts and Moslems did not yet exist: they were all alike, Egyptians."

I have myself seen Coptic churches built by Moslems, and a mosque, built only a year or two before the Occupation, by a Coptic landowner. In the Secular Coptic schools, built by private munificence, in different parts of the country, I have never failed to find Moslem pupils; and no one thinks of excluding Coptic children from similar schools built by the Moslems, especially in the country places.

The history of Islam teems with instances, founded on the teaching of the Prophet, showing clearly that religion was never to be an obstacle to the employment of the best men obtainable in the administration of affairs important to the commonwealth—all the Western prejudice against Islam which comes under the cherished formula of "fanaticism" notwithstanding.

Both under the dynasties of the early Caliphs and the Mamelukes, the Copts were promoted to the highest and most responsible positions in the State, always excepting the Army and the Governorship. Mohammed Ali (the great statesman and soldier, founder of the present dynasty) would never hear of the disqualification in the service of the State of any man of proved ability, whether he was a Copt or a Jew; and there was never in his day any sign of the religious resentment which it is now said would arise under such appointments as he and his successor made.

When one considers the despotic nature of Mohammed Ali's rule, and the methods used to wring from the people through these appointments the taxation he imposed, one finds a conclusive answer to the doubt that the Moslems would resent the appointment of Copts to commanding positions. Mohammed Ali knew quite well the extent to which the Mamelukes before him had given power to the Copts, not stopping short of entrusting them with the collection of taxes, and responsibility for expenditure as well as for revenue.

When Egypt was divided into many states, each ruled by a Moslem Turk with a regiment of soldiers, a Copt was always appointed to the chief civil office as the Governor's Secretary. The duties of this Copt were varied and important. He not only levied taxes, but was responsible for the Budget; and he supervised the surveying of the cultivated land, and generally advised the Governor. Indeed, when Mohammed Ali first took the reins in Egypt he found that the man who was in charge of all the State affairs was Ibrahim el Gohary, a Copt, and he made this man his Chief Secretary or Grand Vizier! According to El Gabarty, the great Moslem historian, this man was the only Egyptian who was privileged to smoke his pipe in the presence of the first of the Khedives.

After the death of El Gohary, Mohammed Ali appointed another Copt, Ghali Doss, as Chancellor of the Exchequer, again with full powers over the taxation and expenditure. Doss was also allowed to appoint all officials in his own department. His son Basalious succeeded him, with such success that he was raised to the rank of Bey, Mohammed Ali making him a member of his Privy Council, which was composed only of his relatives and a few intimate friends. In time that Council came to look upon Basalious as its leader.

It has so often of late years been asserted that no Copt has served in a position where the Moslems would have to submit to his rule, that it may be of use to give the names of men whom I have traced as having filled such posts. Mohammed Ali appointed Risk Bey, a man from Mit Yaish in Lower Egypt, to be Mudir Edara of Kalyobieh province; Makram Agha of Gizeh was made Mudir Edara of Gizeh. The Khedive also appointed Boutros Faltaos to be Governor of Denderah, and Mikhail Abdu to be Governor of Fashn. There is no record that the Moslems showed any signs of resentment to these appointments.

Later, in the time of Said and of Ismail, the Copts continued to fill similar posts, Ismail making it a rule to appoint a Copt to the post of public prosecutor in every province—a position of considerable power, as the men holding it had at certain times to act as judges. They ranked third in the order of precedence with the provincial officials. Among others, Sedarous Takla served in Esneh; Tadros Shalabi in Girgeh; Shehata Hasaballah in Assiout; Abdel Malek Katcout in Minieh: Girgis Yacoub in Beni Souef; and Awadallah Bey Srour in Dakalieh. The last-named gentleman was appointed sub-governor for Behairah, and filled the position with great credit until he retired on a pension just before the British occupation.

In the time of Ismail (who continually asserted that "all were Egyptian alike") the Copts served the State in many high positions, the most striking fact being that the Ministry of War was for the first time given to a Copt (it was Mohammed Ali who first removed the disabilities of the Copts to serve in the army), and Ayad Bey Hanna had full control.

The position of sub-governor of a province was certainly held by a Copt. Even under Arabi a Copt was promoted to be sub-Minister of Justice, a post which actually carried with it the superintendence of the Cadi's courts, and the necessary minor appointments for those courts. The Master of the Ceremonies at the court of Ismail itself was a Copt, Wassif Pasha Azmy.

It was hardly to be expected of Orientals, that when the Moslems saw a chance of getting the succession to all the chief posts in the country, they would do anything to persuade the British rulers that their diplomatic idea favouring this was mistaken and ill-founded. Sir Eldon Gorst's political rôle had been to reverse the Cromer régime, and initiate a diplomatic friendship for the Khedive Abbas to which England had hitherto been a complete stranger. The result was that no single Copt was to be found in the entourage, or even in the service, of the several departments of the Court. Indeed, to speak with the men who surrounded that corrupt Khedive of Egypt was to be led to imagine that one was in an opposing camp, the enemy being the Christian part of the nation.

Under the stern glance of Lord Kitchener, who went to Egypt to remedy the mistakes of the chequered Gorst rule, anything like personal friendship between the Khedivial Court and the British Agency soon perished, and the ground for the dislike of the Copts by the Court changed to the suspicion that they were again trying slimly to commend themselves to the British through their Westernised manners and their Christian faith.

Of late, however, there have not been wanting signs that the authorities are coming to some sort of realisation of the truth, which had guided their predecessors, that the people make up one nation, and that the religion of neither Moslem, Copt, nor Jew should prevent men from being one in patriotism and loyalty, or from equal opportunities in the service of the State, and a share in the honours of that service.

The Copts declare that whereas when the British took control of the country their people occupied a great number of the highest positions in the State, in less than a quarter of a century almost all the Coptic heads of departments have disappeared. They were fully represented on the bench of judges, but gradually the number has been reduced to *nil*; and so in every other department of the State, the process of removing them, and shutting the door against fresh appointments, has gone on until they have been reduced to a state of discouragement bordering on despair.

I have often seen how the effects of this are paralysing the springs of the best part of the Coptic life. I have talked with the fathers of promising sons as to the completion of their education, and in doing so have discovered how it comes about that in a community which sets such a high value on education, so few Coptic youths find their way to our English Universities and Colleges as compared with the Moslems.

"It is useless," these fathers say to me. "I may make great sacrifices to give my boy the best possible education in England, and when he returns to Egypt he will eat his heart out in the work of trivial posts, and will see the men who studied by his side at Oxford or

Photo: Dittrich, Cairo.

THE GREAT COPTIC CENTRE IN EGYPT—ASSIOUT.

Here the wealthy Christian families have built themselves palaces and made gardens by the river side. The domes of the Coptic Cathedral and the minarets of the Mosques may be seen in the distance.

Cambridge, and who in no way excelled him, promoted again and again because they happen to be Moslems. I will not make the mistake which has been made, and leads to so much bitterness, by some of my friends."

I have often talked, long and earnestly, with young men of both religions who have followed this course: with a charming young Moslem, who after a successful career at an English University, has been promoted by rapid strides; and with a young Copt, who was his companion at the University, and whose ability has been placed beyond doubt, but whom Egypt has left unemployed. Not being under the necessity of seeking the crust of lowly service, the latter has almost lost interest in his country and is using his talents in a land where the disabilities of Egypt are unknown—to his parents' grief, who, being of an ancient family, doubly deplore the loss of their son. I can say that everything I learned of this young Copt's failure came from his Moslem friend, who regarded it with genuine sadness; and, in this instance, the Copt said nothing to me, nor did his father, of the disappointment they were suffering through British neglect.

These are some of the facts which might be taken into account when the Copts are pleading for a consideration of their case—facts not to be impatiently dismissed as a part of a case got up out of sheer Coptic vexatiousness, or in an attempt to secure something to which the Copts have no sort of claim.

One of the strangest things, perhaps, in Britain's rule in Egypt is the way the question of the observation of Sunday has been dealt with. Who could believe that a Christian people, on whom the observance of the Sabbath is laid as a Heaven-given commandment, could go into a country where there was already another Christian Church, with many hundreds of thousands of adherents, and promptly make arrangements by which they deprived the Christians whom they employed, and all their children in the State schools, of any chance of observing their Holy Day; giving up at the same time their own Sunday to secular work? But this is what British rule has done.

And to what end? Some one conceived the idea that this was the only politic thing to do out of consideration of the Moslem people, who must alone be thought of because they are in the majority! That this political idea was imaginary and ill-founded may be judged from the effect it has had on the minds of those whose prejudices were thought to demand it. I am more than convinced that there is nothing which has robbed us of respect on the part of the Moslems so much as this very act which we had done to gain their goodwill. Over and over again I have been asked, with great seriousness, by Moslems of every class, in all parts of Egypt, "Have the English Christians any Day of Prayer?" And when I have explained the nature of our Sabbath, I have been met by expressions of surprise that such a religious institution could, under any circumstances, be set aside. They are utterly incredulous when it is suggested that this was done out of consideration for Moslem views.

There is nothing in the Moslem religion that would lead its followers to resent the keeping of a Holy Day in their midst; on the contrary, such an observance appeals deeply to them. I have seen this in Algeria, where the French people have never abated their private and public respect for the Sabbath, and find no difficulty in meeting at the same time the demands of the Moslems for their Hours of Prayer on Friday. Many a pious Moslem sheikh in Algeria has spoken to me of the way this has favourably impressed his people.

The nature of the Moslem Day of Prayer has never called for such a sacrifice as the English officials were led to make for it, for it is in no way a day set wholly apart for religious observance, or even for rest. It is incumbent on the Moslem to abstain from work every Friday until he has made his "great prayer" at noon; after that he is free, by the express words of the Prophet, to "go his ordinary way, for profit or pleasure."

If the Moslem feeling was misread in this matter, it is certain that the protests of the Copts were equally mistaken. A surface judgment had suggested—Lord Cromer expresses this in his great work on Egypt—that the Egyptian Christians were so in name only, and that there was little real feeling for the keeping of the Sabbath behind the grievance they somewhat elfishly urged.

As a matter of fact, with all their contradictions of conduct, I have seen abundant evidence that the Copts have an intense feeling of reverence for the Sabbath, based first of all on the scriptural commands,—and the literal Scripture is at the root of everything in which the Oriental Christian believes,—and then on a sort of supernatural influence which gathered in the early centuries about the Day of God and of the Eucharist, with its rest from toil, even for the fellah and the slave. I know Copts in Upper Egypt who ride for three hours on a donkey's back to attend the Sunday worship; one of them to my knowledge gave up his only means of livelihood rather than violate the Sabbath; though when his Moslem employer saw he was really in earnest he took him back into his service, and has showed him the most perfect confidence ever since.

Those of the Copts who are most deeply concerned to see their countrymen of the Christian faith advance towards a more spiritual realisation of their religion, are justified in speaking as Dr. Fanous has done. Lord Cromer, he said, "hinted that we Copts are not an example of true Christianity. Alas! it is too true; and it is because our education as Christians is neglected. How can we expect the people to follow the precepts of their religion if they are shown that they are of no importance to the authorities, who will themselves put obstacles in the way of our religious observances? We have been taught the habit of neglecting the precepts of our religion."

Unlike the Moslem, the Copt must go fasting to his church; and in contrast to the worship of the mosque, which lasts not more than half an hour, even with the sermon, the Holy Eucharist goes on from before eight o'clock till well on to noon. After that the binding law is that the Christian shall "do no work."

It is a surprising thing that the only plan for meeting the claims of these Holy Days that commends itself to British authority is to give a half-holiday to all the schools and the Government offices on Thursday afternoon and a whole day on Friday; and to ignore, both for the Copts and for themselves, any provision for the observance of the Christian Sunday.

The Law Courts are open on Sundays, and all Christians must attend there when occasion demands, leaving their religious duties—and this applies even to a priest who may be summoned, whose duty was to have been serving at the altar. An adjournment of the Courts is made, however, on Fridays for the Moslems, and the Mixed Courts adjourn on Sundays for the benefit of the European Christians, without any inconvenience. In the national schools no opportunity is given to the students of keeping Sunday. And yet the

General Post Office is closed at Alexandria, and also the Customs offices on Sunday instead of Friday, in deference to a certain amount of special pressure there; and it is found quite an easy matter to allow the Moslems to be absent on Friday until after their noonday prayer.

As a solution of this sore grievance, what is suggested is that the Copts in the Government Departments should work each day an hour longer than at present, in order that on Sunday they might be free to worship. They point out that the Sultan Khalif of Islam adopted long ago the custom of closing the Government offices at Beyrout, and in other places, on Sunday as well as on Friday, with no ill result; and within the last year or two the Turkish Government, after consultation with the Sheikh-el-Islam, the chief religious authority of the whole Moslem world, decided to admit the claims of Sunday.

As for the schools, it is asked that, instead of the Thursday half-holiday, the Coptic pupils might have the necessary time on Sundays to attend the Holy Eucharist. This would mean, even then, a certain loss of school time, but it is pleaded that this would be insignificant as compared with the wrong of bringing up the rising generation in complete detachment from the practice of their religion; and all the time doing violence to the consciences of the parents, many of whom are keenly apprehensive of the evil results which they see accruing from this practice.

The British official answer (showing the attitude of mind the authorities bring to any discussion of this question) may be found in the following words: "It cannot be denied that, on the face of it, the Coptic desire to worship their God on the Christian Sabbath is not only just but laudable; yet it is not a demand with which the British authorities can comply, so long as they only represent the occupying power. Mohammedanism is the State religion of Egypt, and since the officials have too much work to do to be able to adopt the Beyrout system, there is nothing for it but to continue the observance of Friday as the only day of rest in the week."

It is questionable if such callous expediency as this can ever, under any circumstances whatever, be justified where vital principles are at stake. But what can be said of justification so shallow as to fall back on the plea of Islamism being the State religion—when all the best teaching of Islam is opposed to the thing here implied of it.

As for our "only representing the occupying power," such a pale ghost dissolves at the first instant that the British authorities feel the need of asserting the sovereign and autocratic power, which they know perfectly well they do in reality possess, to carry out any project whatsoever, the most trivial as well as the most important, on which they are intent. It is this sort of pretence which brings upon England the scorn of men of other nations, and hampers our influence as a Christian people. There is an unctuosity about it which supplies our foes with their bitterest sneers.

England could without doubt settle this grievance, if she cared to. It *would* be done, if she could first believe in the sincerity of the advocacy which asks for redress, and could then bring herself to be as interested in the moral and social development of the Egyptian people as she is in the material gain which so handsomely accrues from her rule.

Of the remaining Coptic grievances I shall say

nothing. If the strong man ever appears in Egypt, with aspirations towards the spiritual uplifting of the nation, with no special application to either Islam or Christianity, he may confidently be expected to readjust the position of the Coptic people with regard to the historic and moral considerations already set forth. Then the sore grievances as to education, and the incidence of the taxation respecting it, the religious instruction of the children, the just representation of the Copts in the Councils of the Government, will automatically disappear.

As for the national Moslem celebrations, I doubt if another word of dissent would ever be heard, for in such details the minority must always submit. Pre-Occupation history, if appealed to on one side, must also be left to settle Coptic objections to the expenditure on the Holy Carpet Pilgrimage, so dear to the great majority of the Moslem population.

If such a man as I hope for does not appear, and the British Government itself, sitting in London, is never to be moved to look for anything in the rule of Egypt beyond audits, with monetary balances on the credit side, I do not see that any arguments can be of use.

With deep conviction I trust and believe that both the inspiration and the man *will* come, when the day is ripe. And to those who know something of the soul of Egypt there are many signs of a rare harvest, to be garnered in God's good time.

Addenda

THE BURYING OF THE PICTURE IN THE ALTAR

ON Holy Thursday the picture of the Crucifixion is taken down from its place in the church, and put upon a special stand, and round it are placed crosses, censers, and candles. A silver Gospel case is also placed on the stand, covered with a great quantity of rose petals. On Good Friday the service goes on from nine o'clock till sunset, and at one point the picture is taken and carried in procession three times round the church. Another picture, of Christ in the tomb, is now buried in the altar, with a small wooden cross. Small pieces of myrrh are laid upon the cross, and then a quantity of roses and petals are put in to bury the whole, which is covered with a large veil.

The congregation, in the belief that when our Lord descended into Hades all the imprisoned souls fell down on their faces to worship Him, are now required by the Church to make four hundred prostrations, each hundred directed to a cardinal point. They then break their fast, with an infusion of myrrh in vine-leaves.

The Easter service begins at sunset on Saturday, when the Liturgy of St. Gregory is recited with special pomp. Immediately before the service of the Holy Eucharist the doors of the sanctuary are closed, and the deacon, after chanting a long hymn, strikes the closed doors on the western side and says, "Open ye, O Kings, your doors," etc., to make an entrance for the King of Glory. The priest inside the sanctuary demands, "Who is the King of Glory?" and then opens the doors. The picture is then brought out from the altar, and all the clergy and cantors then carry another picture of our Lord, rising from the dead, in procession round the church, chanting, "Christ has risen!" This service ends about midnight.

THE BREAKING OF THE BREAD

The method of dividing the Host is as follows:

1st. The priest divides it up into a right third, and left two-thirds.

2nd. He places the right third upon the left, two-thirds in the form of a cross. He now severs a piece of the third, to which the *Ispadikon* is attached, and places it in the paten towards the east, and another piece, to be placed to the west. He also severs a piece from the right third and places it to the right, and puts the remaining part to the left in the paten, thus forming the figure of a cross.

3rd. He divides the piece of two-thirds into two divisions, and places the entire *Ispadikon* in the centre of the paten.

4th. The remaining third in his hands is also divided. He now takes in his hands the third placed to the left, and puts in its place the last third that was divided.

5th. He also divides the third that is in his hands, and puts it to the right of the paten.

6th. He now collects all these divisions together in the centre of the paten, and rubs his hands together to get rid of any crumbs that might have become attached to them.

Bibliography

THE following books bear upon the subject, and some of them have been consulted:

Egypt and Israel. Professor Flinders Petrie. (Society for Promoting Christian Knowledge.)

Among the Huts in Egypt. M. L. Whately. (Seeley, Jackson, & Haliday.)

Ragged Life in Egypt. M. L. Whately. (Seeley, Jackson, & Haliday.)

More Ragged Life in Egypt. M. L. Whately. (Seeley, Jackson, & Haliday.)

Dr. Liddon's Tour in Egypt and Palestine. (Longmans, Green, & Co.)

Copts and Moslems under British Control. Kyriakos Mikhail. (Smith, Elder, & Co.)

Egypt and the Christian Crusade. Charles R. Watson. (Published in America.)

In the Valley of the Nile. Charles R. Watson. (Fleming H. Revell Co.)

The Eastern Church. A. P. Stanley. (J. M. Dent.)

The Patriarch of Jerusalem. Ven. Archdeacon Dowling. (Society for Promoting Christian Knowledge.)

Ancient Coptic Churches of Egypt. A. J. Butler, M.A. (Clarendon Press.)

Egypt and Syria. Sir J. W. Dawson. (Religious Tract Society.)

The Story of the Church of Egypt. E. L. Butcher. (Smith, Elder, & Co.)

Christian Egypt: Past, Present, and Future. Rev. Montague Fowler, M.A. (London Church Newspaper Ltd.)

Folk-lore of the Holy Land. J. E. Hanauer. (Duckworth & Co.)

Blessing of the Waters. Marquis of Bute, K.T., and E. A. Wallis Budge, M.A. (Henry Frowde.)

Upper Egypt, its People and Products. Dr. Klunzinger. (Blackie & Son.)

Thäis. Anatole France. (The Bodley Head Press.)

Dictionary of Christian Biography. (John Murray.)

The Paradise of the Fathers. Translated by E. A. Wallis Budge, M.A. (Chatto & Windus.)

The Egyptian Church. Archdeacon Dowling. (Cope Fenwick.)

The Abyssinian Church. Archdeacon Dowling. (Cope Fenwick.)

The Coptic Church. Archdeacon Ward. (The Faith Press.)

The Rites of the Coptic Church—Baptism and Matrimony. Translated by B. T. A. Evetts. (David Nutt.)

The Encyclopædia of Religion and Ethics.

Yearly Reports of the Anglican and Foreign Church Society. (S.P.C.K.)

Index

Abbas, Khedive, and Sir Eldon Gorst, 335.
Abd-el-Sayed, the Rev., on the Bishop of the Fayoum, 286.
Ability, the special, of the Copts, 331.
Abraham, the first recorded Hebrew visitor to Egypt, 148.
Absolution, the prayer of, 195.
   attitude of the people during, 198.
   to the Son, 198.
   to the Father, 203.
Abu Nerus, carnival of, 66.
Abu Sifain, the picture of, 293.
   the saint's picture at, 217.
   the casket at, 215.
Abydos, temple at, 172.
Abyssinia, chief Bishop of, visits Egypt, 304.
Abyssinians, Epiphany, ceremony of, 66.
Acolytes, the, at the altar, 181.
Adib Bey Wahba, the miracle of, 304.
Administrators, Government, the Copts' claims to be, 329, 330.
Adoration of the Host, 201.
Advent service, the, 220.
   the Fast of, 223.
Aggrandisement, self-, of early Copts, 321.
Agriculture, skilled, 4.
Akhmin, the home of the recluse Shenouda, 292.
Alexander, Pope, destroying an idol, 281.
Alexandria, the burial-place of St. Mark, 176.
   Apollos of, 230.
   the date of Coptic Easter always decided at, 234.
   loses its position as the first See, 234.
   the Metropolitan of, 255.
   turning an ancient temple there into a church, 281.
   Judaism there, 319.
   St. Simeon Stylites at, 323.
Altar, the high, 175, 176.
   prayer for preparation of the, 195.
   the neglect of the, 226.
   the, stained with blood in the theological feuds, 236.
   burying the picture in the, 345.
Amelineau on Coptic courage, 326.
American Mission, debt of the Copts to, 83.
   the, and the villages, 241.
Angel, the guardian, 198.
   invocation to the, 202.
Angels, disputing as to whether they have wings, 232.
   supplication in the name of, 281.
Animals, care in beckoning, 73.
Ankh, the ancient, transferred to the Christian Cross, 295.
Annianus, St. Mark's first convert, 229.
Anonymous, gifts to the Church must be, 206.
Anthony, the monk, a saying of, 271.
   called by hearing the Scriptures read, 193.

Apis, the bull, 74.
Apollos, an Alexandrian, 230.
Apostates, the bitter remorse of, 323.
   the glorious story of their return to the faith, 324.
Apostles, the Fast of the, 223.
Arabi Pasha, 326.
"Arabian Nights," the, live again in the bazaars, 155.
Arabic, reading the Scriptures in, 192.
Arabs, the reception of the invading, 237.
Arian controversy, 232.
Arius, and his definitions of the Trinity, 233.
   to be restored to priesthood, 234.
Ark, the, on the altar, 177.
Armenians, a mixture of, 314.
Arsenius, the plot of, 255.
Asceticism, Egypt the home of, 317, 320.
Assiout, a great wedding at, 119.
   burning the church pictures at, 219.
   the itinerant teachers of, 241.
   the Patriarch at, 261.
   early connections of Bishop Abraam with, 301.
Assumption of the Virgin, the Fast of, 223.
Athanasian Creed, the, 200.
Athanasius the Great, 228, 233, 234.
   plotting in the time of, 255.

Baboon, the story of the, 75.
Babylon in Egypt, 229.
Backsheesh, 11, 43.
Bagdad, a Patriarch summoned to, for healing, 293.
Baking the Eucharistic cakes, 213.
Balcony, the use and antiquity of, 39, 40.
Baptism, customs and rites of, 95.
   ideas of infant, 101.
Baptist, St. John the, story of relic of, 221.
Baramous, the monastery of, 255.
Barsoum, the monastery of, 137.
Basalious, Coptic Chancellor of Exchequer, 334.
Basil, St., Liturgy of, 169.
   Liturgy proper of, 201.
   prayer of the kiss of, 201.
Basin, the, used by the priest, 182.
Baskets, making of, in monasteries, 151.
Bath, the infant's first, 90.
   visit to, enjoined after healing, 295.
Bazaars, the workers in the, 155, 156.
Beans, the story of the, 30.
"Beating the board" to summon worshippers, 224.
Bedouin, visit to tents of, 49, 57.
   the pride of the, 58.
Bells, the use of, in church, 197.
   distasteful to Moslems, 224.
   no church, 224.
Beni Hassan, inscription on a tomb at, 185.
Berber, the brave Copt of, 325.

23

Bible, the life of, reproduced, 43, 47.
  material sanctity of the, 100.
  as a talisman, 178.
Bibliography, 347, 348.
Bird life, 7.
Birds, fearlessness of, 72.
Birth, the customs attending, 82.
Bishop of the Fayoum, the, 180.
Bishop's blessing, a, 275.
Blacksmith, the, and his primeval implements, 159.
Blackwood's Magazine on the Copts, 328.
Blessing, the, of a Bishop, 275, 276, 277.
Blind cantor, the, 196.
Blood, the Patriarch must never have shed, 251.
Blyth, Bishop, suspected by the Patriarch, 311.
Boasting of monkish achievements, 186.
Bolsters, the, containing the relics, 220.
Bones of the saints, 220.
Books never used by the church congregation, 183.
Botros, Abd el Schahid, courage of, in the Arabi rebellion, 326.
Boutros Faltaos, a Coptic governor, 334.
Box, the incense, 182.
Boys as deacons, 190.
Bread, native, resembling stones, 81.
  the elaborate ceremony of breaking the Eucharistic, 346.
Breathing, the priest's use of, 98.
  ordination by, 263.
Bricks without straw, 47.
British Museum and its Coptic treasures, 253.
  Coptic Church treasures in the, 225, 226.
British political attitude towards the Copts, 327.
"Broom of the Nunnery," the story of, 108.
Bruce, the traveller, visited Egypt without knowing of the existence of the Copts, 306.
Burseem, or "taste of the spring," 9.
Burying the sacred picture, 177.
Butcher, Mrs. E. L., the misleading statements of, 107.
  the prejudice of, 309.
Butler, Dr., on the Egyptian School of Painting, 215.
  quoted, 308.
Byzantine persecutions, the horrible, 237.

Cafés, the Street of the, 160.
Cairo, the welcome of, to the returning Patriarch, 261.
  Old, the prophet Jeremiah's tomb, 316.
Cakes, the Eucharistic, distributed in church, 212.
Calendar, the Coptic, 66, 231.
Camel, a story of a, 75.
  bone of, as a shop sign, 165.
Candelabra, the church, 173, 181.
Candle-maker, the, 161.
Candles, religious use of, 161, 163.
  used at wedding festivals, 164.
Canopy, the baldaquin, 176.
Cantor, the blind, 196.
Carelessness of the Church treasures, 150, 173.
Carnival of the high Nile, 66.
Carpenter, the, how he works, 155.
Cathedral, the Cairo, 169.
Cavity, the, of the altar, 176.
Celibacy, unknown amongst servants, 17.
  of the nuns and monks, 238.
Censer, the song of the, 199.
Censing of the people, 190.
  the ceremony of, 199.
Chains, use of the, to bring the new Patriarch to Cairo, 254.

Chalcedon, the Council of, 231.
  the stormy Council of, 235.
Chalice, the, 177.
  the ceremony of mixing the, 204.
Characteristics, personal, 313, 314.
Charm, the Scriptures as a, 178.
  the, given by the Patriarch, 248.
Charms found in Christian graves, 134.
Childlessness, horror of, 86.
  overcome by Bishop's prayers, 304.
Children, the charm of the, 79.
  love of, 93.
Choir, the Coptic, 169, 196.
Chrism, use of, 97, 98, 99.
  the use, and the making of, 214.
Christ, disputes as to the nature of, 235.
Christianity, easily understood by ancient Egyptians, 132, 170.
Christmas Eve, the Fast of, 223.
Church revenues in the hands of the Patriarch, 248.
  services, days of the, 220.
Churches, the plan of the, 171.
  neglect of, 225.
Circumcision, practice of, 102.
Claims, the Coptic, 329, 330.
Claudius Bey Labib on origin of Copts, 312.
Clement, St., the Liturgy of, 182.
Clergy, degeneracy of, not due to fasts, 223.
Clerk, the native, 41.
Clocks, story of|the stopped, 32.
Coffee, discovery of, 16.
  making, 50.
Collection, the threefold, 212.
College, a theological, founded and abolished, 256.
Colour prejudice unknown, 315.
Commemoration of the dead, 131.
Communicants, absence of, 205.
Confession, is it disliked by Orientals, 205, 206.
Confirmation at the time of baptism, 102.
Constantine, the Emperor, 231.
Constantinople, rivalry of the Coptic Church with that of, 234.
Controversy, the Arian, 232.
Conversation, charm of, 32.
Convert, the first, of St. Mark, 229.
Copt, the derivation of the name, 311.
Coptic, prayers in, 183.
  reading the Scriptures in, 192.
Coptos, the town of, 311.
Corn-dealer, the, 158.
Corn-mill, the modern, 58.
Corporal, the silk Eucharistic, 177.
Councils, the forming of the new, 255, 258.
Country Copts, the isolation of the, 240.
Craftsmen, Oriental, 147.
Craven, the Copt not a, 322.
Creed, the Athanasian, 200.
Crocodile, stuffed, as a shop sign, 165.
Crocodiles, sacred, 74.
Cromer, Lord, and the *corvée*, 6.
  abolished the whip, 146.
  and the Patriarch, 245, 247.
  acts against the Patriarch, 259.
  defeated by Cyril v., 261, 262.
  on the sole difference between Copt and Moslem, 310.
  on the Copts' claim as a Christian, 329.
  on the keeping of the Sabbath, 339, 340.
Cross, the flat hand-, 179.
  always tattooed on the wrist, 181.
  sign of, on the forehead, 207.
  the hand, as used in blessing, 274.
  belief in magic of, 295.

Index 351

Cross, mention of, repugnant to English officials, 328.
Crotch, the dervish's, 158.
Crowning, the, in the wedding ceremony, 115.
Crucifix, the, unknown to the Copts, 179.
Crusaders, the, and the Copts, 305, 306.
Crutch, the use of, in the Church, 184.
Cures, marvellous, by Bishop Abraam, 303.
Curtains, the baldaquin, 176.
Cymbals, the use of, 191, 197.
Cyril the Fifth, Patriarch, sketch of, 245.
Cyrillus, Patriarch, burning of the pictures by, 218, 219.

Danke, the Moravian missionary, 232.
Darkness, fear of, 162, 163.
David and the rule about the shedding of blood, 251.
Deacon, position of, at the altar, 195.
Deacons, little boys as, 190.
Death, rites and customs concerning, 122.
Degeneracy of clergy not due to fasts, 223.
Deir-el-Bahri, sacred picture at, 216.
Deir-el-Baramous, Bishop Abraam and his disciples at, 302.
Deir-el-Meharak, the Bishop of, against reform, 261.
Delta, the levelling of, 4, 45.
  the geology of, 4.
  the handsome race of the, 55, 63.
Denon on Coptic characteristics, 313.
Depopulation, mistaken ideas of, 237.
Devil, the, largely ignored in the pictures, 218.
Devils, casting out, 265, 287.
Dimiana, Sitt, the *moolid* of, 141.
Dioscoros refuses to agree with the Council of Chalcedon, 235.
"Dipping" in the Scriptures, 178.
Dispute, propensity to, 63.
Disputing, love of, 232.
Divination, belief in, 282, 283, 291.
Divorce uncommon with the Copts, 118.
Dogma, a great dispute of, 232.
Dome, the vision in the, at the Monastery of Barsoum, 137.
Doss, Ghali, Coptic Chancellor of Exchequer, 333.
Dowry, the correct, 110.
Drink, intoxicating, 30, 32.
Drollery, love of, 19.

Ears cut off, to avoid Patriarchate, 255.
Easter, date of Coptic, always decided at Alexandria, 234.
  the change of the Western date of, 234.
Eating-places, how they differ from those of the West, 161.
Ecumenical Councils, the first of the, 233.
Eggs, ostrich, in church, 174.
Egypt, St. Peter in, 229.
Egyptians, the Gospel to the, 317.
El-Baramousi El-Saghir, the Rev., on the Bishop Abraam, 301.
Elijah, Abba, the monk who established a nunnery, 296.
Endowments of the Church, the laymen's views of the, 264.
Engagement for marriage, 105.
England, Church of, and the Coptic Church, 310.
  impartiality, how it is unbalanced, 309.
  dislike, reasons against, 322.
Epiphany tank, the, 209, 211.
  the services of, 210, 211.

Ethnology, the, of the bazaar workers, 156.
Eucharistic cakes distributed in church, 212.
Eutyches excommunicated by Greeks and Romans, 235.
  the views of, 235.
  estimate of population, 313.
Evening service, the, 195.
  prayer, preceding the Sabbath, 207.
Evil eye, the, 25, 26, 81.
  and the ornaments of Gideon, 74.
Ewer, the, used by the priest, 182.
Excitement, a scene of, at the celebration of the Holy Eucharist, 207, 211.
Excommunication, a rule of, 289.
  of Coptic Church by Rome, 235.
  of the Bishop of Sarabon, 258.
Excommunications, wholesale, of Cyril v., 260.
Exile of the Patriarch, 259.
Exorcism, 265.
  story of the Bishop of Fayoum and, 287.
Ezra, the story of the scroll of, 316.

Fanaticism, 61.
Fanning of the holy elements, 182.
Fanous, Dr., on the unity of the people of Egypt, 239.
  on Sabbath observance, 340.
Fast of Ramadan, 221.
Fasting for the Holy Eucharist, 175, 183.
Fasts, the Coptic, 221.
  the genuineness of the Eastern, 222.
Fatalism, 124.
Father, the, Prayer of Reconciliation to, 201.
Fayoum, the Bishop of, 180, 224, 268.
Feasts, the seven Coptic, 224.
Fellaheen, the qualities of, 62.
Fetish of Scripture reading, 193.
"Fixed price" a modern introduction in Europe, 164.
Food, willingness to share, 61.
  the, of the poor, 81.
  offerings to the dead, 133.
  the, of the handicraftsmen, 156.
Fortitude, Oriental, in ordinary calamity, 123.
Fox, stories of the cunning of, 76.
Francis of Assisi, St., unaware of existence of Coptic Church, 306.
French invasion, Coptic courage at the time of, 325.
Friday, Good, one of its ceremonies, 177
Friends, Society of, introduced the "fixed price," 164.
Furniture, destruction of, when death takes place, 126.

Gabarty, El, the historian, 333.
Gabriel, the angel, 190.
Gardener, the monastery, with only one garment, 154.
Gardens, Egyptian, 28.
Garnault on the oracles, 291, 292.
Gauge, the Nile, 67.
George, St., and the Dragon, 218.
Ghost, an early monastery, 296.
Gideon and the camel's ornaments, 74.
Gifts to the Church must be anonymous, 216.
  to the bride-elect, 111.
Ginn, fear of, in the dark, 162.
  protection of the Cross against, 180.
Gipsies, the Egyptian, 296.
Girdle, ceremony of the loosing of the infant's, 101.
  the Coptic, 189.
Girl preacher, a, 241.
Godparents, close relationship of, 96.

352 Index

Gohary, Ibrahim El, Coptic Grand Vizier, 333.
Gordon, Lady Duff, the Patriarch's rudeness to, 250.
Gorst, Sir Eldon, dislike of the Copts, 329.
Goshen, the land of, 46, 47.
Gospel-case, the sealed, 100, 177.
Gospel to the Egyptians, the, 317.
Gospels as a cure for headache, 297.
   the first, circulated in Egypt, 317.
Governor, a Coptic, 334.
Gratitude, how it is shown, 61.
Gravity of the Oriental, the, 19.
Greek Orthodox Church, the, 234.
   the translation of the Gospel into, 230.
Gregory, St., the Liturgy of, 185.
Grief, the Oriental in, 122.
Guardian angel, 198.
Guilds of the ancient workers, 156.
Guiltiness, the, of sin, 185.
Guimet on a sacred picture, 216.
Gulah used by the priest, 182.

Hadrian, the Emperor, on the Copts, 148.
Haikal, the (or screen), 170.
Hand-cross, the flat, 179.
Hands, the bleeding, of Theodore's, the monk, 151.
   laying, on the sick, 265.
   Oriental use of the, 198, 199.
   the washing of the priest's, 196, 200.
   the washing of the, 31.
Hanna, Ayad Bey, Minister of War, 335.
Harat-az-Zuailah, venerated picture at, 217.
Hareem, the, 20, 21, 23.
Harness-makers, the, 42.
Head, the native, never uncovered, 52.
Headache cured by touch of Gospels, 297.
Head-covering of the priest, 189.
Healing, a great church service of, 293, 294, 295.
   power of the saints, 221.
Hebrews, the Gospel to the, 317.
Helba, belief in virtues of, 88.
Helowan, the monastery near, 137.
Heraclius, the Fast of, 223.
   his intervention declined, 236.
Herbs, use of, 294.
Heredity, belief in, 85.
Heresy, "the soul-destroying," of the Copts, 249, 310.
Heroism shown by the Copts, 323, 324, 325, 326.
Hiding of the Copts from Western Christians as well as the Moslems, 305, 306.
Holy Ghost, the Coptic dogma of the procession of, from the Father, 233.
Holy Week, the Fast of, 222.
Hope of the future, 343.
Hospitality, duty of, 29.
Host, the adoration of the, 201.
   the elaborate ceremony of dividing the, 346.
Houses, tomb, visits to, 132.
Hyena, superstitions about the, 76.
Hypnotic suggestion, the monk's surgical operation by, 296.
Hypnotism of the Patriarch's prayers, 251.

Impassibility, efforts to attain, 291.
Incense, morning, the service of offering, 183.
   box, the, 182.
India, the Gospel sent to, 230.
Infants, unbaptized, beliefs about, 101.
   in church, liberty of, 171.
   partake of the Communion, 100, 205.
Inlay work, skill in, 149.
Instruments, musical, 37.
Intrigue, the mistake of, 256.

Invasion, the Arab, 237.
Irrigation water, the stealing of, a great sin, 185.
Isis, the robe of the priests of, 188.
   traces of the cult of, 210.
   the boat of, in Christian picture, 216.
Islam, conversions to, 239.
   the absorption of the village Copts by, 240.
Ismail, story of his cattle raids, 319.
   on equality, 334.

Jackals in Christian picture, 216.
Jacob, the Copt who resisted the French invasion, 325.
Jacob's experiment with the flocks, 86.
James, St., healing based on his teaching, 294.
Jaundice, a cure for, 77.
Jeremiah, the prophet, buried in Egypt, 316.
Jerusalem, the pilgrimage to, 209.
   entry denied to Copts by the Crusaders, 305.
Jesus, the early stories about, 298.
Jewellery, the women's, 24.
   skill in making, 148.
Jewish element in the Coptic race, 315, 316.
Jews, ascetic brotherhood of, 319.
   denied entrance to the Coptic Church, 317, 318.
Joseph, a scene reminiscent of his time, 158.
Judaism, Alexandrian, 319.
Justification, an Egyptian trait, 186.

Kallini Pasha on the Patriarch's Council, 289.
Khamseen, the, 20.
Khedive, the, sought as the ally of the Patriarch, 258.
   the, sought to override the Patriarch, 258.
   the, and the *Wakfs*, 263.
Kiss of peace, the, given by congregation, 201.
Kissing the Gospel, 191.
   the hand of the priest, for purification, 297.
Kitchener, Lord, changes made by, 335.
Kultah, Saint, the picture of, 293.

Labour, forced, 5.
Ladies, Coptic, and domestic efficiency, 271.
Lamps, holy, 174.
Land reclamation, 45.
Lane on the Copts, 107, 293, 306.
Language, the dead Coptic, 170.
Laughter never loud, 19.
Laymen, reading church lessons, 194.
   their attempt to assert themselves, 255.
Left hand, the, dishonourable, 198.
Leider, Mr., the C.M.S. missionary, 232.
Lenten Fast, the great length of, 222, 223.
Leonides, one of the first martyrs, 230.
Light, love of, 162.
Litany, a beautiful, 190, 191.
Liturgy of St. Basil, 169, 185.
   of St. Clement, 182.
   of St. Mark, 185.
   of St. Gregory, 185.
Loaves, the three Eucharistic, 182, 195.
Longevity, instance of, 48, 49, 50, 51.
   and the fasts, 224.
Lord's Prayer, how used, 207, 208, 247.
Lots, casting of, to find the new Patriarch, 252.

Macarius the monk and the mosquito, 72.
   and the friendly panther, 73.
Magic of the Gospels, 178.
   the, of the Cross, 180.
   the Church's teaching about, 298.
Mahdi, the, and his Coptic prisoners, 324, 325.
Makram Agha, a Coptic Mudir, 334.

Index

353

Marcian dethrones the Patriarch, 236.
Marcus Simaika Pasha on Coptic resignation, 123.
   and the proper marking of Eucharistic cakes, 213.
   and the Coptic Museum, 150, 226.
   and the Patriarch, 263.
Marcus the cook, 27.
Mareotis, Lake, ascetic brotherhood of Jews there, 319.
Mark, St., buried at Alexandria, 176.
   St., Liturgy of, 185.
   hymn to the Apostle, 190.
   St., the coming of, 228, 229.
   ben el-Konbar, an early reformer, 294.
Marriage, often very happy, 106.
Martyrdom of St. Mark, 229.
   of Leonides, 230.
   of Diocletian, 231.
Martyrs, the chief Coptic, 143.
Martyrs' relics, 220.
Maspero on the oracles, 292.
Matarieh, the Holy Family at, 299.
Mat-making in the monasteries, 151.
Mats, the altar, 181.
Maundy Thursday, the tank for, 211.
Meat, the offence of eating it all the year round, 250.
Mediation, the Coptic view of, 185.
Medicine, often studied by the clerics, 293.
Melkite and Jacobite feuds, 195.
   authority defied, 236.
Memphis, the sanctuary for the sick there, 292.
Menelek, King of Abyssinia, his gift to the Patriarch, 246.
Mercurius, St., converted Vasheh, 216, 217.
Mercy, belief in God's, 217, 218.
Messenger, the native, 43.
Midnight prayer in the church, 220.
Mihrab, the Moslem niche, adopted from the Copts, 175.
Mikhail, the angel, 281.
Mimicry, children's love of, 80.
Minieh, the Bishop Abraam at, 301.
Minority, baptismal innocence presumed during, 206.
Miracle of the Monastery of Barsoum, 137.
Missionaries, Western, attacks of, on the Coptic Church, 250.
Mohammed Ali and Coptic state service, 318, 332; 333.
Monasteries, the work in the, 151, 152.
   ignorance of the monks of the, 225.
   the revenues of, in the hands of the Patriarch, 248.
   dislike of, by reformers, 253.
Monasticism, depopulation due to, 238.
Monk, the, who sold shoes, 153.
Monkeys, reasons for detestation of, 74.
Monks, how they earned their bread, 151.
   their practice of standing, 184.
   the boasting of the, 186.
   weeping for their sins, 187.
   ignorance of the, 225.
   the immense number of, 238.
Monophysite controversy, the, 235.
Monotone, the musical, 196.
Moolids, or saints' birthday feasts, 136.
Morality of the Copts, 107.
Morning incense, the service of offering, 183.
Morocco, story of the Sultan of, 32.
Mosaics, skill in making, 149.
Moslems preferred by Patriarch to Protestants, 250.

Moslems seeking the ministration of the Christian Bishop, 282.
   Coptic provocations to, 321.
   the, on Coptic ability, 331, 332.
   the, on our non-observance of the Sabbath, 338.
Mosque, equality of the worshippers in the, 54.
Mother-in-law, the ancient joke of, 71.
Mudirs, Coptic, 334.
Mummification practised till the fifth century, 133.
Museum, Coptic, at Old Cairo, 150.
   British, and its Coptic treasures, 253.
Musical instruments, 37.
Mustapha Pasha Fehmi acts against the Patriarch, 259.

Names used by the Copts, 91, 101.
Napoleon on the Egyptians, 146.
   and Coptic troops, 325.
Natron valley, the monastery in, 255, 315.
Nature, the people's love of, 64.
Neglect of the churches, 225.
Negro blood, traces of, 315.
Nestorius on the two natures of Christ, 235.
News, how it travels, 12, 13.
Nicæa, Council of, the point of separation, 218.
   Council of, and the Copts, 228.
   Council of, on standing for prayer, 184.
   the Creed of, 191, 233.
Niche, the decorated, in the churches, 175.
Nickname, Moslem's, for the Copt, 312.
Nile, the rising of, 65.
   boatmen of, 65.
   the, as a subject of conversation, 65.
   prayers for the flood, 68, 69.
   the miracles of, 68.
   the beneficent water of, 70.
   prayers for inundations of, 194.
   blessing the waters at Epiphany, 210.
Nineveh, the Fast of, 223.
Nitria, the monastery in, 259.
Novatian heresy, the, 230.
Nunnery, the, under Abba Elijah, 296.
Nuns, strenuous and self-denying, 154.
   the immense number of, 238.

Oblation, the prayer of, 197.
Occupation, the Christian, strange results of, 240.
Official posts, great, held by Copts, 334, 335.
Oil of healing, the, 215.
   the consecrated, or chrism, 214, 215.
   holy, use of, 97, 98, 116, 293, 294.
Ombos, the crocodiles in the Temple of, 74.
Omdurman, courage of Copts at, 324.
Oracles, the people's love of the, 291.
Ordination, the Patriarch's sole power of, 263.
Origen, 230.
   story of conversion of, 192.
Orphan, care of the, 93.
Ostrich eggs hung in the churches, 174.
Ovation, the, given to the returning Patriarch, 261.
Oven, the church, 213.

Pachomius the monk, 238.
   story of the gardener of his monastery, 284.
Palm Sunday, curious services on, 211.
   leaves, uses of, 150, 154.
Paphnutius the monk and his tunics, 284.
Paten, the, 177.
Patriarch, and young engaged couples, 105.
   the, at the monastery of Barsoum, 137.

354 Index

Patriarch, Cyrillus, burning of the pictures by, 218, 219.
   the present, piety of, 224.
   Athanasius, the, 233.
   Dioscoros, the, 235.
   regarded as sovereign of their country, 237.
   the hypnotic power of his prayers, 251.
   how elected, 252.
   a, and the cup of coffee, 257.
   the triumph of, 261.
   the passionate attachment to, 261.
   the sole power of, 263.
   the, defied by Bishop Abraam, 289.
   the intrigue of, with France, Turkey, and Russia, 260.
Patriarchate, the, dread of, 254.
Patriarchs, mention of names of, in the Holy Eucharist, 203.
Patriotism roused by the disputes of the churches, 236.
Pedlars for the monks and nuns, 152.
Pentapolis, the city of St. Mark, 228.
Persecution of Severus, 230.
   of the Arabian invaders, the, 237, 321.
Peter's, St., First Epistle dated from Babylon, 229.
Petrie, Professor Flinders, quoted, 231.
Pharaohs, are the Copts the descendants of, 305.
Philo on the Jews in Egypt, 316, 319.
Picture, sacred, in Church of St. Michael, 70.
   burying the, in the altar, 177, 345.
Pictures, of the church, 215.
   church, burned in Cairo, 218, 219.
   church, readmitted by the present Patriarch, 219.
   private prayer before, 219.
Pigeon towers, the, 14, 15.
Pilgrimages, Copt and Moslem, 16, 165.
Piterius, the visit of, to the nunnery, 108.
Poison, Scripture reference to, 265.
Politan, the Patriarch, 293.
Politeness, Oriental, 11, 12.
   native, a story of, 60.
Population, increase of, 5.
   of Egypt, the, 239.
Posts, great, held by the Copts, 333.
Poverty of the monks, 284.
Prayer, a, translated from the Coptic, 194.
   private, 219, 220.
   washing before, 219.
   hours of, 220.
Prayers of the Patriarch, hypnotic power of, 251.
Praying before the church pictures, 217.
Preacher, girl, my visit to a village with, 241.
Prejudice, yielding to Western, 308.
Presbyterian zeal against church pictures, 219.
Pride "that apes humility," story of, 187.
Priest's prayer for his own forgiveness, 204.
   neglect of church treasures, 225.
Prime Minister, the Coptic, 330.
Prospharin, one of the altar veils, 177.
Prostration of the congregation, 203.
Proverbs, 33.
Ptah Sotmu, sanctuary of, 292.
Public Prosecutor, the Copt as, 334.
Pulpit, the, 174.
Purification, service of, 97.

Quartets, the congregation divided into, 199.

Raisins used for Eucharistic wine, 214.
Ramadan, the Fast of, 221.
Real Presence, the, belief in, 197.
Reclamation of the land, 45.

Redemption, the Coptic view of, 185.
Reform, the Patriarch suspicious of, 249.
   hopes of, 254.
Reformation, the English, hated by orthodox Copts, 250.
   the English, distasteful to the Patriarch, 311.
Reformers and the church pictures, 218.
Relics of the saints and martyrs, 220.
Repentance, no word in Coptic for, 187.
Repetition of the Scriptures, a fetish, 193.
   Oriental love of, 280.
Repudiation of sin, 185.
Resting, different forms of, 18.
Revenues of the Church and monasteries in the hands of the Patriarch, 248.
Riaz Pasha and the Patriarch, 261.
Risk Bey, a Coptic Mudir, 334.
Ritual, love of, 84.
Robe, story of the Bishop's, 283.
Rome and the Epiphany service, 210.
   excommunication by, of the Coptic Church, 235.
Rosary, the general use of, 19.
   the Coptic use of, 280.
Rosellini on origin of Copts, 313.

Sacrament, the mode of administering the, 206.
Saints' tombs, 136.
   reading the Lives of, in church, 194.
   held in remembrance in the Eucharist, 203.
   relics, 220.
Sakieh, the, 43, 64.
Sanctuary, the church, reverence for, 170.
Sarabon, Bishop of, excommunicated, 258.
Sayce, Professor, on religious antagonism, 332.
Scents of rural Egypt, 6.
   love of, 28.
School, the first great Christian, 230.
Screen, beauty of that at the Church of Abu Sifain, 149.
   the *haikal*, 173.
Scriptures, the reading of the, 192.
Sealed Gospels, the, 177.
Secretiveness, Oriental, 305.
Serapion, Abba, reading the Scriptures, 193.
Serapis, St. Mark's protest against the feast to, 229.
Sermon, the place of the, 200.
Serpent, the, in symbolism, 188.
Serpents, Scripture reference to, 265.
Severus, the persecution of, 230.
Shadoof, the, 43, 159.
Shafika, the Coptic singing woman, 107.
Sheep roasted whole, the, 35.
Sheikh, the, and the girl preacher, 243.
Shenouda, the recluse of Akhmin, 292.
Shoemaker, a, the first Christian convert, 229.
Shoes, the story of the monk who sold, 153.
Shopkeepers, Oriental, 146.
   not wholly mercenary, 165.
Sick, the solemn service for the, 217.
   the, visits of to ancient temples, 292.
Sickness cured by laying on of hands, 265.
Signs, shop, 165.
Silversmith, the, and his primitive tools, 155.
Simeon Stylites, a Coptic saint, 323.
Sin, the Coptic view of the guiltiness of, 185, 187.
   repudiation of, 185.
Singing, native delight in, 36, 37.
Slave-holding, 315.
Sleep, scorn of, 290.
Slippers, the story of the Prophet's, 75.
Smith, Professor Elliot, on personal characteristics of the Copts, 314.
Sobhy, Dr., views on origin of Copts, 312.

Index

Sociability, native, 32.
Soldiers, why the Copts are not, 323.
Songs of the fellaheen, 55, 56.
Soul of the recently dead, sending away the, 130.
Souls, the, "under the altar," 176.
Spiritualism born in Egypt, 296.
Spoon, the, used in the Eucharist, 177.
   the Eucharistic, how used, 205, 207.
Staff, the bishop's, 188.
   the bishop's, used to stir the waters, 212.
Standing, the monks' practice of, 184.
   for prayer, 184.
Stanley, Dean, on the liturgy, 185, 187.
   mistaken ideas of, 309.
Statues, none in the Coptic Church, 216.
Stirring the waters for the Epiphany, 212.
Stole, the priest's, 189.
Stones, magic, 77.
Straw, bricks without, 47.
Street cries, the, 157.
Strenuous, when the people were, 160.
Suez Canal, the conservative way of the labourers on, 150.
"Suggestion," the young monk surgically operated on by hypnotic, 296.
Sunday, the claim for its observance, 329.
   the non-observance of, under British rule, 337.
   the passionate attachment of the Copts to observance of, 339.
   Coptic suggestions for keeping, 341.
Superstition, an early effort to suppress, 294.
Supineness of modern days, 160.
Surplice, origin of the, 188.
Synod, the Patriarch's, 259.
Syrians, a mixture of, 314, 315.

Tabernacle, the, on the altar, 177.
Table-rapping in the fourth century, 296.
Tank, the Epiphany, 209, 211.
Taor, the nun, 154.
"Taste of the spring," the, 9.
Tattoo used to mark the cross on the wrist, 180.
Tent-peg, story of the, 34.
Terrors of the judgment never pictured, 217, 218.
Tewfic Society, the, 257.
Tewfik Bey, the Coptic hero, 326.
Textus cases, the, 178.
Thebais, the city monasteries of, 238.
Thebes, the monastery at, 238.
   the nunnery at, 296.
Theological College, a, founded and abolished, 256.
Thieves, Sitt Dimiana's power over, 144.
   a Bishop's power over the, 282.
   Shenouda's power over, 292.
Thor, the monk, 238.
Thoth superseded by Enoch, 281.
Throne, the church, 175, 176.
Tolerance, religious, between Copt and Moslem, 53.
   instances of mutual, 332.
Tomb-houses, visits to, 132.
Torture never represented in the church pictures, 217.
Treasures taken from the churches, 225.
   church, neglect of, 253.

Tree, a sacred, 77, 78.
Triangle, the use of, in church, 197.
Tribune, the church, 175.
Trinity, the Holy, view of, 185.
Truth, difficulty of finding the, 307.
Tunic, the priest's embroidered, 189.
Turban, the priest's black, 189.
Turkish decoration accepted by the Patriarch, 262.

Uniat Church, the, 257.
Unitarianism, views leading to, 233.
Usury, Coptic, 318.

Vasheh converted by St. Mercurius, 216, 217.
Veil, the woman's, 21.
Veils, the Eucharistic, 177.
Vestments, the interest of the, 188.
Villages with no church or priest, 240.
Virgin, festival of a, 69.
   use of the picture of the Blessed, 190.
Virgin's Well, balsam from, for chrism, 214.

Wailing women, 126.
Wakfs, the Moslem, 263.
War, a Coptic Minister of, 335.
Ward, Mr. John, on Coptic customs, 307.
Washing before prayer, 219.
Water, of the Nile, 70.
   "the gift of God," 157.
   the stealing of, a great sin, 185.
   thrown upwards by the priest at the Holy Eucharist, 206.
   scattered over the congregation, 207.
   Holy, views about, 209.
   from the priest's hands, magic of, 297, 298.
Waters, blessing of, 210, 211.
Water-wheel, the making of, 43.
Wealth in the hands of the Copts, 3.
Wedding, rites and customs of the Coptic, 112.
Well, the holy, at Harat-az-Zuailah, the story of, 299.
Whately, Miss, an anecdote by, 186.
   a story of her visit to a remote village, 241.
   on Coptic morals, 310.
Wheelbarrows never used for proper purpose, 150.
Wheelwrights, the, 42.
Whip abolished by Lord Cromer, 146.
Whistling, distastefulness of, 162.
Wife, the, how chosen, 104.
Wind, Arab hatred of, 20.
Wine, the giving of, to mothers, 88.
   the Eucharistic, 214.
Wissa-Fanous, the costly wedding of, 118.
Woman saint, a, 108.
Women, seclusion of, 21, 22, 104.
   the work of the, 59.
   screened by the Jews, 319.
Writers who do the Copts great disservice, 308.

Yussef, the late Sheikh Ali, on Coptic ability, 332.

Zagreet, the women's cry, 125.
Zephyr, "smelling the," at Easter, 234.

PRINTED BY
MORRISON AND GIBB LTD.
EDINBURGH

THE Middle East COLLECTION
Arno Press

Abbott, Nabia. **Aishah:** The Beloved of Mohammed. 1942

Addison, Charles G. **Damascus and Palmyra.** 1838. 2 Vols. in 1

[Adivar], Halidé Edib. **Turkey Faces West.** 1930

Baddeley, John F. **The Rugged Flanks of Caucasus.** 1940. 2 Vols. in 1

Barker, Edward B. B., ed. **Syria and Egypt Under the Last Five Sultans of Turkey.** 1876. 2 Vols. in 1

Bell, Gertrude Lowthian. **Syria:** The Desert & The Sown. 1919

Bowring, John. **Report on the Commercial Statistics of Syria.** 1840

Brydges, Harford Jones. **The Dynasty of the Kajars.** 1833

Churchill, [Charles H.] **The Druzes and the Maronites Under the Turkish Rule from 1840 to 1860.** 1862

Denon, Vivant. **Travels in Upper and Lower Egypt.** 1803. 3 Vols. in 1

Donaldson, Bess Allen. **The Wild Rue:** A Study of Muhammadan Magic and Folklore in Iran. 1938

Eton, W[illiam]. **A Survey of the Turkish Empire.** 1798

Forbes-Leith, F. A. C. **Checkmate:** Fighting Tradition in Central Persia. 1927

Fraser, James Baillie. **Narrative of the Residence of the Persian Princes in London, in 1835 and 1836.** 1838. 2 Vols. in 1

Fraser, James Baillie. **A Winter's Journey (Tâtar) from Constantinople to Tehran.** 1838. 2 Vols. in 1

Gobineau, Joseph Arthur. **Romances of the East.** 1878

Islamic Taxation: Two Studies. 1973

Kinneir, John Macdonald. **A Geographical Memoir of the Persian Empire.** 1813

Krusinski, J[udasz Tadeusz]. **History of the Late Revolution in Persia.** 1740. 2 Vols. in 1

Lane-Poole, Stanley. **Cairo:** Sketches of Its History, Monuments, and Social Life. 1898

Le Strange, G[uy], ed. **Don Juan of Persia:** A Shi'ah Catholic, 1560-1604. 1926

Leeder, S. H. **Modern Sons of the Pharaohs: A** Study of the Manners and Customs of the Copts of Egypt. 1918

Midhat Bey, Ali Haydar. **The Life of Midhat Pasha.** 1903

Miller, Barnette. **The Palace School of Muhammad the Conqueror.** 1941

Millspaugh, A[rthur] C[hester]. **The American Task in Persia.** 1925

Naima. **Annals of the Turkish Empire from 1591 to 1659 of the Christian Era.** 1832

Pasha, Djemal. **Memories of a Turkish Statesman, 1913-1919.** 1922

Pears, Edwin. **Life of Abdul Hamid.** 1917

Philby, H[arry] St. J[ohn Bridger]. **Arabia of the Wahhabis.** 1928

St. John, Bayle. **Village Life in Egypt.** 1852. 2 Vols. in 1

Sheil, Lady [Mary]. **Glimpses of Life and Manners in Persia.** 1856

Skrine, Francis Henry and Edward Denison Ross. **The Heart of Asia: A History of Russian Turkestan and the Central Asian Khanates from the Earliest Times.** 1899

Sykes, Mark. **The Caliphs' Last Heritage: A Short History of the Turkish Empire.** 1915

Sykes, P[ercy] M., ed. **The Glory of the Shia World.** 1910

De Tott, Baron. **Memoirs of Baron de Tott.** 1785. 2 Vols. in 1

Ubicini, M. A. **Letters on Turkey.** 1856. 2 Vols. in 1

Vambery, Arminius. **Arminius Vambery:** His Life and Adventures. 1914

Vambery, Arminius. **History of Bokhara.** 1873

Waring, Edward Scott. **A Tour of Sheeraz by the Route of Kazroon and Feerozabad.** 1807

MODERN SONS OF THE PHARAOHS

A STUDY OF THE MANNERS AND CUSTOMS OF THE COPTS OF EGYPT

BY

S. H. LEEDER

AUTHOR OF "VEILED MYSTERIES OF EGYPT"
"THE DESERT GATEWAY" ETC.

ILLUSTRATED WITH PHOTOGRAPHS BY THE AUTHOR,
ALPHONSE EFFENDI GRIESS, JAMES SCOTT, M.A.,
P. DITTRICH, CAIRO, AND LEKEGIAN, CAIRO

" 'TIS time new hopes should animate the world,
New light should dawn from new revealings
To a race, weighed down so long, forgotten so long."
BROWNING.

HODDER AND STOUGHTON
LONDON   NEW YORK   TORONTO

916.2
L454m

75-3349

MODERN SONS
OF THE PHARAOHS

ONE OF THE MOST GORGEOUS C
Which united the prominent families of Wissa and Fanous. The photograph shows
The wedding t

WEDDINGS OF RECENT YEARS.

gnificent Egyptian pavilion used on ceremonial occasions, with its myriad lights.
e at Assiout.

Dedication

TO

CANON HAWKINS

WHO, IN SPITE OF TOTAL LOSS OF EYESIGHT,
CONTINUED FOR NEARLY A QUARTER OF A
CENTURY, WITH UNDIMINISHED EFFICIENCY
AND CHEERFULNESS, TO SERVE HIS CHURCH,
AS VICAR OF LYTHAM IN LANCASHIRE

IN ADMIRATION
AND GRATITUDE FOR A
NOBLE EXAMPLE